Walking

Through

Walls

Walking

Through

Walls

A Memoir

Philip Smith

ATRIA BOOKS
New York London Toronto Sydney

ATRIA BOOKS
A Division of Simon & Schuster, Inc.
1230 Avenue of the Americas
New York, NY 10020

First Atria Books hardcover edition September 2008

ATRIA BOOKS and colophon are trademarks of Simon & Schuster, Inc.

For information about special discounts for bulk purchases,
please contact Simon & Schuster Special Sales at
1-800-456-6798 or business@simonandschuster.com.

Designed by Kate S. Moll

Manufactured in the United States of America

1   3   5   7   9   10   8   6   4   2

Library of Congress Cataloging-in-Publication Data
Smith, Philip.
Walking through walls : a memoir / Philip Smith.
p. cm.
Contents: Redneck mambo—War on sanpaku—The human ray gun—Devil
be gone—Spirit talk in Overtown—Meet the preacher—Psychic shopping—
Pink or gray?—Dios mio, Dr. Siegel—In shock—Futurama—Into the etheric—
Another angry doctor—The goddess debuts—The mad scientist—Mister magic.
1. Smith, Lew (1904–1981). 2. Smith, Philip. I. Title.
BF1027.S65   2008
130'.92—B22   2008015502

ISBN-13: 978-1-4165-4294-0
ISBN-10:   1-4165-4294-9

This book is dedicated with eternal gratitude to Esther Rand Smith, my beautiful and brilliant mother, who not only gave me this miraculous opportunity to visit planet Earth but the full love and content of her own lovely soul.

Contents

Author's Note ix

Prologue xiii

one • Redneck Mambo 1

two • War on Sanpaku 19

three • The Human Ray Gun 35

four • Devil Be Gone 57

five • Spirit Talk in Overtown 69

six • Meet the Preacher 84

seven • Psychic Shopping 107

eight • Pink or Gray? 122

nine • *Dios Mio,* Dr. Siegel 140

ten • In Shock 163

eleven • Futurama 178

twelve • Into the Etheric 199

thirteen • Another Angry Doctor 221

fourteen • The Goddess Debuts 242

fifteen • The Mad Scientist 274

sixteen • Mister Magic 297

Epilogue 323

Acknowledgments 331

Author's Note

My father knew that one day this book would be written and wanted to make sure that whoever took on the task had all the resources he would need. He documented all aspects of his work, and much of this book is based on the hundreds of hours of audiotapes, testimonial letters, extensive notebooks, photographs, diagrams, artifacts, and over five thousand pages of spirit dictation that he generously left behind.

The majority of names in this book have been changed to protect the innocent and the not so innocent.

At night my spirit guides take me up to visit laboratories on other planets and in other dimensions. Lately I've been spending a lot of time on the seventh plane, the eleventh plane, and the twelfth plane.

—Lew Smith, 1970, in a recorded audio interview

Prologue

It was late July.

The summer mangoes had dropped from the trees and were lying rotting on the ground, ripped open by feasting bugs and birds. Their intoxicating, sweet smell mixed with the heaviness of the night-blooming jasmine. This languid perfume created a thick, rarefied atmosphere that at times made breathing difficult. In Miami nature is often a mix of colorful abundance and dark decay.

This evening I was walking home from a friend's birthday party. We had listened to the new Rolling Stones album, *Aftermath,* then turned off the lights and pretended to make out with the nearest girl. Some party. But then, this was 1966, and I was only fourteen.

It was long after eleven o'clock. I should have been home hours ago but was having too much fun to leave the party. As I approached my father's house, I realized that I had forgotten my keys. The porch lights were on, my father's car was parked out front, but the house was completely dark. He must have gone to bed early.

Not wanting to startle him, I knocked somewhat timidly. A tornado of mosquitoes brought on by the summer rains swarmed around my head.

I knocked again, this time louder. "Pop, it's me, open up." No response. Not hearing any movement from inside, I became concerned that something was wrong. I decided to walk back to my friend's house to use his phone to call my father. As I turned to leave, I heard the front door's dead bolt click open. Relieved, I spun around ready to greet my father and apologize for coming home so late.

As I stood there, the front door remained closed. I was wondering if the sound I had heard was just a very loud cricket or a buffo toad looking for a mate. Then, ever so slowly, like in some black-and-white horror movie, the door creaked open. From the shadows emerged a tall man with grayish skin. I had never seen this guy before; he had the stature and demeanor of Lurch. Without any introduction, he looked at me with a cool stare and said in a flat, robotlike voice, "We are currently in communication with the master souls of the eleventh plane. Your father is deep in trance and cannot be disturbed."

Lurch began to back away and close the door. He then paused and asked, "Why did you even bother to knock? After all, you are your father's son. Haven't you learned to walk through walls yet?"

Walking

Through

Walls

one

•

Redneck Mambo

"My, aren't you a cutie!" She leaned closer to me and took a drag off her cigarette. As she exhaled, her ample sunburnt breasts, spilling out of her black fishnet one-piece, bobbed up and down against my face. Dressed in my blue blazer, bow tie, khaki shorts, and freshly shined Buster Browns, I was, at six years old, an irresistible magnet for drunken middle-aged women looking for love. Mom always insisted that if I were going to sit at the bar and drink that I at least be well dressed.

I was at my favorite bar, the kind that was very popular in the 1950s throughout the Caribbean: below ground with a big picture window looking directly into the front of the pool. For hours I would watch would-be Esther Williams types engage in aesthetic swimming routines or drunken couples attempting to make love in the shallow end of the pool completely unaware that some of us had a front-row seat.

At the moment, the hotel's live mermaid was doing her aquatic show while sucking on an air hose. I lived for the mermaid. She was my fantasy come true—a sleek woman in a tight flesh-colored bathing suit, wearing very red lipstick, who did artistic somersaults and blew bubbles at you through the window. For some reason, possibly due to the Gulf Stream or immigration, mermaids did not exist back in my hometown of Miami. Mermaids were strictly a foreign phenomenon.

Being a gentleman, I restrained myself from telling this aggressively drunk woman that her breasts were blocking not only my view of this very important show but my air passages as well.

The Bahamian bartender gave me a wink and a smile. I was a regular, and he had witnessed my powerful little-boy charm on women many, many times. I was the Cary Grant/Hugh Hefner of my first-grade class—suave, debonair, and just a bit naughty when necessary. I knew the difference between Manischewitz and Bordeaux.

He poured my third drink: a planter's punch packed with dark rum. Delicious. On these weekends away, my parents would often park me at the bar. What better babysitter than a bartender and an open tab?

At the time, I spent many of my weekends in tiki bars throughout the Caribbean, accompanying my mother and father on business trips. Nassau, Havana, Port-au-Prince, Kingston, and the Caymans were each just a short hop from Miami. In 1958 round-trip airfare to Nassau was around twelve dollars. Sometimes we would fly over for the day just to bring back duty-free liquor for one of my parents' parties.

Pop was an internationally known interior decorator who, through no real effort of his own, specialized in making pretty for Caribbean dictators, prizefighters, minor celebrities, assorted mobsters, and just plain rich folk. Because Miami did not have a great demand for decorators, my father's clients existed largely outside of U.S. jurisdiction. Wherever there was offshore banking, Pop seemed to have clients. Once they had quietly exchanged one passport for another, his customers would discreetly retire to their Lew Smith–designed villas, usually the kind with an ever-ready seaplane parked out front. In the fifties, the only thing those Miami rednecks knew about decorating was driving the wife over in the pickup and grabbing whatever piece of colonial furniture with brown plaid upholstery was on sale at Sears during the Midsummer Spectacular.

When my parents visited Havana, Mom would usually step off the plane and head straight for the casino, from which she would often emerge the next morning after beating the pants off every English expat at blackjack. With her gold cigarette holder, emerald earrings down to her shoulders, and style for miles, Mom was a brilliant gambler and always walked away with a win. Gangster Meyer Lansky regularly bought her breakfast after a night at the tables; he was probably hoping to recoup some of the house losses with a little snuggle behind the bar. While Mom was shaking the dice, Pop was doing business with President Carlos Prio or sugar mogul Willie Lobo. President Prio had given my father his signed personal calling card to keep with him at all times as his passport against any type of trouble. With just a wave of the card, Pop could slip right past the gauntlet of bodyguards packing plenty of heat who thought nothing of icing a potential political rival. The card magically opened every door not only throughout Havana but also in Miami after Prio fled. Pop often visited the ex-*presidente* at his home on one of Miami Beach's exclusive private islands to make Prio comfy at his palace in exile.

In addition, Pop's services were sought after by plenty of legitimate clients—foreign developers with funny-sounding names and even funnier accents who were building new beachfront hotels throughout the Caribbean. These guys usually gave my father free rein on any project. Their attitude was "just fix it," as if designing a tropical-themed resort was basically a plumbing problem.

Back then, Miami was not much more than a big ol' cracker swamp due east of the Everglades. Dixiecrats, blacks, and coral snakes summed up the population, in that order. Miami was still the Deep South. Tropical apartheid ruled. The local A&P on Bird Road had three bathrooms upstairs above the meat counter: one for men, one for women, and one for colored. All that back-of-the-bus, separate-drinking-fountain, Woolworth's sit-in stuff that everybody thinks was limited to the redneck South of Alabama was alive and well in Miami—correctly pronounced at the time as "My-am-*uhhh*." If you were black and found walking along the pink sidewalks of Miami Beach after 5:00 p.m. without an official permit or a letter from your employer, you were immediately thrown into the back of an intimidating black-and-white police car and escorted off the island.

However, blacks weren't the only ones whose access was restricted on Miami Beach. Entire islands, such as Indian Creek, along with the various social clubs such as the Bath Club, the Surf Club, and the Indian Creek Club, did not welcome Jews. Guards and property associations kept them at bay. Additionally, many of the best hotels and apartment buildings were for "restricted clientele"—some by implication, others by not-so-little signs on the front lawn that clearly stated NO DOGS, JEWS, OR IRISH ALLOWED. Mom, who had lived her entire life in New York City, had never seen anything like this before.

Occasionally, for sport, Mom loved walking into a hotel, registering, and then telling the guy that she was Jewish. She stood there until they either broke out laughing or threatened to kill her. She usually got off easy due to her emerald-green eyes, Nordic nose, and blond hair, all of which confused the desk clerk as to whether this was a *Candid Camera* event or the real thing. It was not unusual for her to be met with a forceful shove from a foul-mouthed cleaning lady telling her to get out or else. Pop, never one for confrontation, quickly put an end to her freedom-fighter routine for fear that she would end up dead in the back alley of one of the hotels. Most of the hotel owners had mob connections and thought nothing about making a quick phone call to rid the premises of a pesky little Jew.

Just as my mother and father started their new life in Miami proper, Miami Beach was about to enter yet another one of its many incarnations as it began to cater to the movers and shakers of the day. Rather than flappers and polo players, certain sections of the Magic City, as it was touted in tourist brochures, were now becoming the winter haven for the Rat Pack and the newly emerging Jewish middle class. Mobsters and elderly Jews began to soak up the sun at hotels promising some crass class, such as the Roney Plaza, the Shore Club, and the Delano.

The Carillon, Deauville, Eden Roc, and Fontainebleau—with their sweeping, audacious curves and free-form pools—eventually grabbed the high-rolling clientele just waiting to have their names announced poolside: "Paging Mr. Sy Bernstein. Paging Hy Lefkowitz—please report to the main cabana for an important phone call." After each announcement on the PA, heads would turn to see who was the VIP from Brooklyn.

The exotic scents of suntan lotion, cigars, and kosher pickles mingled in the warm air. By the late sixties, Sy and Hy would be replaced by Manuel and Alfonso. The kosher pickles would be replaced by yuca and *ropa vieja*. However, the suntan lotion and cigars would remain constants.

In eighty-five-degree weather, wives of Jewish lawyers paraded around the lobby in smart little mink wraps to combat the "cool inside" frigid air-conditioning. Everybody came down during season, from Frank Sinatra to boxer Jake LaMotta. The joint was jumping, and the palms were swaying.

During the long summer months, when most of the city was deserted, the hotels would run unbeatable weekend specials in order to keep their doors open. Mom convinced my father that we should take advantage of these offers with three simple words: "Let them cook." Basically, we had the place to ourselves. I'd splash in the pool as the searing sun bleached the landscape and its inhabitants. At night Mom would sneak me into the Boom Boom Room for a whiskey sour and a floor show of "Live from Las Vegas: Girls! Girls! Girls!" It was very important to her that I understood and embraced sophistication, so as not to end up as another Jewish schlub accountant but rather a jet-set playboy who intimately knew the likes of Paris, London, and Havana.

Whenever a favorite singer or comedian came to town during the season, Pop would take Mom to one of the hotels, such as the Eden Roc or the Carillon, for dinner and a show. At intermission some sexy blond photographerette would temporarily blind the happy couple with the flash from her maximum-sized Graflex camera. Several drinks later—Manhattan for him, whiskey sour for her, usually with small, brightly colored paper umbrellas imported from Japan perched jauntily in the fresh-fruit garnish—Pop would reach for his wallet to purchase the black-and-white souvenir of their evening. These documents show my father in a sharkskin suit and my mother in a little black cocktail dress and pearls, smiling—actually beaming—for the camera. Pop was delighted with his beautiful little blonde, and Mom was thrilled with her dashing decorator husband. After the show, Mom would screw up her courage and ask the star to autograph whatever was available: a napkin, a business card, or the drinks menu. When she got home, she would wake me from my sleep, tell me all about the show, and present me with the latest autographed treasure for my scrapbook.

While my parents were enjoying their drinks, listening to Dean Martin or laughing at Shecky Greene, farther up the strip at the cheesier hotels, brilliant but naughty comediennes like Belle Barth (whose famous live album was titled *If I Embarrass You Tell Your Friends*) would sit at the piano in smoke-filled rooms, tickling the ivories and telling bawdy jokes with a studied finishing-school innocence for the entertainment of lower-middle-class patrons munching fat cigars and getting plastered on cheap scotch. Bloated salesmen and young studs on the make stimulated by the toilet vaudeville usually had two or three blondes on their arms, waiting to "go back to the room." Nearby, at Place Pigalle, Belle's competitor, Pearl Williams, "Direct from New York's Lower East Side," told jokes like, "Did I tell you the one about the drunken cop who fell off his whistle and blew his horse?" Her live routine was captured on an "adults only" album titled *A Cruise Is Not a Trip Around the World,* which was quite a mouthful back then and can still shock today with its clever and scandalous innuendos. And then there was Tubby Boots, an obscenely overweight nerd in thick black glasses who dressed in shiny purple boxer shorts with tassels pasted on his nipples, which he could swing in wild syncopation to the beat of the swing band that accompanied him.

The real miracle of Miami—which still exists to this very day— was the opportunity for anybody from anywhere to suddenly show up and reinvent himself. Supposed Guggenheims, du Ponts, and Rock-efellers, as well as princes and princesses, were always washing up on the social scene only to end up convicted of fraud, embezzlement, or, more often than not, murder. There is a radiant quality to the light that makes people feel as if their past and their soul have been com-pletely sanitized. All is forgiven. They are suddenly swept clean of any personal history and wholly convinced that they have always been who they now say they are. The fabled Miami light encourages even the most humble man in the street to start again, or at the very minimum to mythologize the past.

Countless Cubans who were once sweeping the streets in Havana or serving *fufu* and arroz con pollo in some shack on the outskirts of town now publicly bemoan the loss of their sugar plantations, sum-merhouses, maids, and chauffeurs with the arrival of *El Comandante*. They swear on their beloved mother's grave—who, by the way, hap-pens to be buried in the "good" section of the Havana cemetery, near the mausoleum created by Lalique (far away from the section for both Arabs *and* Jews)—to one day overthrow Fidel and reclaim what is rightfully theirs. Only in America, and, especially, only in Miami.

It was in this miraculous light that my father was able to convince the ultrarich that he was just the man to fluff their pillows, hang their drapes, and ease them away from their addiction to anything rococo or European baroque. In no time at all, he was designing tropical-fantasy interiors that combined the best of Oriental splendor and high-style fifties moderne.

Pop brought an enlightened sensibility to his clients, introducing them to current styles and educating them to new possibilities. When he sketched a room, and no such furniture existed in the market, he quickly designed it and had it custom fabricated. Everything from high-style, free-form modernism to Zen-inspired minimalist furniture began to fill the better homes in South Florida. His commercial work for restaurants, bars, hotels, and even hairdressing salons tended to be more adventurous and experimental than anything else seen at the time. For one Miami Beach hotel, he created a prepsychedelic black-light lounge where his mobiles were painted fluorescent glow-in-the-dark colors along with the eye-popping murals. Drunken patrons appeared as Martians bathed in the purple light.

As often as possible, he hired local artists to produce large works and sculptures for these public spaces. Pop felt an obligation to generate commissions for starving artists and believed that their work contributed an important creative twist to his projects. One artist in particular, Jon Keller, created bizarre murals, screens, and sculptures for his interiors. Jon, whose skin was so thin and ethereal that you could see the blue veins running through her face and arms, lived in a wooden shack on stilts in the black section of the Grove. She was married to King Louie, a Chinese man who worked as a waiter at the local Formosa restaurant. King was never around much, so Jon focused on her surrealistic-inspired work, which seamlessly blended Fellini and Dalí into a classical yet alien aesthetic of floating ghosts, Minotaurs, and busts of patrons with dramatically rearranged physiologies.

Often my parents would leave me at Jon's shack for babysitting while they went out on the town. Jon was oblivious to the aggressive wildlife of snakes and daddy longlegs that would try to make friends with me as I slept on her floor. Eventually Jon's barbiturate-induced fantasy life superseded her reality, and she killed herself. Back then suicide had a kind of shocking chic, akin to martyrdom, that it does not carry today. Jon was typical of the tortured yet wildly creative souls with alternative visions of reality who surrounded my father at the time.

In addition to the Caribbean, Pop's other happy hunting ground for clients was Palm Beach, a galaxy away from Miami. PB's star-studded social life was often covered in the *Miami Herald*'s "For and About Women" column, where reporters breathlessly gushed, "Under a mammoth canopy of silk in flamboyant sunset hues and in an atmosphere of Oriental, eye-popping splendor, Society with a capital *S* danced the hours away Sunday night at the Royal Poinciana Playhouse Celebrity Room. It was the fifth annual Polo Ball for the Damon Runyon Cancer Fund. Honorary chairman, the Duchess of Windsor, never looked prettier. She and the Duke danced with a number of different partners to the music of the Marshall Grant and Guy Lombardo orchestras. Mrs. Joseph P. Kennedy laughed and chatted with the Duke, Elsa Maxwell was everywhere. Joan Crawford and Joan Fontaine were introduced by emcee Walter T. Shirely. Mr. and Mrs. Herbert A. May were there, and so was Mrs. May's movie-star daughter, Dina Merrill. Bearded Joshua Hecht, star of *Fanny,* threw back his head and sang songs from Broadway musicals. The entire crowd sang 'Happy Birthday' to Frank Hale, and the Playhouse president blushed. Pastel blonde Cee-Zee Guest was at the same long table with the Duke and Duchess, the Sanfords, the Mays."

Unlike Pop's glamorous clients, we lived in an area forgotten by the tax collector, known as "unincorporated Dade County." Anything called "unincorporated" told you all you needed to know; the area was more jungle than suburb. Located just a few miles outside of the city proper, our neighborhood was basically raw land filled with miles of poison ivy, saw palmettos, deadly coral snakes, and night-vision possums that slept like bats, hanging upside down in poinciana trees. Wild lime and kumquat trees dotted the landscape, sprouted from seeds dropped by migrating birds. After the summer monsoon rains, rickety old trucks passed through the barely paved streets, spewing acrid smoke filled with DDT, shortening our lives while trying to eradicate the population of skeeters the size of black widow spiders.

When we first moved there, we had no telephone for the first year, as the phone company just plain forgot to run a line out to our neck of the woods. The water was undrinkable, so that, just like women in

Caribbean countries, Mom spent most of her time boiling our drinking water because our well had been polluted by one of several hurricanes passing through, along with the constant decay of the natural sulfur in the rocks.

There was a homesteading feel to the place. All the houses were on sprawling rural plots of land oriented to catch the tropical breezes, with large open areas protected by metal screens that were annually blown away by the first winds of any hurricane. Everybody, except us, had Florida rooms, a kind of screened-in porch where you sat out the worst of the summer with slightly rusty fans and a pitcher of ice water. We had a curious house built in the shape of a pentagon. All of the rooms opened onto an enormous Japanese garden with a small waterfall, shrimp plants from Hawaii, and a pond stocked with large gold and black koi. The garden, my father's idea of Bali Hai, was designed by a Mr. Kobyashi, who on Easter Sunday, just a week after completing the garden, was shot in the head during a robbery that netted the thieves all of two dollars. According to the report in the newspaper, "Kobyashi was murdered by three Negro bandits, who, after holding him up in his Northwest section nursery and florist shop, became irate because of the small amount of money they found on him and shot him."

Our neighbors, whom we hardly ever saw and made every effort to avoid, were good old rednecks who drove beat-up Ford pickups with gun racks on the back window and Confederate flags fluttering from the antenna. They all had long-drawn southern accents and deeply rooted beliefs as to the God-sanctioned inferiority of Yankees, Jews, and blacks. We fit the first two categories. In our neighborhood, Klan membership outnumbered subscriptions to *Life* magazine by about twenty to one. Guaranteed, we were that one and only *Life* subscriber for miles. Given our geographical and religious liabilities, there was no chance in hell that we would ever be invited next door for some deviled eggs or a cool beer out back under the pines. We did not mess with our neighbors, and they didn't mess with us.

I'm not sure that the Carters next door could even read. Sometimes at night I saw Mr. Carter leave the house in a shimmering white gown as he headed off to his Klan meeting. His lanky son, Billy, with a perfect blond crewcut, had dropped out of high school and never seemed to do a lick of work. There was a lemon-yellow trailer parked at the rear of the property. Presumably, this was the spaceship that brought these aliens down from Loxahatchee or whatever hick planet they were from. Billy locked himself in there day and night. Young blond cheerleader types came and went with great frequency. I knew something naughty happened in there. Annie, his first-grade sister, would set pinecones on fire and tell me she was "burning the chocolate babies."

Me? I was a happy little kid running around in the backyard, climbing almond and banyan trees, picking wild bananas, and watching the stars that seemed just a few feet away. Pop was fascinated by the fecund nature that surrounded us and at times overtook us. It was not unusual that strangler vines, enormous frogs, blackbirds, and assorted moths the size of your hand would find their way in through cracks in the screen and start to take over our home.

Pop loved to watch the garden snakes spiral up the rake handle as he worked in the yard. The pretty ones, like coral snakes, were the ones that killed you fast. He made me memorize each name and picture of all the poisonous snakes from his pocket-size snake identifier book. At least once or twice a month, I would wake up and find some stray garden snake crawling in my bed. How they got in was a mystery we could never solve. But they liked my warm bed a lot more than the dew-soaked late-night earth out back. Like a good scout, I trapped them in a brown grocery bag and threw them in the garbage. In the morning, Pop opened the can and released them back into the wild. To him all life was precious, even a snake's. Sometimes for entertainment he brought them in the house so he could watch them slither along the cool terrazzo floor. Mom would run screaming into the bedroom.

Science, nature, and invention always fascinated my father. Pop used the backyard not only to explore nature but to look toward the heavens. For years, he would take me outside at night and we would scan the starry skies with an old pair of binoculars. Over time I learned all the constellations and would get excited when we would spot planets such as Venus or Mars. I remember one night when Pop became silent as he slowly tracked a moving object for several minutes. He had never seen anything like this bright light traveling across the sky. For someone born in 1904, witnessing a man-made object sail through space was a miracle he could never have imagined. Night after night we would watch Echo, NASA's first experimental communications satellite, which was not much more than an inflated Mylar balloon, silently letting the world know that significant changes were about to arrive.

Meanwhile back on earth, life couldn't have been better. Slowly my mother was transforming herself into hostess with the mostess. Mom took to cutting out the latest recipes from *House and Garden* and *Vogue* for her nights of entertaining. Small and incandescently beautiful, she did modern dance, read the society column, and entertained poets and homosexuals. You get the picture: Gertrude Stein meets *Hee Haw*.

On Sundays, with great regularity, she gathered Miami's best and brightest, often as many as forty people, for champagne and lobster Newburg served in a copper chafing dish. Tiki torches lit up the backyard, and couples gathered in the shadow of the black smoke from the hurricane lamps burning kerosene. Mambo and calypso music played from the stereo system. Japanese paper lanterns illuminated the lanai.

Probably 80 or 90 percent of the guests were decorators. Since my father was the only heterosexual decorator in Miami (and quite possibly in the entire world), my parents' parties tended to be large gatherings of gay men. At the time, there were no gay bars in Miami, and "the boys," as my mother referred to them, had to meet somewhere. That somewhere was either my parents' house or the Coconut Grove Pharmacy, known locally as the Coconut Grove Fagacy, where on weekends men in tight white jeans would sit around the U-shaped soda fountain counter seductively sipping chocolate milk shakes with red straws while keeping one eye cocked on the men's room to see who went in but did not come out.

At our Sunday afternoon get-togethers, the men always cooed about how adorable I was, which drove my mother insane with both fear and pride. I am sure she had visions of me being raped out back by the gardenia bush. On the other hand, who better to appreciate her darling, witty, and charming offspring (as she called me) than Miami's most talented and tasteful homosexuals? They always brought me imaginative presents, such as never-before-seen seashells with strange twists and spikes in vibrant colors and exotic Japanese Kabuki dolls in glass boxes. What I really remember is that all the men seemed to wear plaid pants in a rainbow of colors. One man in particular not only specialized in a diverse collection of patterned pants but also loved to steal one of the many hats that my mother wore during the party. After a few drinks, he would rip the hat off her head, place it ever just so on his head, and for the rest of the evening tiptoe around as if he were wearing high heels. Often, after everyone had left, we found him in one of the bedrooms either dancing by himself with his eyes closed or collapsed on my bed sobbing about some lost love. Such were my male role models at the time.

Perhaps one of the boys whispered something in her ear, but Mom suddenly got the brilliant idea that I should audition for TV commercials. I guess she decided to lay the early groundwork for my future stardom—plus, she figured, the extra cash from the residuals wouldn't hurt, either. My mother clearly entertained the idea that all of us should be in the public eye and live off of our assorted talents. I don't know what product she thought I was going to sell, but she truly believed with all her heart that I was camera worthy. However, my performance was less than stunning. During the screen test, I couldn't remember my name. Whenever they asked me questions, I stuck my entire hand in my mouth, swiveled back and forth, and made bathroom noises. Sadly, her career as a stage mother was disappointing and short lived.

Not wanting to totally let her down, I surreptitiously entered the Channel 2 children's Christmas card contest. My hand-drawn menorah drowning in glue and expressionistic glitter tied for first prize with some girl's prim drawing of a Christmas tree. My passionate desire to be an artist was quickly surfacing. The night that the television station

called to announce my prize was the first and last time I ever won any
contest. I probably won not because of artistic merit but because mine
was the only Hanukkah card submitted. I'm sure my mother felt that
maybe, just maybe, public acclaim was right around the corner. My father was pleased that I was showing signs of artistic promise. For him,
being an artist was one of the most important things anyone could do
with his or her life. The ability to transcribe invisible sensations into
tangible works of art was nothing short of a miracle, even if it had to
start with a glitter menorah.

The holiday card winners were to be featured on an after-school
television special to discuss the artistic themes of our festive creations.
This was my first brush with stardom and major media exposure. Unfortunately, auditioning for commercials did not do much to improve
my lackluster television persona. During the broadcast I stared at the
floor and talked to myself while the little blond girl in the nice party
dress smiled and stole the show.

After my television debut, my proud parents took me out to a
swanky adult restaurant with pink lighting and an aquarium filled
with slow-moving lobsters. There was a Shirley Temple for me, a
whiskey sour for Mom, and a double Manhattan with two cherries for
Pop. Having finally gotten her son on TV, I'm sure Mom was hopeful
that I was headed toward the bright lights and the big city.

Soon after the broadcast, Mom decided that we needed to maintain some semblance of northern decorum around the house while
curing me of my recently acquired cracker accent. During my forma-
tive years in nursery school and kindergarten, I had been taught by
single women from Tennessee. As a result, I had become completely
unintelligible to my parents as I slurred my words in that southern
kind of way. Even today I unconsciously slip into "yes ma'ams" and
"y'alls" more often than I care to admit. After two drinks I can begin
to sound like some Confederate who never left Pensacola. Mom was
growing increasingly concerned that I would end up living in an old
plywood shed out by the Everglades, raising chickens and goats and
eating fresh-caught rattlesnake for dinner. So she shipped me off to

the Playhouse Country Day School in the hope that the stern Bible-thumping principal and his wife would erase the bluegrass influence and get me ready for some smart prep school in the Northeast.

At the Playhouse, I was surrounded by boys and girls whose Baptist and Methodist parents, unlike our neighbors, spent their Saturdays doing something else besides shooting coons. I met church mothers who ran bake sales and fathers who owned gas stations or sold insurance. Since my parents were both self-employed in the style industry, I had no idea that such exotic people existed. These kids had fathers who looked like the ones I saw on TV. Their mothers were demure and acted like good wives—preparing pitchers of Kool-Aid and getting the Slip 'n Slide or the Water Wiggle working in the backyard. Ignoring such standard maternal duties, my mother could often be found cha-cha-cha-ing with the best of them till 3:00 a.m. in some dive off Collins Avenue.

Mom also loved anything calypso. We had a stack of steel drum and Harry Belafonte albums. Often, I would come home from school and put on my all-time favorite song, "Mama Look A Boo Boo," from *Belafonte at Carnegie Hall.* I would sing and play rhythm on one of the brightly painted voodoo drums that several years earlier Pop had brought back from Haiti.

The story of Pop's trip to Haiti was one of Mom's favorites. During her dinner parties, after the plates had been cleared, she would open a fresh pack of Camels, screw a smoke into her cigarette holder, flip open her Dunhill lighter, and take a long drag. She was now ready to entertain her guests with this epic.

One afternoon, as she often recounted, she came running into my bedroom, threw some clothes on me, and scooped me up in her arms. I was around three years old at the time. Mom put the top down on the convertible as we drove Pop to the airport for yet another "client meeting" in some sun-parched, impoverished country surrounded by water the color of glass. This time, the country was Haiti, land of forbidden voodoo and Barbancourt rum.

Just a week before, Pop received several phone calls at the office from the Haitian ambassador to the United States and from the commercial attaché. The president of Haiti, Paul Magloire, needed the public rooms of the palace freshened up ASAP, since he was expecting a visit from U.S. vice president Richard Nixon to review the troops. What that really meant was that Dick was going to drop a pot of foreign-aid money on Magloire, which would never see the light of day after it landed silently in his Swiss bank account. What they didn't tell my father was that the Haitians had already gone through one decorator, an Italian. Seems the poor guy was unable to get the job done in time and, as a result, had disappeared without a trace. His body was never found. Rumors circulated that he was either killed by the president's secret police or was the victim of some pretty powerful voodoo. Most likely it was a combination of the two—voodoo first and murder later. It would have been helpful if my father had been informed of this minor detail before he agreed to take the job.

Given the fact that the palace redo was a top government priority, the Haitian ambassador sent an old Pan Am prop plane with the interior ripped out to pick up my father in Miami and fly him to a barely paved landing strip known officially as Port-au-Prince International Airport. My father's presence at the palace was a matter of utmost urgency. Met by a solid-black Cadillac and whisked through customs without even opening his suitcase, Pop was personally greeted by the smiling president back at the palace. President Magloire spoke to him in heavily accented English, a gesture reserved only for those foreign guests of great importance. My father took a look around and realized he needed a few basic things, like a tape measure, pins, electric sewing machines, and a few hundred yards of the best French silk. Pop sent a telegram to my mother with a laundry list of items needed to get the job done. With barely any phone service, a telephone call was out of the question.

Back in Miami, Mom headed over to their office on fashionable Lincoln Road and began throwing bolts of fabric and boxes of tools out the window to the waiting Haitian army officer downstairs. The ambassador called Pan Am and had them bump everybody off the next flight back to Haiti and fill the plane with the necessary materials for the palace makeover. Like a pro, Pop worked around the clock and completed the job in less than a week despite the country's erratic delivery of electric power, which made sewing somewhat difficult.

With the job finished and the palace sparkling, the president held a celebratory dinner in honor of my father. After the guests had finished their first glass of wine, Mrs. President announced her vision that with a proper palace she could become the reigning Queen Mother of the Caribbean basin. She invited Pop to stay on and redo the place, top to bottom. No thanks, he said, got to get home to my wife and kid back in the States. Smiling in a way that only madam dictators can, she said, "Oh, but you must." At that moment the president's elite team of thugs and murderers swarmed the dinner table, and my father found himself looking at twelve American-made machine guns. Backup arrived with machetes drawn. He was taken hostage, bound, gagged, and pistol-whipped until he agreed to make the palace the shining star of the Caribbean. Threats against my mother and me were also uttered with "We have people back in Miami that can do great harm to your family." Until that moment, he had no idea of the serious occupational hazards and risks of being a decorator. I seriously doubt that anyone in the high pantheon of interior decorating, from Billy Baldwin to Sister Parish, was ever pistol-whipped over a job—that is, unless they wanted to be.

Never one to let a few machine guns or guards keep him down, Pop waited until his personal guard was asleep, and, just like in the movies, climbed out the bathroom window. He hailed the first local donkey to come along and paid the owner to get him to the airport pronto, where he boarded the next flight to Miami. While the plane's three propellers (one wasn't working) spun furiously in preparation for takeoff, my father's gun-toting friends from dinner suddenly stormed the plane and once again pointed their weapons at his head. He was handcuffed, blindfolded, and pushed into the backseat of a waiting army jeep. It was back to the palace for several more months of sewing, measuring, and making French fantasia.

Back home, Mom was preparing for widowhood as weeks turned into months with no word from her hostage husband. There was not the usual phone call asking us to pack our bags and join Pop that afternoon by the pool. Nor was there the sudden knock at the door from some rich person's representative telling us to be ready in ten minutes for our ride to the airport. There was nothing but silence from the great republic of Haiti.

Mom spent the next six months pleading with the U.S. State Department, the FBI, and the U.S. embassy to launch a search-and-rescue mission for her husband. For some reason, hunting down a missing decorator was just not one of the government's top priorities. Every U.S. agency slammed its door in her face. I was constantly asking annoying and unanswerable questions such as "Where's Poppa?" Mom did her best, inventing countless explanations as to why my father wasn't around. I was beginning to get used to the idea that I was now a fatherless child.

Under the watchful eyes of armed guards, Pop made Mrs. Magloire the most splendid palace imaginable. Marble and mahogany, silk and brocade were flown in from all over the world, thanks to an unlimited budget that magically appeared in the poorest country of the Western hemisphere. The palace renovation was a testament to the critical importance of American foreign aid. Rest assured that our tax dollars purchased the finest-quality draperies and silk ottomans that money can buy.

Finally, when every inch of that palace had the divine Lew Smith touch, the president shook my father's hand, gave him a glass paperweight containing his official portrait as full and final payment for services rendered, and sent him back home.

Having secured his freedom from decorator detention, Pop returned to his daily routine of satisfying the needs and fantasies of the mega-rich. I was content growing up in my own private jungle, chasing wild rabbits in the backyard. Life, for the very last time, was completely normal.

two

•

War on Sanpaku

Fast-forward to October 1962—the height of the Cuban missile crisis. I was ten, listening to the air-raid sirens screaming war from the roof of the Loews Riviera movie theater, which was over two miles away. Mom was in the kitchen making meat loaf for what she imagined might be our last supper. She had rushed home from work at my father's design studio to the terrifying accompaniment of piercing air-raid sirens that filled the city. Talks between the superpowers and Fidel had not gone well that day. With all the sirens going off, I was convinced that the world was about to end, and we were all going to die.

My favorite radio station, WFUN-AM, was broadcasting nothing but a single piercing tone followed by a recorded message: "This is an alert from your emergency broadcast station. Stay tuned for further instructions." Of course, there were no further instructions, because there was nowhere else to go. Unlike most of the country, Miami did not have real bomb shelters. The water table was too high. If you dug down a couple feet, you hit brackish green-gray water, despite the fact that *Miami* was the Seminole word for "sweet water." Because of this elevated ground water, there are no cemeteries on Miami Beach. The bodies would quickly contaminate the water, and what would all the tourists drink? As a result of our unfortunate proximity to ground water, we had no place to hide in an underground bomb shelter and enjoy canned peas and powdered milk like the rest of the country.

Usually Mom liked me to talk to her while she made dinner. As soon as she came home, she would find me in my bedroom looking at picture books of archaeology or modern art and say, "Come talk to me in the kitchen." That night was different. Instead of seeking me out, Mom just opened the front door, threw her pocketbook on the black-and-white zebra-patterned lounge, and went right into the kitchen. After a while I wandered in, a bit perturbed that she had not issued her usual invitation.

The big pink Philco refrigerator was humming noisily as she squished meat, eggs, and crumbled Saltine crackers in a large Pyrex bowl. Just as I was about to announce my presence, the sirens wailed again. They seemed to be either louder or coming closer. I was now officially scared. Having spent several years in school perfecting my "duck-and-cover" routine that would protect me in the event of nuclear war, I quickly climbed into the cabinet under the sink, huddled next to the Ajax, and waited for the war to start while Mom chopped onions.

Soon Pop arrived, looking sharp in his gray suit. He wore his usual Rooster tie with its horizontal stripes in muted tones, held in place by his free-form gold tie tack. All of my father's clothes seemed to come from another era. Thinking back, I now realize that he dressed as if it were still 1930. He wore dark, elegant, pleated pants, and if you looked close enough, you could see the small, subtle patterns floating throughout the weave. On several occasions I had asked why his pants were so baggy. I was trying to understand the purpose of those strange folds of fabric on the front of his pants. All of my school pants were Perma Press and pleat free, giving me that sleek sixties look. The pleats seemed to precede him as he entered a room and made him appear bigger than he actually was.

He was a compact man with a dark mustache, at a time when few, if any, American men wore mustaches. It gave him a distinguished European air that women found attractive. His salt-and-pepper hair was turning grayer by the day on a head that seemed round and free of sharp angles. When he smiled, his face flushed with happiness. His voice was melodious, and he spoke with a precise and kind intonation, as if he had read endless amounts of poetry during his youth. This camouflage carefully hid his lack of any real formal education.

As the sirens continued to wail, the atmosphere became claustrophobic. All my senses had been short-circuited by the noise, which seemed to be closing in on me. I decided to stay under the sink. Peeking through the doors of my makeshift bomb shelter, I watched my parents talking in very serious tones. It seemed almost as if they were going to have a fight. I cracked the door a little farther to hear what my father was saying but without jeopardizing my safety. "There's something I've been meaning to tell you. I have some bad news we need to discuss before this war starts."

All chopping stopped. There was an immediate and strained silence in the kitchen. Pop just stood there while my mother stared at the iceberg lettuce on the counter waiting to be washed. Dinner was on hold.

"I have *sanpaku*."

"You what?" my mother asked, still staring at the lettuce. Her face had a look as if she had stepped barefoot on a piece of glass. "What is this *sanpaku*, like cancer?" She began to slowly pull the outer leaves off the lettuce. In that split second, she must have imagined herself as a young widow with a child to take care of and no real income to speak of. Perhaps being vaporized by Castro's nuclear weapons was not such a bad option after all. I could tell that Mom was not in the mood for this conversation. The threat of the bombs was upsetting her, and I think she was already overwhelmed preparing for her last night on earth.

My father attempted to explain this mysterious disease. "There's too much yang in my body. My system is being poisoned with an acidic pH. If I don't correct this, my body will succumb to disease, most likely cancer. And it's not just me. You're toxic. Philip is toxic. We're all toxic." My father's voice began to rise in intensity, which it rarely did. He was clearly upset. Something very serious was going on.

This toxic stuff worried me; whatever toxic was, it did not sound good. I decided that bombs or no bombs, I needed to join the family predinner conversation. Jumping out from under the sink, I pleaded with my father, "Poppa, what's toxic? Am I going to die too?" I started crying and hugging his legs.

"See what you're doing? You're scaring the kid. Now he's going to have nightmares and will have to come sleep with us. Thanks a lot." Mom got tough and angry when she was upset. Pop was the opposite: the angrier he was, the calmer he became. To her credit, my mother was seeking some clarification about this mysterious disease that was killing her husband. "Can you please start at the beginning and explain to me exactly what it is you're talking about? Don't we have more important things to worry about right now instead of this toxic nonsense? What did the doctor say about this? You have about another five minutes until Castro wipes us off the face of the earth, so start talking." The air-raid sirens had revved up again, and the noise was getting on everybody's nerves.

Pop was shouting to make himself heard over the piercing wail. "You know I don't believe in doctors. What do they know? You think a doctor is smart enough to know that I'm sanpaku? You know what your wonderful doctors do? They give you some pills that make you sicker than when you walked in the door. Then they give you more pills to counteract the first pills, and when those don't work, they start shooting you full of things like cortisone that rot your insides, and then you die. Look what happened to my brother Ruby. He's dead now, thanks to the brilliant doctors and their goddamn medicine. And while the doctors make money, and the drug companies make money, and the insurance people make money, you have the privilege of dying as they take your last dime."

Doctors were always a big source of contention between my parents. Mom thought they were gods who had created germ-free modern living, and Pop thought they were nothing but ignorant devils. Ever since I could remember, Pop kept his medicine cabinet filled with thick brown bottles of homeopathic medicine, which he imported from England, with strange-sounding names like Allium cepa and Rhus tox. The moment anyone got sick, Pop pulled out his enormous *Materia Medica,* the diagnostic bible of homeopathy, and began prescribing tiny, sweet white pills. I don't know where or when he learned to diagnose and prescribe homeopathy, but as far back as I can remember, this was his preferred method of treatment.

At the time, it was nearly impossible to get homeopathic medicine in this country. Usually when his shipment of pills arrived by freighter months after he'd ordered it, it was immediately impounded by customs. Pop would then receive a call from some customs agent requesting that he come down to talk to them. I remember our frequent trips to the Miami docks to try to claim his packages. After a lengthy interrogation by officials from customs and often the Food and Drug Administration, the bottles were usually destroyed, and my father was warned that he could serve jail time for importing unregulated pharmaceuticals into this country. But he would just order them again and again until some sleepy customs agent handed him the package and waved him through.

However, when I was sick, I wanted to be treated by a real doctor in a white coat with a cold silver stethoscope around his neck—not by my father, in a pair of madras shorts, opening a brown bottle, shaking out some small white tablets, and saying, "Here, put these under your tongue." All the kids at school went to doctors to get shots, pills, and lollipops. What I really wanted was a penicillin injection like everyone else.

When the oral polio vaccine was first being tested, Pop was

convinced that it was part of a government-sponsored medical experiment on unsuspecting American children. "They are putting the polio virus into your body. Anything can go wrong," he said. "You could become paralyzed or even die. Don't go near that stuff. You cannot put that virus in the human body and expect everything to be okay." He was not entirely crazy. When the Salk vaccine was first being administered, portions of the virus were still live and actually created several hundred new cases of polio. But Mom was not about to risk me losing the use of my legs or becoming a poster child for the iron lung.

In protest over whether or not I got the vaccine, she threatened to leave him, then actually moved out, into a pink motel romantically perched on a small waterway just a few minutes away, near the University of Miami. Every day Pop drove me over to see her sitting alone in this small room, and we begged her to come home. My mother had brought nearly a dozen suitcases, several hatboxes, and an assorted collection of wigs in order to camp out in style. The small room was filled with her luggage, which contained about eight months' worth of wardrobe changes. It was considered wildly chic and very a-go-go in the sixties to have numerous wigs in various styles and colors to change your mood, your look, and your mind at a moment's notice. No matter what her wig of the day looked like, Mom always remained a blonde. Her combined annual wig and hat bills must have been equal to the gross national product of Bimini. During our time in the cramped hotel room, my parents engaged in high-level talks about vaccine theory and their marriage. On several occasions my mother would just collapse into a flood of tears. Three days later her walkout achieved its goal. I was back at school, drinking cherry-flavored vaccine out of a tiny paper cup, the kind normally used for urine samples. It was delicious. Immunization against a deadly virus never tasted so good.

"Are you going to die from sanpaku?" I asked as the tears streamed down my face.

My father bent down to look at me and pointed to the bottom of his eye. "You see this little bit of white under my eye?"

I looked cautiously because I was afraid that if I peered too closely,

I would see thousands of sanpaku germs floating around that might jump out and bite me. Just below his dark brown iris, I noticed a bit of white. That didn't strike me as unusual. Everybody had white in their eyes. "Uh-huh," I responded slowly.

Excited that I had seen the white, he explained, "Whenever you see white at the bottom of your eyes, that's how you know you're sanpaku. Normally, when you look straight ahead, your lower eyelid should just touch the bottom of the iris. If it doesn't, and any white is showing, this indicates a high level of toxicity created by the Western diet. It needs to be corrected immediately by balancing your pH levels to reduce your acidity, which causes all this cancer. You don't need a *doctor* to tell you that you are sanpaku. The body tells you what you need to know, if you only know how to listen to it." The word *doctor* was emphasized for the benefit of my mother, who was measuring out the oil and vinegar for the Good Seasons salad dressing with her back to us. She pretended not to be listening to our conversation, which she didn't want to hear anyway.

I wasn't about to rush into the bathroom and self-administer my own sanpaku test. Pop had already told me I was toxic, and I didn't need any additional information on this subject. "So will the doctor give you some medicine that will make the sanpaku go away?" I asked. This disease seemed so serious, I figured that just this once, he would have to see a doctor.

"I'm going to use macrobiotics to cure my sanpaku."

Macrobiotics sounded like some sort of new and advanced form of antibiotics. Whenever other kids at school were sick, they got to stay home and take big pills. Not me. I had to stay in bed shivering with a high fever because my father believed that the fever was nature's way of heating the body to cook the germs and render them harmless. In the process, he claimed, the immune system was enhanced.

As part of his new anti-sanpaku campaign, Pop announced, "In the morning we all start our ten-day macrobiotic brown-rice purification fast to get rid of the sanpaku. This will equalize the acid-alkaline balance in our bodies. Next we'll have three days of coffee enemas prepared with spring water to remove the poisonous residue from our bodies." This did not sound like something I was going to enjoy. Suddenly my fear of nuclear weapons was replaced with an even stronger fear of coffee enemas. I looked over at my mother, who did not seem very excited either. My father was not winning any converts to his new purification program. She had not made any more progress on the dinner preparations. It looked like we would not be eating before midnight, if at all. I knew that it would be easier to get those missiles moved out of Cuba than it would be to get my mother to remove poisonous residue from her body. To her there was nothing more pleasurable than a cigarette and a dry martini—any time of day or night. Smoking was almost a religious rite. Any comments about her tobacco use were considered heresy and punishable by death. There was not a chance in hell or in heaven that she would suddenly become macrobiotic in the interest of cleansing her body of toxic sanpaku.

Trying to stop him in his tracks, my mother exclaimed, "For God's sake, we may not even be alive in the morning! Why don't you just drop this nonsense right now? You and your crazy ideas." Mom had heard enough. With that, she slammed the oven door on the meat loaf and retreated to the bedroom to enjoy her favorite meal—a fresh pack of Camel cigarettes and a pint of Howard Johnson's bright-green pistachio ice cream—while watching *To Tell the Truth*. Mom was a true believer in contradictions and extremes. To her, life was about style, and style was born from extremes.

When I woke up the next morning, I was surprised to find that despite the end-of-the-world nuclear war that had just occurred, everything looked the same. I looked around and didn't see any of the radiation damage I had heard about at school. Nothing was glowing. There were no large craters in our front yard, no mushroom clouds on the horizon.

Just like every other morning, Mr. Woodpecker was trying to peck a hole in the side of our roof. The malaleuca tree outside my window was giving off its customary morning medicinal smell that made me feel as if I was living inside a dentist's office. The air had that particular October clarity and brilliance found only with the tropical light of Miami. The fact that my father was on the verge of toxic death and that my mother was confused and angry seemed to be just a bad dream as the morning light flooded my bedroom.

I went out to the lanai, an architectural import from Hawaii that allows you to live completely open to the tropical elements and still have a stable roof over your head, to start my day. As usual, the parakeets that we let fly around the house were perched in the trees of our indoor garden, chirping away. Then, approaching the dining table, I noticed that my regular bowl of Trix had been replaced by a bowl of cold brown rice. This was neither a good sign nor a pretty sight. Rice was only for dinner, and it should be snow white. Somehow in this new world order of Castro versus the United States of America and the invisible dangers of sanpaku, our meals had been mistakenly inverted. I had never even seen brown rice before. To me it looked like a bowl of small worms. I wondered where my father got this stuff— certainly not at the local Food Fair.

Pop sat at the other end of the table, quietly chewing his brown rice. He was so engrossed in his anti-sanpaku breakfast that he didn't even notice me. Gone was our normal routine of cereal, eggs, Canadian bacon, fresh orange juice, and toasted bialys. Between last night and this morning, my father had become a different person. Instantly I knew that all my fun as a kid was about to end.

At the age of ten, I was not about to sit down and simply be the only acid-balanced, nontoxic macrobiotic kid in all of Miami. I wanted a breakfast that was multicolored, made noise, and had been seen on TV. I took another look at that rice and laid my head on the table and closed my eyes, hoping it would all just go away. If nonviolent protest worked for Gandhi, it sure as hell was going to work for me. Or so I thought. As the minutes passed, I peeked to see if the rice had been removed. Nope. That rice was going to sit there as long as I did. I was not going to get my way on this one. It was unusual for my father to be so adamant about something so small. When it came to the day-to-day details of my upbringing, he largely deferred to my mother. She was mainly concerned with tangible, external aspects of my character. First and foremost I should always be a deferential gentleman, which included holding doors open for ladies of all ages, never arguing over money, always picking up the check, and treating everyone with respect. My father, on the other hand, cared only about the intangible, internal aspects of my being such as indulging and fostering an unlimited imagination, learning to listen to and heed my own inner voice, always being honest with myself and others, and, above all, following my dreams, the most precious of all commodities.

Not acknowledging that something was terribly wrong at our breakfast table, Mom arrived and automatically went into her everyday routine: Folgers instant coffee with two saccharin tablets and a Metracal shake, accompanied by Camel cigarettes before, during, and after. She liked any food that came in a jar and could be mixed with water or swallowed as a pill—one of the major offshoots of the nascent space program. To her all this instant stuff was terribly sophisticated and very modern. After a perfect, modern breakfast for a modern mom, she was ready for the world.

She probably got this idea from reading something in *Life* magazine about some minor starlet who started her day with this exact breakfast regimen. In her mind she was constantly auditioning for whatever dramatic role was necessary at that particular moment: glamorous wife, nightclub swinger, civil rights activist, patron of the arts, socialite. In addition to her long nights in offshore casinos, Mom eventually marched on Washington with Martin Luther King Jr., spoke knowingly about Pollock and de Kooning, and investigated starting a halfway house for drug addicts. She liked being in the forefront of the tides of cultural change. There was a particular cinematic logic to her thinking and how she lived her life—as if she were on camera twenty-four hours a day.

While in starlet mode, she wore sunglasses at all hours of the day and night. Glamour was her first name, and style was her last. Mom had an incredible radar for the latest fashions and somehow by osmosis was able to integrate them into her wardrobe, her speech, or her mannerisms as required. She always knew which way the fashion winds were blowing long before they ever hit the pages of *Vogue*.

At this point in their marriage, Mom perfectly complemented my father both personally and professionally. She was attractive, vivacious, and very comfortable around people with large sums of disposable income who wanted a new bedroom designed for the yacht or a whimsical folly created in back of the house facing the Gulf of Mexico.

My mother enjoyed the social whirl of the small, incestuous fraternity of the decorating world. As second in command, she would do the books, handle difficult clients, and occasionally make grand, sweeping pronouncements that determined the direction of a particular design scheme. At just the right moment, Mom would interrupt a client conference that was going nowhere due to indecision and say with absolute confidence, "Why, Mrs. Parker, I think your house done in black-and-white with a touch of red would be *too* divine."

Mom became a destination for all the decorators along the street. As if on some predetermined flight plan, they would come zooming into Pop's office with their wings flapping and drop the latest gossip on my mother. She worked the office like it was her private booth at the Brown Derby. Squeals of delight escaped her mouth as some decorator whispered to her, ". . . and then Marty said to Mrs. Worthington, 'Excuse me, Mrs. Worthington, but the Salvation Army wouldn't take those chairs even if you paid them, so let's just save you the effort and throw them in the trash right now. After all, that's all those chairs are anyway, nothing but *trash*. Now, I want those chairs out of here *immediately* . . .' "

"Oh, I don't believe he said that; he didn't really, did he? So what did Mrs. Worthington say?"

"Well, that's just the beginning. So then Mrs. Worthington said to Mary—I mean Marty . . ."

And on it went. As the gabfest continued, my father would sketch out new designs for furniture or talk on the phone with clients. My mother was all ears while Pop ignored the gossiping magpies and focused on serious issues, such as whether the piping on a sofa should be magenta or mustard. Occasionally when he went out to meet with a new client, my mother, left alone in the studio, not only held court but would often attract new clients. She had a way, which she never really appreciated, of convincing people with just a few simple phrases that there was a better, chicer, more glamorous way of designing the dining room than what they currently had. And while they were at it, a new sunroom, cabana, and draperies for all twelve rooms wouldn't be such a bad idea, would it?

If it hadn't been for my mother, my father would have been just a plain old heterosexual decorator dressed in dreary suits. Instead she convinced him to wear custom suits and artisan-made jewelry, and drive jazzy cars. She set the tone for all of us. Her style was accepted and admired by my father and his circle, but the outside world was another story.

Those southern hicks had no idea what had just whooshed by them as she glided through the A&P with her black patent leather heels, oversized sunglasses the shade of midnight, her black patent leather pocketbook the size of a small footlocker, massive gold and jade earrings, rings on practically every finger, a small pillbox hat wrapped in black iridescent feathers that looked like crows' wings, and, of course, her gold cigarette holder with an unlit Camel projecting from it. Believe me, at just four-feet-nine, she did not go unnoticed.

From the moment she woke up until she turned off the switch of the Venetian chandelier above their bed, my mother lived as if she were constantly walking into a movie premiere—hers. Any movie was a glamour event, even at the downscale Tropicaire Drive-in Theatre, where an entire car packed with eight people watched a movie for fifty cents, or for free, if you had ten RC Cola bottle caps. At the Tropicaire, we would put down the convertible top, hook the speaker to the window, and watch the movie under the stars. Paradise.

Mom, wearing her darkest sunglasses, always sat straight up in rapt attention, completely absorbed in the film, while Pop and I would swat mosquitoes. Mom was too engrossed in the movie to be bitten.

The bugs knew enough to leave her alone. She explained her natural immunity simply as, "I'm too sour for them." Eventually I would fall asleep in that little concave area where the top went down while my parents sat through double features such as *Gypsy* and *Hatari!* Though Mom pulled off her starlet pose with great panache, occasionally it was a bit too much even for my father. At times, for what he felt was her own good, he would admonish her in an attempt to bring her back to earth. "How can you see a thing with those damn glasses on?" he would say. His practicality only encouraged her to buy another dozen pair. This, in essence, was the yin and yang of my parents' relationship. Mom was always ready for her close-up, while my father was ready for his blast-off to other dimensions.

When Mom got dressed in the morning, it required more effort, concentration, and theatricality than any Broadway star preparing for opening night. Pop had already risen with the birds, had his breakfast, and left for the office. For my mother, her first two waking hours were spent slowly digesting her black coffee and cigarettes. The social column was usually read out loud to no one in particular, with appropriate emphasis when either her or my father's name appeared.

Even her dinner parties made the *Miami News*'s "Party Camera" column, with "Buffet supper celebrating completion of their pentagon-shaped dream house was given by Lew Smith and his wife Esther." The black-and-white photograph shows Mom dishing out her creation to a waiting line of hungry decorators. Below the story is another photograph of "Mr. and Mrs. Rufus Mimms swinging in Lew Smith's backyard." Hmmm.

If my father had a particularly favorable write-up, she'd lean over to his side of the bed, pick up the phone, and dial the office. "Guess what Kay wrote about your new designs for the Allen residence? Uh-huh, yes . . . but she didn't mention that fabulous revolving bar that you had designed at poolside. Ummm, only three photographs, but at least one's in color on the front page. No, she didn't show the master bedroom, only the living room. Okay, enough chitchat, I haven't even put my face on yet, let me go . . ." After the daily news briefing, she then would fiddle with the crossword puzzle for a half hour while the gold cigarette holder dangled from her red lips long after the cigarette had been extinguished.

There were times when she would throw the society page across the room in a fit of rage. After having just had lunch with Frank Lloyd Wright at an American Institute of Architects event, she was justifiably furious when the paper mistakenly quoted the maestro. "Listen, what he said to me during dessert was that he thought Miami was nothing but a future slum. You don't think they'd put *that* in the paper, do you? Of course not. They're nothing but a bunch of cultural illiterates. They wouldn't know great architecture if it fell on them. But that's exactly what he said to me. And instead they print some meaningless trash. Did they mention that little pat on the back that he gave to Alfred Browning Parker, which should have been more of a hug? After all, he was one of Frank's best students at Taliesin. No, they're too stupid to understand the symbolism of that gesture. Alfred is a genius. And he knows how to pick them; that's why Alfred works with your father on the interiors. Honestly, I need to get that editor on the phone . . ." But that call would have to wait; she needed to focus on her jewelry fitting. Would it be black pearls and jade or just plain emeralds today? Mom was lucky: her sea captain brother, Max, used to roam the world and would pick up a few precious "rocks" in every port. My father would then have one of his jeweler friends fashion them into massive gold-encrusted works of art that doubled as both conversation pieces and lethal weapons.

My mother did not have to color-coordinate her jewelry to that day's outfit, since she wore the same black dress every day. Her closet was filled with rows and rows of identical little black cocktail dresses, all made by her mother from an old Dior pattern that she had bought from the back pages of *Vogue*. It was a kind of uniform, as she served in the fashion army on the front lines of style.

It would often be close to noon before the blackout shades in the bedroom were finally lifted to admit the white-hot glare of the Miami sun. With half the day now gone, she was just about ready for her cameo appearance at my father's design studio as bon vivant, confidante, and personal secretary to Mr. Lew Smith, interior designer to the stars.

One night my father was attending a meeting of the Designers and Decorators Guild, where he was acting president. I was lying in bed with my mother, watching Johnny Carson as he interviewed some starlet about her new celebrity crash diet that consisted only of coffee, cigarettes, and pills. While she looked great, Johnny made it very clear that he did not think this diet was a good idea, and neither did I. But here was a live report from *Valley of the Dolls,* and Mom was all ears. She shushed me to be quiet whenever the starlet spoke. Mom's intense interest made it evident that she was taking the exact same diet medication as someone on TV. I used to fish the slim, clear compartmentalized plastic box out of Mom's enormous pocketbook and stare at the beautiful assortment of green, yellow, and pink pills. They looked identical to those candy dots on long white strips of waxed paper that I devoured by the yard. The starlet's pill diet confirmed for Mom that she was in sync with the Hollywood elite even though she was living in Miami and married to a kooky decorator.

It didn't take a brilliant analyst to realize that the recent arrival of brown rice and coffee enemas was going to present a serious image problem for my mother. At the time, tragic starlets dined on what could kill them—not what was going to lead them toward longevity. There was no way Mom was going to find brown rice even remotely glamorous.

In an effort to convince her that some celebrities were interested in keeping their looks through diet and exercise, Pop bought her a copy of Gayelord Hauser's book *Look Younger, Live Longer.* Hauser was the 1950s health and fitness guru to many of Hollywood's stars from the golden era. Among other things, he advocated steaming one's face daily with boiling water seasoned with an herbal laxative mixture, Swiss Kriss, in order to remove the impurities from the skin and create movie-star radiance. Mom couldn't be bothered. She was too busy reading her stack of assorted trashy detective novels.

As a last resort, Pop tried to appeal to her Hollywood sensibility and informed her that Mae West was a devotee of daily enemas. Wrong role model. He didn't realize that Mom thought Mae West was vulgar. He would have scored more points if he had mentioned Audrey Hepburn. Problem was, now that I think about it, I doubt that Audrey Hepburn would have enjoyed having a coffee enema for breakfast. Despite his relentless efforts at conversion, Mom deftly managed to escape the joys of macrobiotics. However, I wasn't so lucky.

three

•

The Human Ray Gun

"*Sir,* that is *not* a jacket."

The sniffy maître d' raised his eyebrows as high as they would go and grandly pointed to the framed sign behind his podium. Executed in elegant cursive script, it read "Gentlemen Must Wear Jackets."

My father and I were standing before the maître d' of a posh French restaurant in Coral Gables. We were wearing matching Nehru jackets made of a shimmering gold brocade fabric left over from one of his Palm Beach jobs. I had accessorized my outfit with a primitive lead casting of the ankh, the Egyptian symbol for life—purchased by mail from the Psychedelicatessen head shop in New York—as well as a few strands of multicolored peace beads that I strung up myself. Mom was off to the side in her black cocktail dress, sunglasses, and patent leather heels, studying the menu with unusual intensity. Her gold bracelets clanked as she turned the pages.

Pop looked down at his gorgeous creation and couldn't understand what the maître d' was saying about jackets. It was as if he were speaking a foreign language. Unfortunately, I understood what he said perfectly. Now at the age of thirteen, I was a flawless translator of the experiences that transpired between my family and the overwhelmingly hostile outside world. What he was really saying was, "This restaurant does not serve freaks—go away."

We would have had a better chance of being seated if we had presented ourselves as loud, gregarious performers who had just finished taping *The Jackie Gleason Show,* but instead we were too blissed out to be in showbiz. Our peace-love-om-shanti-shanti routine was new in town and had never been seen by the Miami establishment. By now Pop had a whole closet filled with Nehru jackets. There was no chance that he was going to return to his earlier incarnation of a suit and tie for dinner. In 1966, he was digging the Nehru scene. What he should have said to the maître d' was, "Hey, daddy-o, I'm, like, in the guru groove and looking for some cool cordon bleu, can you dig it?" We would have eaten out more often if he had just gotten the vocabulary down.

"But this *is* a jacket," my father protested. In his mind, he was better dressed than the maître d' in his crummy black suit. Not to mention that the fabric in that Nehru jacket alone was worth more than what we would have spent eating out for the next month.

"*Sir!*" The maître d' leaned forward. The conversation was over. We would just get in the car and go somewhere else where we were not wanted.

When we *did* manage to break through the security detail at the front door, it never failed that the entire restaurant fell silent as we walked to our table. People stopped eating and eyed us with concern. Miami had never seen a live impersonation of the Addams Family up close. I seemed to be the only one who noticed that we were the center of attention. Pop was perfectly content being transcendental, and Mom was happy to finally be out of the house. The maître d' always scrambled to find us a table as far away as possible from the other diners. I'm surprised that they didn't hold tablecloths in front of us while we ate or stick us in the kitchen next to the dishwasher.

Ever since Pop had begun his macrobiotic transformation, we rarely ate out. It was difficult, actually impossible, to find a restaurant that served *hijiki* seaweed as the main course and *umeboshi* plums for dessert. As a result, we ate at home—where I ate what Pop ate, and Mom ate whatever she wanted. Mom didn't care if she went straight to macrobiotic hell.

For my mother, dining out was a pleasure; it was elegant and an adventure. She loved knowing the chefs at the various restaurants and asking for the secret recipe for the salad dressing or the key lime pie. For example, at the restaurant on top of the Miami airport, Mom felt like she was eating at Chasen's when the chef came over with a wooden salad bowl the size of a satellite dish and prepared his special Caesar salad with fresh eggs just for her. As he narrated each step and ingredient, she pulled out her huge black Parker fountain pen and took notes.

There were exceptions. No matter how many times we went to Joe's Stone Crab and she wandered back into the kitchen to beg the chef for his key lime pie recipe, she could never duplicate it at home. Turns out he intentionally left out just one ingredient, which he would never tell my mother, and the secret died with him.

As I had anticipated at the start of our evening's adventure, we ended up back at the house, where Pop and I had leftover brown rice from breakfast, and Mom boiled up two kosher hot dogs. This was typical not only of our attempts to eat in restaurants but to interact with the outside world. Because we were on our own planet, we were treated like unwelcome aliens wherever we went.

Over the next few months, the contents and the atmosphere of our house began to change. Just as my father's thinking had become more transcendental, so too did his interiors. Our once modernist house began to look like an opium den as seen through the lens of a Technicolor Hollywood movie. Heavily perfumed smoke from burning pots of incense in thick bronze antique Chinese censers now mingled in the hot, humid air with Mom's ever-present pale blue cigarette smoke. Brown rice in heavy cast-iron pots was constantly cooking on the stove. Ceiling fans slowly mixed this eclectic potpourri into an intoxicating, strange ether. All of this scented haze gave the house a languid, dreamlike feeling, as if time had stopped in our own private universe. Low-hanging Japanese rice-paper lanterns softly lit the living room, while casually tinkling wind chimes stirred by the slow-moving tropical breeze added to the esoteric sound track. Strange surrealist sculptures, such as a pair of fractured hands holding a bleeding heart, were carefully placed in front of cryptic Balinese calendars—illustrated with mythical sea monsters devouring cowering humans. Calder-esque mobiles made of assorted metals by my father hung from the ceiling and moved slowly in random, hypnotic rhythms.

Every morning as my clock radio alarm went off, I would slowly open my eyes to the sounds of the Beach Boys and the weather report, which rarely varied from "seventy-four degrees and sunny." I would lie in bed for another few minutes, dreading the idea of getting up and going to school. As I finally got out of bed, I could hear the distant strains of Japanese *shakuhachi* flute music or Ravi Shankar's sitar coming from the living room. This was the new background music for my father's morning ritual. He now awoke early to practice his yoga asanas, pelvic "fire" breathing, meditation, and Buddhist chants. Somehow he had discovered the one and only yoga teacher in all of Miami, who taught him at age sixty-two to stand on his head and sit in full lotus position. This was the first I had ever heard of yoga or seen it practiced. When I mentioned to a teacher at school that my father started his morning with an hour of yoga, she didn't know what the word meant.

With his exercises completed, he fired up the blender for one of his special health drinks, which included wheat germ, liquid lecithin, raw eggs, brewer's yeast, honey, apple cider vinegar, juice, and yogurt. Occasionally he would be inspired and throw in something green: a cucumber, a stalk of celery, or an entire aloe leaf from the backyard, for "good digestion." The result was unpalatable, as I was often forced to attest. If Mom stumbled into the kitchen while he was mixing up his "mess," as she called it, she dramatically rolled her eyes, grabbed a can of Metracal, and fled before she could be offered a glassful of vital green froth. She then retreated to more important matters, like putting on her makeup.

As soon as I heard the *toot-toot* of the yellow school bus, I was ready for my Academy Award–worthy performance of a normal, average kid. When the school bus door swung open, I greeted my fellow classmates with a beaming smile intended to say, "I have just woken up in a household where Mom served bacon and eggs, and my father finished the morning paper before he left for the office to sell life insurance policies." What that smile and the rest of the day actually required was that I would have to radically rein in every one of my natural eccentricities, seal my lips about my wacky parents, and with great strain appear to be just a normal kid.

Of course, having a lesbian golf pro and an aristocratic Cuban pedophile as teachers did not exactly help to reorient my compass toward normality. My homeroom teacher, Miss Davis, better known as Bobbi, started class every Monday by showing off her weekend tournament wins. One week it was a diamond ring that she would flash in our faces; the following week it was a new car, and so on. Bobbi was aggressive and proud of her overt athleticism. Every single day she dressed in her signature color—turquoise—complemented by her closely cropped brassy blond hair with dark roots. Her tops were always tight and stretchy, which fully displayed her large, tapered, and very pointy breasts. They were so sharp that some of the boys worried that if they accidentally bumped into Miss Davis's chest, they could have their eyes poked out, while others had trouble concealing their boners as she walked by.

Bobbi decided immediately that she didn't like me and classified me as a "discipline problem." In order to demonstrate who was in charge, she would dig her nails in my arms until I began to bleed, pull me out of my chair by my hair, and, on several occasions, "acci-dentally" throw me down the stairs. During phys ed, which consisted of volleyball, she insisted on always playing opposite me. The result was that all her returns were spike balls that bonked me on the head every time. Eventually my mother grew concerned about my patches of missing hair and constant black-and-blue marks. When she called the principal, he told her that I had a balance problem that needed to be reviewed by a medical professional. My story of a sadistic teacher seemed too fantastic to be believed by anyone.

Concerned that I was fabricating this persecution complex, they herded me through a vast array of medical evaluations, including ses-sions with a child psychiatrist who showed me Rorschach tests that all looked like caricatures of gyrating African dancers. After endless weeks of assessments, all the psychiatrist ended up with was a diag-nosis that I had an acute sensitivity for color that he had never seen before. His prescription: get Philip a dog; he needs a friend.

Mr. Rodriguez was part of the first wave of upper-class Cubans who fled Castro's revolution and found a job teaching us classical penmanship. Before we began the day's adventure of exploring the more cursive aspects of the alphabet, Mr. Rodriguez would peer at me through his thick black glasses and, after several minutes of this silent visual interrogation, publicly declare my budding Beatle haircut a disaster. I was then ordered to the bathroom, where we would have a little hairstyling session with his big black comb. Gently, he would part my hair to the side and slowly comb it into a more traditional style. He would step back and admire his salon skills and then pat my head and say, in his heavily accented English, "Now, isn't that bet-ter?" Only then would he notice that I looked a little rumpled. Over the next several minutes he would tug on my shirt and carefully tuck it in until I looked like a little cadet. We would then return to class to resume the day's lesson. No one ever seemed to notice that the two of us would disappear from class every day for a good half hour and that upon return I looked remarkably different.

During recess, while the other kids roughhoused in the play yard,

I would wander out into the back alley behind the school, where there was a body shop. The walls were filled with blond pinups from *Playboy*. I would stare at them while the guys fixed cars. The mechanics would jab one another and point at me. They loved this idea of a little kid gawking at their nudie shots. Thus was the cycle of my day: watching Pop stand on his head, lesbian male-o-phobia, pedophilia, macho mechanics, and then home to a nice hot dish of macrobiotic adzuki beans and organic brown rice.

Macrobiotics sparked Pop's appetite for physical and spiritual transformation that could be achieved through dietary extremes. This was a strange concept in the time of TV dinners and where the only fresh vegetable sold in supermarkets was iceberg lettuce. Every few days Pop embarked on yet another obscure-sounding fast that was meant to purify a specific organ or internal system. For example, his beet fast was intended to cleanse the liver, the organ dedicated to filtering all of the toxins in the body. The grape fast would rebalance his acidity-alkalinity. It was not unusual for him to follow a ten-day rice fast with a fifteen-day juice fast. Once this phase of fasting was complete, he would then slowly prepare himself for solid food by drinking cups of hot water with the juice of half a lemon squeezed into them. It might then be another three or four days before the first morsel of brown rice entered his mouth. Once he began eating again, each mouthful of solid food had to be chewed one hundred times before swallowing. This was an idea that he found in one of his ancient books on yoga philosophy: "All digestion begins in the mouth. The enzymes in your saliva must thoroughly mix with your food so that you can extract optimal nutrition from everything you eat." Each meal became a major project in the reconstruction of the body and mind.

I alternated between being curious and being totally uninterested in Pop's evolving diet fanaticism. At times I wanted to be a supreme thirteen-year-old yogi, and at other times I wanted to be a typical kid and eat as many Snickers bars as I could. Every so often I joined Pop on a ten-day fast, which pushed my already skinny body toward emaciation. He had convinced me that I needed to purge myself of all toxins, which, left untreated, would eventually induce disease and death. During the first three days of any fast, I felt dizzy, unable to concentrate, and horribly hungry. Mom usually ignored any dietary extremism on our parts and continued to eat as she always had. She categorized these dietary adventures as a type of father and son outing.

I begged Pop to let me stay at home during a fast. Nope. I had to go to school, as fasting was supposed to be part of one's everyday life and nothing out of the ordinary. By the fifth or sixth day, I emerged from the clouds with a sense of mental clarity and a renewed stream of physical energy. On Saturdays we visited Nancy, the colonic specialist in a crisp white uniform, who irrigated my young colon with a big smile.

My normal appetite was always being curtailed, either through fasts or the dictum that the stomach should never be completely full. While other kids stuffed themselves with sweets and hamburgers, I had to carefully calibrate my eating according to strict yogic principles so that at the end of any meal my stomach would be filled with one-third food, one-third liquid, and one-third air.

During this time of various fasts, my father frequently mentioned his goal of eventually becoming a breatharian, a practitioner of an esoteric form of yoga. This was one of the few goals that, fortunately, he never achieved. Breatharians are those who have refined their body's mental and metabolic processes to the point where they are able to live solely off rarefied magnetic particles in the air known as *prana*. They breathe, but they do not eat. I could just see us at dinner parties as the hostess passed along her favorite dish: "No thanks, we'll just have some air" or "We're already full from breathing."

These ongoing fasts seemed to be the official launching pad for my father's grand philosophical search. Possibly the lack of food altered his brain chemistry and encouraged him to begin asking larger, deeper questions about his own life. He began an aggressive reading program on every aspect of esoteric spirituality. In order to keep up, he enrolled both of us in the Evelyn Wood Speed Reading Dynamics made popular by the late President Kennedy. So many books, so little time. At night we would sit in class moving our fingers across and down pages while supposedly retaining everything we read at a thousand words a minute.

In 1966 he began reading everything he could about the philosophy of yoga, which led to an interest in reincarnation. One metaphysical topic led to another. Over time his exploration of the arcane began to unfold as if he were following a well-defined syllabus. His esoteric books were not easily purchased. To obtain these long-out-of-print titles, Pop patiently wrote letters of inquiry to small, dusty bookstores in New York or London that specialized in wacky, hard-to-find books. Most of these were published in the early 1920s during the last great wave of interest in spiritualist matters. Weeks and often months passed between when he mailed his request and the time he found a package wrapped in brown paper and string waiting in our mailbox.

Through his readings, Pop became fascinated with the idea that he had been here before and would be back again. Mom wasn't buying any of it. She believed that we have only one life to live, and we'd better make the best of it. When she tried to have civilized discussions with him about her views on these topics, they went nowhere. At this point in his path, his views were so far out that he was looking for agreement, not logic, and certainly not dissension.

One evening, just at twilight, my father and I were sitting in near darkness. As we continued to talk, we must have looked like talking-head silhouettes shrouded in black. We could barely make each other out. He began explaining the concept of reincarnation, which I had never heard before. Suddenly my life seemed a little less solid. I began to feel completely transparent as I imagined the ghosts from my past lives surrounding me. The idea that this was not my only life really scared me. I didn't want to have another life either as an Egyptian prince or as a high priest in Atlantis; I wanted this one. He laughed when I told him that I didn't like this subject. The laugh made me uncomfortable. It was the kind of Vincent Price all-knowing laugh that implied, "You foolish young thing, you can fight this strange idea all you want, but one day you will succumb . . ."

His curiosity about reincarnation naturally led him to the provocative mythology that surrounds the pyramids. Pop was especially fond of an out-of-print book from England on the secret science of the pyramids. This was not your average pyramid power book positing that the pyramids acted as landing cones on the runway for errant flying saucers but instead a scientific treatise the size of a large city's yellow pages. *The Great Pyramid: Its Divine Message,* printed in 1925, featured complex fold-out tables with such dense titles as "Pyramid Noon Reflexions During the Winter Half of the Year," providing the reader with numerous calculations of the sun's altitude along with azimuth of apex ridge of "reflexion." Another chart offered information on the "Precession of the Equinoxes—The Solar Year in 4699 BC." "The Sed Hebs of Dynasties XVIII and XIX" detailed the genealogy of specific Egyptian dynasties.

Pop read this book as seriously as if he were in Bible study class trying to gain enlightenment from the book of Revelation. He must have felt that this book contained some missing key that would illuminate his life. Over time he filled several notebooks with quotes and observations from the book. I would flip through the book and carefully pull out the diagrams of the secret chambers within the Great Pyramid and imagine becoming an archaeologist. In my father's growing library, this book was like a magic carpet that transported me to other worlds.

The prophetic messages supposedly contained in the Great Pyramid led my father to read about Edgar Cayce, the famous sleeping prophet. During the 1920s Cayce, a simple churchgoing man, was able to diagnose and provide remedies for various illnesses while asleep in a deep trance. Once he went into a trance, associates would bring by "patients" with difficult-to-treat ailments. While in this state, Cayce was able to contact some other form of intelligence that allowed him to prescribe numerous effective treatments. Clearly this was an ability that Pop wanted to acquire. Cayce became an early role model for my father, who was fascinated with the idea that you could obtain from invisible sources information that could heal people. Years later Pop became close friends with Edgar's son, Hugh Lynn, who would visit and stay with us during the winter.

As my father's curiosity and explorations expanded, he would eventually follow a trail that led him to the theosophical teachings of Krishnamurti and Madame Blavatsky. Over time his affiliation with the Theosophical Society would grow, and he would become one of its frequent lecturers on healing. Each of these philosophical stopping points was critical in his evolution as a psychic. It seemed as if Pop was enrolled in some sort of supernatural PhD correspondence program.

I was extremely hesitant to talk to any of the kids at school about ectoplasm, the akashic records, the mystical sect the Hunza people, or any of the other arcane topics that Pop discussed with me based on his readings. Out of necessity I developed a dual personality. During school hours I needed to appear as normal as possible, in order to avoid being beaten up or laughed out of class. However, as soon as I came home and opened the front door, it was like walking onto the set of *I Dream of Jeannie* or *Bewitched*. For me these TV shows were like documentaries rather than fantasy sitcoms. At last there were other people who, like me, lived in a parallel, paranormal universe. Major Tony came home from his day job at NASA to find his genie ready, willing, and able to put spells on people, read minds, and alter reality.

After school, along with my homework, my father provided informal lessons in metaphysics. He would casually discuss subjects like Atlantis, astrology, kundalini, and Buddhism the way that other dads talked about baseball players or politics. These subjects had a captivating quality, as if I were listening to the latest installment of *One Thousand and One Arabian Nights*. Soon I knew more about chakras and reincarnation than I did about Tom Sawyer or American history. Our conversations about multiple incarnations and life in other dimensions made it somewhat difficult to actually focus on my algebra homework. When at home, I lived in my own imagination as I daydreamed about mystical beings and supernatural feats of power.

In an effort to mimic my father's new interests in religious spirituality, I signed up for an evening one-on-one Bible study class. I really did it for the free illustrated Bible, which had great pictures and was the reward for finishing the course. My parents watched in horror as a former Fuller Brush man with a limp would come to our house twice a week at seven o'clock at night and make me memorize psalms from the New Testament. Since I only wanted the free Bible and wasn't doing really well with the apostles, I quit after five weeks. I just wasn't that interested in the door-to-door salesman's version of Jesus's Good News.

As my father continued to teach me about the ins and outs of reincarnation, it made me feel as if this life didn't matter that much. After all, it was just a preview for the next one. Because everything was predetermined by God, spirits, and karma, I assumed that it made no difference whether I studied or not or whether I excelled or not, because God had a plan for me. The problem was, I didn't know what the plan was and felt powerless to change it. As a result, my school performance began to plummet. I figured if my destiny was to be an honor student, then God and His spirit cohorts would make it happen for me. Learning to read cues and affirmations from my environment as omens, my beliefs were often reinforced when my mother would spontaneously break out in her favorite song: "Que Sera, Sera"—whatever will be, will be . . .

Mom continued to work hard at being a supportive wife, as if her husband had merely taken up golf or tennis. While she rejected most of his "wacky ideas," she did her best to go along with his new interests. On nights when he disappeared for yoga lessons, she expressed her delight that whatever this thing called yoga was, it was helping him relax from the tensions of the office. Ever practical, she focused on the end result of his metaphysical curiosity.

She endured the first wave of "kooky friends," which included the yoga teacher, astrologers, and other seekers, with a good-natured hostess smile and a feigned interest in the conversation. Over time the smile disappeared, and her conversation turned to logical and incisive questioning of their belief systems. Typical of one of her stop-the-conversation-cold questions would be, "So, if I understand you correctly, what you are saying is that the reason someone gets cancer is because they did something terrible in their past life such as raping their daughter or killing their next-door neighbor? Therefore the cancer in this lifetime did not occur because of the current medical explanation of mutant cells rapidly multiplying but instead is due to a karmic payment for past sins? Am I on the right track here?" She quickly entered the no-win zone of these metaphysical, meandering conversations. In no time at all, she realized that she was better off playing the silent cook rather than the happy hostess.

The ever-widening gulf between my parents was especially apparent in the bedroom. Secondhand books on Buddhism, levitation, hypnosis, Rosicrucianism, magnetic healing, UFOs, and reincarnation continued to pile up on the table next to Pop's side of the bed, while Mom stuck to her lurid novels and biographies of screen stars and Rat Pack comedians. The separate piles of reading material beside the bed were indicative not just of different interests but of two lives that were diverging.

But now time had passed, and their differences had hardened. As if in one final attempt to acknowledge and accommodate their growing estrangement, Pop created a special mattress that catered to their individual tastes: firm and ascetic on his side, and soft and cushy on hers. There was something very Hollywood about this his-and-hers mattress invention. In a nod to Eastern sleeping habits, the bed, a gold-leafed extravaganza, was just a foot off the floor, whereas standard American beds seemed to be getting higher and higher until you needed a ladder to climb into them. The gold metal headboard of swirls and curlicues designed by my father anticipated the free-form psychedelic aesthetic that was about to sweep the country.

During this period of change, my parents continued to work together at the design studio. While much of the day-to-day work remained business as usual, Pop's decorating sensibility took a turn toward the mystical as well. Maybe it was his daily meditations or the early tremors of the mid-sixties shaking all around us, but suddenly he found the staples of traditional decorating—such as fabric and wallpaper—terribly old-fashioned and conventional. Without ever dropping a tab of acid, he was inexplicably drawn to things bright and shiny, especially iridescent jewel-toned colors.

One day Mom was wearing some vividly colored Mardi Gras pop beads (so unlike her) that her sister had given to her. They caught my father's eye. Suddenly he had a decorating epiphany that these beads could become a new way to make modern draperies. Perhaps this inspiration was brought on by one of his many previous incarnations, specifically the one where he was a Persian talisman maker, as revealed to him many years later in a message from one of his spirit guides. Thanks to the magic of reincarnation, a new decorating trend—beaded curtains—was born that would sweep the country and keep me in bell-bottoms for years to come. From this moment forth, fabric was banished from his decorating vocabulary, to be replaced by plastic and glass beads from around the world. The beaded draperies, created with his brilliant sense of color, design, and texture, combined the best of hippie regalia and cheap made-in-Japan bamboo curtains with a majestic sense of antiquity. Pop was high-low decades before this would become a cultural idiom.

His timing could not have been more serendipitous, or prescient. Haight-Ashbury, Maharishi Mahesh, Timothy Leary were all about to unleash their love seeds of a new consciousness on the world. "Turn on, tune in, drop out" was about to become the mantra for a new generation wanting to explore anywhere but here. Somehow Pop sensed that this happening be-in was imminent. He was changing as fast as he could to be in tune with the coming youthquake. For a man in his sixties, he was definitely a hipster ahead of the crowd.

The *Miami Herald* named Pop "the King of Beads." His office took on the look of a psychedelic candy store. Thousands of bottles containing brightly colored beads lined the shelves, waiting to be artfully assembled into curtains and room dividers for the forward-thinking idle rich. His clients would line up to spend thousands of dollars for a designer version of what would be hanging in every stoned hippie's Haight-Ashbury crash pad.

On weekends we all sat down at the long dining room table, which he had designed of expanded metal mesh, and strung long strands of jeweled combinations that seemed worthy of Harry Winston, all destined for wealthy homes in Palm Beach, Miami, and the Caribbean.

Eventually none of us could string fast enough to supply the needs of his design-starved clients. My father's beaded curtains had become a "must-have" accessory for the competitive rich. To keep up with the demand, Pop discovered a family of dwarves living one block off the poverty-stricken Tamiami Trail, which led to nowhere except the alligator-infested swamps of the Everglades. This family, who desperately needed any kind of work, was more than happy to set out beads on their individual metal TV tables decorated with pictures of grapes and ivy, and string, string, string. Pop was their sole source of income.

There was an unspoken but prevailing social stigma attached to being different in any way, and this included being handicapped. You simply did not see handicapped people out in public. They certainly did not hold regular, visible jobs; instead they stayed home and hid. Pop was always looking for a way to help those who were less fortunate. However, Mom's compassion stopped at the door on this one. She was unable to socialize with the dwarves and covered her eyes when the mother dwarf came to answer the door. If Pop asked her to run into their house and drop off some money or pick up their handiwork, she would refuse.

Each of us was finding ways to adjust to and accommodate Pop's new metaphysical personality. To her credit, Mom tried to creatively incorporate brown rice into her best French recipes and feigned interest in a book on Krishnamurti lectures. After school I was teaching myself yoga asanas from a small pamphlet, printed in India on newsprint, with out-of-register black-and-white photos of men and women in tight bathing suits assuming the poses. One particular set of photographs demonstrated a nose-washing technique that involved pushing string up one nostril and somehow getting it out the other. All we had in the pantry was plain old kite string. I passed on this one. In

the mornings, I was meditating (*ommmmm*) and listening to scratchy
recordings of consciousness lectures by various yogis. I didn't understand a word they were saying, but just listening to the sound of their
thickly accented Indian voices made me feel holy and enlightened.

Early in June, just as we all thought we were finally finding our
equilibrium, Pop suddenly disappeared. After several days of not
hearing any chanting, I realized that I had not seen him in a while. No
good-bye, no explanation, just gone.

Mom seemed perfectly content that Pop was MIA. Her daily
routine continued as if nothing had changed. Every morning she got
dressed and went to the design studio. I figured that maybe Pop was
on another business trip to New York or California or Jamaica (Cuba
was out by then), and someone forgot to tell me. Finally I asked. Her
response was simply that he was "away." Weeks turned into months—
but no Pop.

As usual, I found ways to entertain myself, which is the nature of
being an only child. In addition to painting everything in my room
fluorescent orange and green (including myself), I discovered electric
bananas. I thought my father would approve of my method of obtain-
ing cosmic consciousness through the fruit of Mother Nature. Perhaps
I could convince him to light up with me one day.

I loved the idea that I could get high for free using leftover bananas. The process involved scraping out the inside fiber of the banana
peel and then drying this "tobacco" in the oven. After I had dried my
Chiquita stash, I then crushed several aspirin, added a bit of tobacco
from my mother's Camels, and tossed the ingredients together as
if making a psychotropic Caesar salad. I must have read about this
recipe for a low-cost legal high in one of the San Francisco or New
York alternative publications that I subscribed to, like *Ramparts* or the
East Village Other. This was the problem of living in a hick town like
Miami: I believed everything I read in any newspaper or magazine as
long as it was from somewhere other than Miami. Donovan would
memorialize this ridiculous ritual in his hit "Mellow Yellow."

After a few puffs, my skin would begin to tingle in an unpleasant way, as if there were bugs crawling up and down my arms, and the room began to spin. This creepy sensation was followed by a drenching cold sweat, which was the signal that I was to collapse into bed and remain there for the rest of the day—feeling nauseous. I would then switch on my black light and stare at the psychedelic posters that were tacked to the ceiling. Somehow I convinced myself that this "high" was fun and enlightening. I liked the idea that I didn't have to risk arrest by buying marijuana in the Grove. It was safe, it was legal, and it didn't work. I would remain slightly comatose until about five o'clock, at which point I crawled out of bed and started all over again. This was how I spent my summer vacation as a thirteen-year-old—sick to my stomach.

One afternoon late in August, I was just about to emerge from another wasted day in bed when I noticed a shadowy figure standing in the doorway of my room. "Wow," I thought, "I'm finally hallucinating. Maybe it takes time for the banana chemicals to build up in my system. Far out!" This stuff really worked. A full-fledged hallucination achieved with only natural ingredients available at your corner grocery. This formula could revolutionize the drug trade. No more arrests. No more guns. Just miles of banana plantations making millions of people nauseous while hallucinating. Maybe I could start selling it in nickel bags.

To be honest, I was a little disappointed with my vision. I had hoped to see mind-expanding prismatic colors. But I was still happy that my summer of long, hard work perfecting the natural high had finally paid off. I looked again, and as my eyes slowly focused, the figure looked a bit like my father. But he was much thinner, so it couldn't have been my father. The thought occurred to me that maybe this was not a hallucination but actually my father, teleporting in from his presently unknown location—an occurrence that wouldn't have surprised me in the least. I shakily got out of bed to go and touch the hallucination/teleportation.

I was sweating and so weak from months of not eating properly and smoking my aspirin-banana combo that I collapsed. My hallucination caught me. It *was* my father standing there. He held me for a minute while I recovered, then said, "Get some food and meet me in the backyard. I want to show you something. Hurry before it gets dark."

I went into the kitchen, which had gone to hell in Pop's absence. Mom and I had been happily eating sirloin steaks, canned Le Sueur peas, and instant mashed potatoes from a box. In the freezer I found a carton of Sealtest ice cream, the kind that contained three neatly divided sections of strawberry, vanilla, and chocolate. I quickly forced a couple of spoonfuls of chocolate ice cream down my throat. The sugar stabilized me, and I wandered out back looking for my father. I had a pounding headache.

My father was standing at the side of the house, looking up at the sky. His hand was shielding his eyes from the afternoon sun's glare. "Look at those clouds. They are especially beautiful today."

I looked around. The landscape wobbled and spun. I was much more interested in throwing up than looking at the clouds. Once I regained my balance, I saw that they were, in fact, especially cottony and full. Miami specializes in extraordinary cumulus cloud formations, possibly due to its unique location in the Gulf Stream. Finally, as my cognitive functions began to fire up from the sugar rushing through my body, I realized that I had not seen my father all summer and asked, "Where were you?"

"I met someone. A very special man, and we went away together."

"What, like on a vacation or something?"

"To his ashram."

"His what?"

"A place where you study. He showed me some new things, some new ideas about how to think about life. Let me show you one of the things he taught me. You'll like this. Pick a cloud, any cloud, and watch me do something to it. Just point to one."

I scanned the sky and found the biggest, puffiest cumulus hanging low on the horizon. "That one," I said, pointing. "Do something to that one." I had no idea what Pop was planning but imagined that maybe he could make the cloud change colors or even talk. The banana residue was affecting my thinking.

"The one with the little gray spots at the end?"

"Yeah, that one."

"Okay. I'm going to punch a big hole right in the middle of the cloud and make it look just like a doughnut." Who needed to smoke bananas and aspirin when they had a father who talked about punching holes in clouds? This was very trippy stuff. He cautioned me, "It takes a few minutes for my thought beam to reach the cloud, so just be patient." A deep silence fell over my father. About a minute later, he took several deep breaths and let them out. In slow motion he carefully placed his fingertips on his temples and began to stare at the cloud. He looked like one of those ads in the back of comic books for X-ray glasses that let you see ladies' underwear through their dresses.

I looked up at the cloud. Nothing much was happening, and I began to lose interest. At that moment, I had no patience for my father's attempts to defy the laws of physics and wanted to get back in the house. I was eager for my next dose of bananas. It was also getting to be four o'clock—time for *Gilligan's Island*.

Minutes passed. Pop looked like a statue, just staring at the cloud. I glanced around the yard for a distraction, slapped a couple of mosquitoes, and waited impatiently for us to go back inside. The lychees were just coming into season, and the seaside mahoe tree had blanketed the yard with yellow-and-russet-colored flowers. The mockingbirds and the mourning doves were chattering loudly to announce the end of the day. My father just stood there staring at the cloud. His eyes were squinted, his jaw tight. I looked back up at the cloud, and it was completely intact. Nothing had changed.

I started to feel my dizziness return. I turned to walk back in the house, but when I took a second glance at the sky, I noticed a small indentation—a soft, shadowy gray area—in the middle of the cloud. It definitely had not been there before. Wispy strands of cloud started to emerge from the center like a trail of smoke. After these first few strands floated away, the center of the cloud began to open wide as if it were yawning. Slowly the entire central core of the cloud disappeared, revealing a round window onto pure blue sky. A large perfectly formed doughnut hole appeared exactly in the place where I had pointed.

Maybe those bananas were stronger than I thought. I couldn't quite tell if I was still high or if this was really happening. The truth was that nothing my father did these days surprised me. If my father grew another head or began to fly, I would have simply shrugged and lit up another banana cigarette. From everything he taught me, I knew that anything was possible. However, in that moment, I did sense what I can only now describe as a perceptual shift. It was as if someone had, for a split second, shut off the fuse box and then clicked it back on. The world went from color to black-and-white and back to color again in a millisecond. It almost felt as if nothing had happened, but I knew that something very strange and powerful had occurred.

My father dropped his hands from his temples and looked down at me. He was smiling with serene satisfaction. Pointing to the cloud, he said, "There's the hole. Just where you wanted it. What do you think?"

"*Wow,* it's a really big hole. How'd you do that?"

"Mind control. It's a kind of meditation. Once you organize and control your thinking and your mind's energy, then anything is possible. You don't need drugs or anything else to be able to do this kind of work." This was an obvious reference to my chronic banana habit. "You can change reality whenever you want to. What I did just now was to gather up all the power in my mind and project it onto that cloud. I used my mind like a ray gun, cutting a hole in the cloud. Your thought is the most powerful thing in the world, more powerful than a bomb or any other weapon. Thought travels around the world and through the universe instantaneously. Everything in our experience in this lifetime originates in our mind. In the future we will be able to do everything just by thinking. One day we'll be able to drive cars and fly planes just by our thought. This cloud-busting meditation is something I learned from Dr. Mishra."

"Who's Dr. Mishra? I thought you didn't like doctors."

"It's not that I don't like doctors; I wish they were more open-minded and didn't just want to give people pills that create other diseases. Dr. Mishra is a different kind of doctor; he's not a medical doctor but a doctor of philosophy."

I had never heard of a doctor of philosophy before. To me all doctors were *doctors*. Dr. Mishra was the first true metaphysician that my father had met. The few assorted people with esoteric interests that my father had encountered in Miami were all amateurs, but Dr. Mishra was a living, breathing guru from deep in the Punjab. How they met was a mystery, but it was apparent that my father's life was beginning to illustrate the Buddhist saying "When the student is ready, the teacher will appear."

My father's time at the ashram with Dr. Mishra was a revelation for him. It was like consciousness boot camp. At dawn they arose for meditation. The day continued with yoga, vegetarian meals, horoscope readings, and philosophical lectures. Now the stuff of CEO retreats, but back in 1966 this type of activity would invite and warrant a raid from J. Edgar Hoover's FBI. It was during this retreat that my father realized that his goal of greater mental powers and insight was indeed possible. Dr. Mishra had reset my father's compass and sent him off full speed in a new direction.

I looked back up at the cloud. It remained stationary even though the surrounding clouds had now floated away. The perfectly round hole he had created was still there. Unlike the neighboring clouds, which had fuzzy edges and mountains of rough volumes, this cloud was crisp, neat, and looked somewhat artificial. Within minutes the twilight sky was empty except for this one cloud, which hovered like a strange white inflated inner tube. "So, Dr. Mishra taught you to do this just by changing your thinking? How does that work?"

"If you control your thinking, you control your reality. Change your thinking, and you change your reality. It's that simple. Our physical world is nothing more than a manifestation of our thought energy." At thirteen years old, I never gave changing reality much thought. It just seemed to be there—or not there, as in my father's case. But from my father's point of view, reality was something completely pliable that could be shaped like a handful of clay. "Nothing is as solid as it appears," he said. "Most of the obstacles we face in life are only illusions and can be dissipated just like I punched that hole in the cloud. That's why it is important to learn how to use your mind. Once you know how to do this, nothing will ever stop you. When you're ready, I'll teach you to control your mental powers. Life is very different when you fully use your mind's unlimited potential."

The truth was that at that moment I had no interest in learning to punch holes in clouds. What I really wanted to do was lose my mind in some more banana smoke.

four

.

Devil Be Gone

"The world is your oyster . . ."

Mom was starting one of her "you have your whole life ahead of you and, oh, the adventures you will have" talks. She expected great things from me. Since I had no desire to fulfill her dream of becoming the first Jewish president of the United States—which she had bragged about to anyone who would listen since I was a baby—or a rich doctor, it seemed that she was now grooming me for show business. We were sitting on the couch in the living room after dinner.

"You know, when Sammy Davis Jr. comes back to his dressing room after a performance, and he looks in the mirror, he is all alone. At that point, all the lights and the glamour, the applause and the photographers mean nothing. When he looks in that mirror, that is the moment of truth. What kind of person are you? Are you a mensch who can stand up and be counted or just an emotional cripple who lives for other people and needs drugs and alcohol to face the world?

So, yes, all the fame and worldly success are wonderful, but it's who you really are when you're off stage that really counts. Let me tell you a story about Burt Lancaster. You know, Burt is Jewish, and he . . ." Mom was always on a first-name basis with all the stars.

At that moment, my father rushed by us, lost in thought, carrying a two-foot-tall wooden crucifix. Without moving her head or stopping her story, my mother's eyes quickly shifted to the side, fully taking in this man with a mission bearing a cross. I had not perfected her advanced technique of peripheral vision and simply turned my head and looked at my father, wondering where he had picked up this latest accoutrement. I doubted that this was just an accessory for one of the houses he was decorating. He carried that cross as if it were a magic wand.

Mom shot her eyes back to me and continued her story, pretending that nothing out of the ordinary had just happened. However, when her eyes met mine, they seemed to say, "Did you see what I just saw? What the hell is your father doing with that cross?" Given the last few years of his rapidly evolving religious curiosity, neither of us would have been surprised if he had suddenly become a Pentecostal or Baptist when we weren't looking.

That cross was the least of her worries. Now, witches, astrologers, psychics, yogis, and trance mediums were streaming through the house at all hours of the day and night. One woman, Connie, with a beehive hairdo, who only wore purple and smoked Virginia Slims, claimed to be able to speak a variety of languages used by extraterrestrials throughout the galaxy. She was like a multilingual interpreter at the UN and was available for translations for those who had unexpected alien encounters.

It was not unusual for me to walk into the living room and find a group of my father's new friends deeply engrossed in some sort of bizarre psychic activity such as psychometry (the analysis of someone's personality and future by simply holding one of his possessions, such as a set of keys or a ring), aura balancing, or past-life regression. I couldn't even make it to the kitchen without hearing someone talking in an unknown language as he or she revisited a past life.

At the time, my father was fascinated with reports about Filipino psychic surgeons who could supposedly push their hands into someone's body without making an incision, feel around, grab the diseased organ or tumor, and yank it right out. He would show me pictures of their surgeries. In the photographs, there was blood everywhere and a detached hand holding an organic mass of disease. I was terrified that sometime when I wasn't looking, one of his friends would suddenly reach inside my body and pull out my heart or my appendix before I had a chance to scream for help.

Mom had no interest in this ever-changing psychic circus. During these invasions, she would retreat to the bedroom, turn on the television, and begin her marathon of smoking, hoping they would all just go away. Unfortunately, it didn't work. It seemed that the more she smoked, the more these seekers multiplied and took over our house and my father's attention. Most of the time, I ignored the crowd, and they ignored me. It was as if we were on opposite sides of a two-way mirror.

In addition to his interests in meditation, psychic phenomena, and aliens, Pop developed a curiosity about possession—which explained why he was walking around the house carrying that cross. Long before *The Exorcist* popularized the concept of evil possession for the masses, he understood that a lot of strange antisocial behavior was produced by unhappy spirits trapped in the wrong body. In theory, people who die from suicide or murder don't realize that they are actually dead and as a result refuse to naturally progress to the next level of consciousness. They actively look for vulnerable bodies to inhabit so that they can continue to live an earthly existence. Ideal candidates to host their disembodied spirits are people who have been ill, use drugs, or are overwhelmed by anger, grief, or any other negative emotion. Such problems create a weak energy field, as well as an entry point for the spirit to jump into the body and take possession. Bars are a prime example of a low-energy environment where negative entities hang out looking for a host body. As people drink, their inhibitions decline, their guard goes down, and after that fifth shot of tequila, some dead person takes over and starts driving the bus.

Another method of access into someone's body and mind by a dark spirit is a broken aura. Surrounding our physical body is an energy body composed of light, known as an aura. The aura reflects our general state of physical and mental well-being. One's aura can become broken in any number of ways, which results not only in a leakage of our vital energy but also provides an entrance for these negative entities. Once inside our bodies, these dispossessed spirits can make us ill, infect our thinking, and direct us to take actions contrary to our true character. According to my father, many crimes are committed by people possessed by a lost spirit. All of a sudden, a loving mother decides to cook and eat all her children in a stew, or a husband drives his prized Coupe de Ville over the edge of a cliff, killing innocent beachgoers sunning themselves on the sands of Acapulco. Later on in life, Pop would find that many of his patients were chronically ill due to possession.

One Sunday morning, shortly after this first crucifix spotting, I found Pop in his study waving his wooden cross in the air and saying some sort of prayer. He looked like he was swatting flies as he jabbed the cross at various invisible targets. Without any formal training or placing ads in the yellow pages, Pop suddenly developed a nice little sideline of performing exorcisms free of charge. I don't know what self-help manual he read on removing Satan, but he was becoming quite the exorcist.

Within months of acquiring the cross, Pop began to receive calls from nice God-fearing ladies saying that they were suddenly experiencing strange homicidal thoughts, or spontaneous nosebleeds, or hearing eerie noises in the middle of the night. Or they would come home from work and find their sweet, loving husband swearing a blue streak, hitting the kids, and creating a tornado of destruction, breaking everything in sight. Other bizarre stories included their sons' cutting up dead dogs and eating their hearts while laughing, or their daughters' having sex in the cemetery on top of the tombstones or drinking blood.

Like a good doctor, Pop would respond at any hour, day or night, to those in distress. He would grab his big wooden cross, toss it in the backseat of his convertible with the lipstick-red interior and speed off to some cracker-box tract home in the southwest section of Goulds or Homestead, adjacent to the trailer parks just before the okra farms began. What he really needed to complete the picture was one of those portable revolving red lights that undercover cops slap on their roofs when rushing to a crime scene. Or perhaps just a small official-looking sign that he could leave on the dashboard: EXORCIST ON CALL.

Occasionally he would suggest that we "go for a ride" because he needed "to see a friend," without ever telling me where we were headed. If it was anyone else, I would have assumed that he wanted company while going out to score drugs. Instead of taking a look at plastic bags filled with marijuana, I often found myself in homes filled with plastic statues of Jesus or heavy plastic slipcovers on the living room furniture. It was in these homes, within the souls of these good people, that the devil had decided to reside. How else could one explain the spontaneous, irrational behavior that took over these law-abiding citizens?

One day my father answered the phone to hear a woman screaming and crying that her daughter had bitten her face and was running around cursing and spitting. She was talking so loudly that I could hear her panicked voice, though not the specifics, all the way across the room. As he hung up, Pop said, "I need to go help someone right now. I'd like you to come with me." It was a Saturday, and I was just sitting home reading about a light show at the Fillmore West in *Ramparts*. Exorcisms were not high on my list as a weekend activity. I would have much rather helped my father mow the lawn or rake leaves than watch him save another soul. However, duty called, and off we went.

We pulled up to a nondescript little white house way out, just off of South Dixie Highway, with brown grass starved for water, no trees in the yard, and a dented chain-link fence that looked like a couple of cars had backed into it. As we knocked on the door, a mangy German shepherd, the kind you see at the pound or guarding scrap yards, was inside the fence, roaming around and barking.

A plain-looking woman in her mid-thirties, with mousy brown hair and tears running down her cheeks, answered the door. Her face was swollen from the bite, as if she had just happened into a mess of wasps. She did not greet us; instead she stared at us blankly, nodded her head, and glanced to the right, indicating that we should enter. As we walked through the door, we could hear snarling curses coming from one of the rooms and echoing throughout the tiny house.

"You eat dirty pussy, you fuckin' bastard piece of shit! I'll tear your eyes out and swallow them one by one! You'll burn in hell while you drink my piss!" I had never heard anything like this, even from the guys who hung around the 7-Eleven drinking from beer cans wrapped in paper bags. Upon hearing this deep, possessed voice, my father immediately raised his cross and waved it in front of the woman's face and over her head as we entered the living room. Her husband, who looked like the kind of guy who drove a tractor, just sat planted in his La-Z-Boy, staring in shock through his thick glasses.

The house felt dirty, as if there was goo everywhere. I didn't want to touch anything. This was one of those tiny, blank houses that crammed whole families into a living space the size of the garage in a normal-sized house. Divorce or suicide seemed to be the only avenues of escape from this claustrophobic environment. The minute you entered, navigational decisions were thrust upon you. There was no opportunity to wander from room to room. Instead, you either took one step to the right for the living room, two steps forward for the small kitchen—with its white metal cabinets that held dinnerware one got for free in boxes of detergent—or two steps to the left to a cramped hallway containing three bedrooms and the one bathroom that afforded little to no privacy.

We went to the left and found a girl who looked to be about a year older than I was, lying on a filthy baby-blue carpet in one of the bedrooms. Her eyes seemed to have rolled to the back of her head, and all I could see were the whites, which gave her the appearance of being either dead or blind. She didn't seem to notice that we were in the room staring down at her as she thrashed about in violent contortions, completely naked except for her panties. Her alarmingly white body was almost translucent and covered with sores and black-and-blue marks that could have been anything from snakebites to self-inflicted wounds. Her shoulder-length brown hair looked sticky and matted, as if it had never been washed. Pouring out of her mouth was the kind of foam you get from squirting too much detergent into a sinkful of dirty dishes.

She looked like those blubbery manatees that silently patrolled the inner canals of Miami and every so often got caught in a boat's propeller. Brutally gashed all over, they eventually floated to the surface, stinking up the whole canal until some game warden fished them out. I had never seen a naked girl before, especially one with her left hand jammed into her underwear. I just wanted the game warden to come and scoop this one up in a big net and haul her away.

I almost laughed at how ugly she was, but I was too scared and just wanted to go home as soon as possible. The best I could do was to hide behind my father and hope that this would all be over soon. I knew I couldn't cry and distract him, because he was up to some serious business. When I looked at the possessed girl, all I could think of were dangerous snakes—water moccasin, rattlesnake, and python. It seemed like she was going to slither right up, bite me on the ankle, and fill me with her poison. I was hoping my father still had his red rubber snakebite kit that he kept in the glove compartment of the car, in case he had to siphon her venom out of me.

My father was taking this whole scene in his stride. He paused for a moment to assess the situation before getting down to work. With incredible precision, my father planted his feet on the ground about two feet apart as if bracing himself against someone pushing him over. He then lifted the cross and held it firmly in front of him with both hands like a shield that would protect him from a sniper's bullet. He began to recite the Twenty-third Psalm. "The Lord is my shepherd . . . He maketh me . . . all the days of my life . . . forever and ever . . ." Before he got to the "amen," the girl had stopped cursing and was slowly whimpering as she rocked back and forth. Her eyes were now closed. Behind me, her dad watched in dumb astonishment while my father performed his rites.

Next my father repeated his own special exorcism prayer: "Cleanse, clear, fill, encircle this body in the white light of healing protection. Remove all negative energies and entities, and send them to their proper plane . . ." This prayer put the finishing touch on the exorcism. Apparently this was all too much for the devil, and he just up and skedaddled out of that girl.

As she calmed down, my father began to slowly bend closer to her, holding his cross about three inches above her body. He waved it over her from head to toe as if he were disinfecting her. My steady diet of nature shows such as *Wild Kingdom* had me thinking, "Don't get too close, she's going to pounce." I was not far from wrong. Without any warning, she sat bolt upright, as if an electric current had just surged through her body. I thought she was going to stand up and start sleepwalking zombie style. Then, just as suddenly, she collapsed back onto the floor, sprawled out like she was nailed to a cross, and fell into a deep comatose sleep. I felt as if a kind of irritating static electricity had suddenly lifted from the room. The air now seemed clear and calm.

Her mother started weeping uncontrollably. My father looked back at the parents and said, "The devil's gone, she's fine. Let her sleep. When she wakes she won't remember any of this. It's over now." The husband remained silent.

"But how could this have happened?" the mother asked. "She's usually such a good girl. Yes, we have our problems with boys and stuff, but nothing like this, never."

"We are surrounded by dark forces," my father answered. "At any given time, they are looking to find a place to rest, a host that will give them physical form. These are people who died violently but still can't acknowledge that they are dead. As a result, they are desperate to take over someone's body so they can continue to live on the physical plane, here on earth."

"But Melissa didn't do drugs. She is not a bad girl."

"There are a thousand ways this could have happened. Sometimes dark forces can enter the body while you are sleeping. You never quite know how this happens. You always have to protect yourself and surround yourself with the white light of protection: Christ's light." My father smiled at the woman and reached out to shake her hand. She seemed comforted. In some way this explanation had made sense to her.

As we prepared to leave, the woman said to us, "May I offer you some coffee and cake? I can put up some instant coffee, and I just baked some angel food cake." I knew better than to eat anything from a kitchen where the devil had probably been nibbling away at boxes of cereal and spaghetti like a mouse. Thankfully, my father also declined.

Finally the husband spoke up. "Why, preacher, I got to thank you for saving my little girl. Damn! Ah don't know what the hell came over her. She just started screamin' and cussin' like some bobcat caught in a trap. Ah never seen nothin' like this before."

"Frank!" admonished his wife. "Don't talk that way in front of Father Smith—especially after what we just went through."

"She's fine now," my father reassured them. "I'm glad to be of service. God bless you." After the good-byes and handshakes, we left. Boy, was I happy to get out of there. I had seen enough of that creepy naked girl in that room to last me a lifetime. It was getting dark as we got into the car to drive away.

"How come they called you Father? You're not their father."

"Well, it's just a formality. They were being respectful and appreciative. I think that's what they say to their priest, and maybe they think of me as a priest. In the old days, priests used to do exorcisms all the time."

"But you're not a priest."

"Well, in a way I am. I try to help people find God or to do good in life. These are things that a priest does."

If standing over some smelly naked girl with spit all over her face is what it takes to find God, then I wanted no part of it. "Why was that girl acting that way, all crazy?"

"Because she was possessed by the devil."

"I didn't see the devil there. Where was he?"

"You couldn't see him because he was inside of her."

This didn't make any sense to me. "Inside of her? How did he get inside of her?"

"The devil likes to find people who are weak or have problems; this way he can take advantage of them and make them do things they don't want to do. When that girl bit her mother, she didn't mean to do that; she didn't know she was doing it. It was the devil acting through her."

"I didn't think the devil was real. I thought it was just some sort of cartoon thing to make people scared."

My father laughed. "The devil is indeed real and causes people to do things against their better judgment. I don't think he looks like some red man with horns and a pitchfork. That is definitely a cartoon. But there are powerful dark forces out there that can make people do evil."

"How can I keep the dark forces from taking over my body?"

"At all times you need to keep yourself surrounded by the white light of protection. Imagine yourself enveloped by a bubble of white light that can repel any type of negative energy that tries to attack you." As he said this, my father drew an arc over my head with his finger. "This will keep you safe. You have no idea of the number of people I see who are possessed and have a dark entity making them do things against their will. We are all surrounded by possessed people. It's a real problem because you can't easily tell who's possessed and who isn't. And now with so many young people taking drugs, this creates just the type of environment that these lost souls are looking for. The other thing you can do is to say the exorcism prayer, which will instantly get rid of any possession."

"Where do I get that prayer?"

"I'll give you one when we get home. But you don't have to worry. I'll always watch out for you and keep you safe. If you have any problem, I'll be able to fix it."

"When Mom gets mad at you, is she possessed?"

"No, she's just mad. But there are angry people who are possessed."

"Maybe all of us should say this prayer so that nothing happens to any of us."

"I don't think Mom would be interested in this. In fact, I don't think you should discuss what happened today with anyone. Let's just keep it as one of our little adventures."

"Wait till I tell Mrs. Lincoln that I saw the devil," I said. "Tomorrow we're having show-and-tell; I'm going to tell them all about this." Mrs. Lincoln was my ninth-grade teacher. I imagined she would be suitably impressed that my father beat back the devil. Perhaps this story might help improve my homeroom grades, which were somewhat lackluster. I only hoped she didn't have one of her spells when I got to the part about the naked girl rolling around on the floor. Mrs. Lincoln, a good woman who also taught Sunday school, was prone to getting dizzy when things upset her. She was not meant for the modern world. I knew all the boys were going to start to laugh when I told them about the girl with the devil inside of her. I was going to score big points with this story.

"Philip, you can't tell Mrs. Lincoln about what happened today."

"Why not?"

"You can't tell anybody about this. What happened today is a secret. Would you like someone going around telling everybody that you had the devil inside of you?"

"No, but you fixed her. So now that the devil's gone, it's okay to tell people."

"I don't think that girl would want you telling people what happened to her. It was like she was sick, and now she's going to get better. Do you understand?"

I was very disappointed. I thought I would make a lot of new friends telling this to everybody. Finally I could brag about my father. It didn't make sense that he didn't want me to share his victory over the devil with the class. But I agreed. "Okay, but I'll just tell Mom."

"Mom gets very upset when she hears about things like this," he said. "She might not be happy that I took you to see the devil. She would be worried that you might get hurt."

This bothered me. It sounded as if my father had just put me in a very dangerous situation where either one of us could have gotten in trouble. I could have been eaten alive by the devil or had him jump inside of me. I was a little mad that my father had put me at such risk. Clearly he was flirting with danger. I was afraid that if my father kept doing exorcisms, he might come home with the devil inside of him. Then what would I do? It would be the sanpaku thing all over again.

Obviously my mother was not happy with her husband's new-found hobby of exorcism. Had she known how I had spent my afternoon, Mom would have probably grabbed me, gotten on the next plane to New York, and taken me back to her family.

"You don't want to get Mom scared, do you?" he asked.

"No."

"Okay, then, don't tell Mom either. This is our secret. I just wanted you to see this so that you knew what could happen in case the devil got ahold of you."

"Well, I'm not going to let him near me. Besides, I don't want to bite anybody."

"That's good."

"But what if the devil tries to find me and get inside of me when I'm sleeping?" I asked.

"Don't worry, I am always watching, and nothing like that will ever happen to you."

five

·

Spirit Talk in Overtown

"You gonna buy all *that*?"

The black checkout lady wore a little white hat bobby-pinned to her hair that made her look like a nurse. She was staring at me, waiting for an answer. It was a bit like going through customs: I couldn't make my purchase until I had fully declared my intention. Her questioning made me feel slightly criminal.

Too embarrassed to answer, I just sort of nodded my head and looked away.

She wanted an explanation and wasn't going to check me out until she got one. All I wanted was to get out of the Food Fair with my dignity intact.

Unfortunately, this was happening on my first date ever, with a gorgeous Brazilian girl named Maya. She had the most remarkable blue eyes, which seemed to dilate and ratchet wide open when they fixed on you. Once fully opened, her eyes overwhelmed your vision until you couldn't see anything else but this cerulean blue field. The rest of the world ceased to exist. I often found myself stopping in mid-conversation, completely hypnotized by her eyes.

Maya started nudging me, wondering what was going on. She was dressed in tight jeans and a man's shirt, which was unbuttoned at the bottom and tied in a calypso-style knot that showed off her tan, flat stomach. Her goggle-sized amber sunglasses were perched on top of her head, and her feet wore turquoise Greek espadrilles.

"What you doin' with all that?" The checkout lady pointed to the thirty pounds of carrots that I had heaped high on her conveyor belt.

Yes, I was buying thirty pounds of carrots as part of my first date with the most beautiful woman in Miami. I had just turned sixteen and had gotten my driver's license, and with that, the freedom to date. I no longer had to have my father drive me somewhere, which meant that I no longer had to introduce him to a total stranger. "Hi, meet my father, he's from another planet and is a macrobiotic. If you'd like to join us on a fast sometime, I'm sure you'd enjoy it."

I had met Maya at school. She was the only person in the entire high school that would speak to me. Kids picked up on my weird vibe and refused to have anything to do with me. However, Maya just loved it. While stunningly beautiful, she had her own weirdness going on. She could have easily fit in with the prevailing jock-cheerleader culture, but she was curious about a more interesting ride. We hit it off immediately. I had no idea how to ask her out or what to do on a first date, so I said, "Hey, you wanna come over and make some carrot juice?"

She smiled and said, "Yeah, that sounds cool."

Maya responded to the checkout lady's persistent inquiries with a perky but slightly confrontational tone—"We're going to make carrot juice"—followed by her devastating smile.

"You wha—?"

"Carrot juice!" she replied somewhat firmly.

The woman looked at Maya with real pity. Slowly shaking her head, she said, "Ain't no such thing as carrot juice, hon." She raised her eyebrows and rolled her eyes as if signaling the checkout lady next to her that she had a real case on her hands. I was beginning to get a sense of what my father went through on a daily basis. His life was just nonstop public humiliation.

"So, mister, you sure you buyin' all them carrots? I don't want to ring all this up and then y'all change your mind. That's a lotta carrots. We don't sell that in a whole week. No, we don't. No one bought that many carrots, ever. I never seen nothin' like this. That's sure a lot of carrots."

At that moment the woman waiting on line behind Maya poked her and said, "Excuse me, but what are you going to be doing with all those carrots?"

"Oh boy, here we go," I thought. A simple little thing like buying thirty pounds of carrots is turning into a major commotion. As my mother would often say, "Another country heard from."

Maya was enjoying the attention and the controversy that we were creating. I was horrified and wanted to walk out and leave the carrots on the checkout counter. However, I was impressed that Maya was jumping into the fray with great enthusiasm. I had finally found a fellow traveler.

"Oh, we're going to make carrot juice," she answered authoritatively.

"Why, I've never heard of carrot juice." The woman put her index finger to her lips as she pondered the concept of carrot juice. "How do you do that? Do you boil the carrots?"

"No, he has a special machine. I've never seen it, but we're going home to do it right now. Philip, what's that machine called?"

"Um, I think it's an Acme Juicerator." Where were those magic make-me-invisible pills now that I needed them?

"Ohhhh . . ." The lady cautiously looked around to see if anyone was overhearing the conversation. "A *Juicerator*?"

"Yes, that's what it's called, a Juicerator." Maya loved being one of those in the know about the Juicerator.

"Oh, I see, a *Juicerator*. I never heard of that." The woman leaned farther forward and addressed me as the premier carrot expert. "Tell me, do you buy that in the hardware store?"

"Uh, no, I think it comes from California. They drink a lot of carrot juice out there. You should only buy carrots from California. They really know their carrots."

My father had been influenced by an early health pioneer named Paul Bragg, who believed that by juicing you could ingest hundreds of pounds of vital vegetable nutrients in just a few glasses of juice. Leave it to my father to be the only person in the whole city of Miami, not to mention probably the entire Eastern Seaboard, to own a Juicerator. Just the possession of this curious piece of equipment was creating far too many problems for me.

"California? Oh my . . ."

While Maya smiled at the woman, I handed the checkout lady $8.70, a fantastic sum at the time, but I figured this was a date, so I'd better show off.

We carried the four shopping bags of carrots to the car, got in, and headed to my house for an evening of ecstatic juicing. This was the first time anyone from the outside had been allowed into my private universe. I wasn't sure this date thing had been such a good idea. I was afraid that this was probably going to be the last date in my lifetime.

To my surprise and good fortune, Maya loved carrot juice. In fact, she loved carrot juice so much that she wanted to make it again. Having successfully passed the carrot juice test, I thought I could go a step further and invite her to see Sophie Busch. Along with séances and exorcisms, our father-son bonding sessions also included weekly Sunday afternoon trips to visit Sophie Busch, a charismatic preacher woman whose church was located in Overtown. Just north of downtown Miami, Overtown got its name when the city fathers wanted to knock down a large area of the black section of town to put in new roads. Somehow the roads never got built, probably because the suburban white folk farther south were concerned about their neighborhoods being invaded by a sudden mass migration of the black dispossessed. So the city fathers built an expressway *over* the *town* and left the shacks intact. During the twenties, thirties, and forties, the area had a thriving black community and a lively cultural scene. Entertainers such as Billie Holiday and Ella Fitzgerald would do their gigs in white venues and then come back to Overtown and do the real thing till the wee hours.

The place was dirt-poor. Few of the houses had real walls or windows. Instead they were built from leftover wood: old branches knocked down from banyan trees during hurricane season, fallen For Sale signs, and pieces of cardboard with *Modess* and *Palmolive* printed on the sides. You could see through the gaps in the wood right into most of the houses. They looked like birds' nests.

Anchoring the neighborhood was the lime-green Mount Zion Baptist Church, most of its windows blown out either from hurricanes or kids throwing rocks. Next door was Diamond Jim's Pool Parlor, which was painted pink and featured an amateurish painting of a trapezoidal pool table on the side of the building. Down the block was the Sunshine Liquor Shop, with chain-link fencing for windows. Broken glass littered the deserted streets, along with empty Nehi and Orange Crush soda bottles. Stray dogs slept under low-hanging poinciana trees, and old black men sat on empty boxes, staring at the railroad tracks. Amid this desperation was an abandoned wooden warehouse built on stilts that had been transformed by Sophie Busch into her own personal church. The pulpit was nothing more than two sheets of dirty, warped plywood nailed together on two-by-fours standing about a foot off the floor.

The glass in the windows was deep cobalt blue, which was used during the 1930s to alleviate the harshness of Miami's noonday sun. There was no air-conditioning back then, and this tinted glass bathed the interiors in a dark blue light that seemed almost holy and offered some relief from the oppressive oven-hot heat that was otherwise inescapable. The original solar panels still faced east on the building's roof, which was a leftover from the thirties, when solar energy was used to heat most of the water throughout Miami.

Lit by two or three long fluorescent tubes, Sophie's church was filled with an assortment of folding chairs that had been begged, borrowed, and stolen from all over Miami. On a good day, about sixty chairs were set out for the parishioners. By the time services started at four o'clock, there wasn't an empty seat in the house. The late-afternoon starting time gave the regulars a chance to attend their usual Pentecostal or Methodist services before risking transgression by showing up at Sophie's place.

Reverend Busch was a small, very old white lady who probably had been smoking Lucky Strikes since she was nine. She was the kind of girl you would imagine running off with the circus during the height of the Depression and getting by on her wits and sassy mouth. Now, stooped over and frail, she was the embodiment of a kind of harsh southern poverty.

Maya looked around the church with a bit of apprehension. This was not the kind of place or neighborhood for a nice Brazilian girl. Aside from the three of us, there were maybe five or six other white people in the place. The few white men present wore their hair slicked back in a greasy sort of way that was quickly becoming unfashionable. They had thick drugstore glasses and lightly patterned shirts usually finished off with a string tie or lariat. The women wore simple house dresses, the kind you might buy at the five-and-ten, and probably worked as waitresses at Smitty's, a coffee shop on Northeast Second Avenue that catered to day laborers and overweight middle-aged secretaries from the tax department.

Two or three industrial-strength metal fans pushed the humid July air around while black women in straw hats hummed softly, slowly fanning themselves with pieces of paper. A few minutes before the Reverend Busch took to the stage for her service, slightly somnambulant assistants casually wandered among the parishioners, holding large rolls of adding machine tape and a couple of those small yellow pencils that you would find in the library or in the betting section at jai alai. I raised my hand. My father gave me a look of approval that I was participating in the service. A bent-over assistant shuffled over to me and tore off about six inches of paper from the roll. I signaled for him to give a piece of paper to Maya as well. He then handed me two pencils and walked away.

"Write a question that you want Reverend Busch to answer," I said, initiating Maya into my Sunday ritual. "Actually, she doesn't really answer your questions; the spirits do. They tell her what to say."

"Like what? I don't know what to ask."

"Anything. She doesn't care what you ask."

"Do I have to raise my hand when she calls on me? Everybody's going to look at me."

"No, no, no, just write it down. You're the only one who will know when she is talking to you. No one else. It's okay, really. Just ask whatever you need to know, and she'll tell you."

"But what if she tells me something I don't want to know?"

Her question made me realize how different I was from her and everybody else at school. I considered communicating with spirits a normal part of one's daily routine. My father and I listened to them the way other people listened to the news. Whatever they had to say was a direct communication from God, not to be questioned but rather acted upon with all seriousness—or else. For me these spirits were like aunts and uncles. But Maya was scared.

"Look, I'm going to ask a question too," I said, trying to encourage her. "After you write your question, you have to put your initials down. If you want, make up some initials so that even I won't know Reverend Busch is talking to you. It's like going to a psychiatrist, but you get all your problems answered in a few minutes. Just write it down. I won't look; it will be fine. It's good to get the spirits to talk to you. They can help you out."

"But what if they—?"

"I promise, it's all okay. It doesn't hurt. I know you haven't done this before, and it may seem a little weird, but I do this every week with my father."

"Every week? So what do you ask?"

"I don't know. Stuff. Stuff about my parents, stuff about you."

"Stuff about me? Like what? What do they tell you?"

"I don't know. Stuff."

"No, like what? Tell me."

"Look, you'd better write down your question; they're starting to collect the papers now. I need a minute to write my question." With that, we turned away from each other and started writing our secret questions. Trying to keep my father from prying into my business, I reversed my initials and signed the paper "SP" instead of "PS." This way I figured he would not know that the question was mine.

I then rolled the paper back up into a little scroll, with the writing facing inside, and raised my hand for it to be collected by an assistant. When all the papers were collected, each scroll was inserted upright into one of the holes in a twelve-inch square of Peg-Board and placed on the pulpit in the middle of the stage. They looked like birthday candles atop a square wooden cake.

Moments later Reverend Busch clomped onto the stage. The plywood platform on which she stood reverberated and echoed as she walked over to the lectern. For such a fragile wisp of a woman, she made a hell of an entrance. Without so much as a hesitation or a greeting, she immediately began her service with "Lord, thank yew for our blessin's today." A small murmur of "amens" and "uh-huhs" rippled through the crowd. "Thank yew for the wisdom yew give to us. And thank yew, Almighty, for all yew have in store for yur beloved children."

"Uh-huh. Yes. Yes. That's right. Thank yew, Jesus," the congregation responded.

Walking back and forth across the stage, Reverend Busch continued, "All of yew are here today to receive the blessin's that only God can bestow upon yew."

"Mmmm-hmmmm."

"And God sees yew all . . ."

"Yes. Yes, Lord."

"God wants yew to know . . ."

"Praise God. Thank yew, God."

"Yes, God wants yew to know . . ."

"Yeah!"

"God says, He wants yew to know . . ."

"Amen."

In her delivery, Sophie Busch reminded me a bit of Reverend Ike, the black television preacher. As a kid, on Sunday mornings I would watch Reverend Ike's weekly broadcast, which started around six. My parents were still asleep. It must have been my father's influence that encouraged me to watch charismatic religious programs instead of cartoons. Unlike Sophie Busch, Reverend Ike preached one main concept: magic prosperity. Read the Bible and receive your God-given abundance. Prosperity was available through the power of prayer and his ministry. By joining his ministry, you received a small square of red cloth, cut with pinking shears, that was blessed by the reverend and promised to bring an end to your money woes.

After my very own "Reverend Ike Magic Prosperity Prayer Cloth" arrived in the mail, I carried it around with me at all times. At night it was carefully tucked under my pillow to work its magic powers. Eventually it disappeared before I was able to claim my God-given millions. I guess my mom found it in my pocket when doing the laundry and, thinking it was a rag, tossed it out. There went my early retirement.

"And now God has a message for yew . . ."

"Praise God. Say it. Amen."

At this point in the service, Reverend Busch's three-packs-a-day habit caught up to her. All this incantation and preaching had her doubled over in a fit of coughing and wheezing that lasted several minutes. No one paid any attention to this alarming tubercular demonstration. It happened every week. I was hoping she wouldn't die before she got to read my scroll. We all patiently waited until the reverend caught her breath.

Once she regained her composure, Miss Sophie walked over to the lectern, randomly picked up one of the tightly rolled scrolls of adding machine paper, and, without unrolling it, clenched it in her fist. She closed her eyes for just a moment to absorb the question

written on the paper and then raised her fist above her head for all
to see that her hand was still closed. I squeezed my eyes shut and
prayed that it was mine. Then she called out the initials she had
mentally read off the little scroll. It had remained tightly locked in
her fist the entire time.

"J.T.!" she called out to the crowd. No one raised a hand or acknowledged that he or she was J.T. Anonymity was a key part of Reverend Busch's service. She then began addressing J.T. with a specific
message. "Your boy's not doin' too good. Doctor say he got the pneumonia, and you havin' trouble meetin' the bills. I cain't help you none
with the bills. It gonna be rough this year. No way fixin' that right
now. Ain't no money comin' your way. But that boy a-yours is gonna
be okay, and that's the main thing. He needs rest now. Don't let him
go back to that summer school. He'll just up and get sick again. You
keep him away from the other children. By August he'll be just fine.
And you tell the doctor about your difficulties, and he won't charge
you a thing."

Scattered throughout the audience, several people acknowledged
the reading with "Yes. That's right. Jesus says. Thank you, Lord." I
didn't feel that I had to amen like everyone else, because Sophie hadn't
gotten to my question. If and when she did, I would give her a big
amen. But not until then.

Out of the twenty or so scrolls in the Peg-Board, she usually
picked three or four during the course of the service. According to my
father, God directed Sophie to pick the scrolls of those most in need.
Even though I felt included in that group, there was a good chance
that someone needed her more than I did. I was getting nervous that I
wouldn't be one of the lucky ones.

When she plucked the next scroll of paper from the Peg-Board,
Reverend Busch called out the initials "R.K." Holding the little paper
scroll in her fist, the reverend began to speak with a certain tone of
anger in her voice. "Now, R.K., yew listen to me, and yew listen
good and hard. Yew need to stop, and I mean stop right now, all
that runnin' around yew doin'. Every night someone new. Lotta bad

people round you. And then yew just go out and get that abortion one, two, three, like you goin' out for a soda or somethin'. This just bad. Yew need to stay in one place with one person. Keep this up, and yew gonna hurt yurself and everyone around yew. And for what? Now, stop this carryin' on. Yew hear me now? Yeah, I know all the reasons yew cain't. Yew cain't cause-a this and yew cain't cause-a that. But forget all that. Yew know that what I see is nothing but trouble gonna keep banging on yer door unless yew stop, and I mean stop right now. Right this second yew gotta stop, all this here carryin' on. Not tomorrow, not in ten minutes. I say yew stop this all right now. Hear? That's all I'm gonna say. Rest is up to yew. I ain't got nothing else to say on the matter." The congregation remained stone still except for a couple of knowing uh-huhs that rippled through the crowd. These women had been there and seen those man troubles with their own eyes.

None of the subject matter delivered by Reverend Busch seemed to disturb anybody. The attitude was "we all have our crosses to bear, and no one is any better or worse than anyone else." I looked over at Maya and noticed that her face was tight, pale white, and nearly frozen. Her jaw was clenched, and she was staring straight ahead.

"Hey, you okay? What's wrong? You don't look too good."

"I don't think I should have come here. I don't like this stuff. It's just too weird. I don't want to listen to these people's personal things; I think it's wrong. And all these people here . . . I don't know, it's not my thing, I just want to go home."

"Sorry, I shouldn't have brought you; I thought you would find it interesting. Yeah, I guess it can be a little weird. Just pretend you're watching a movie. That will help. I do that all the time." I knew it was a mistake to bring an outsider to something like this. I vowed never to do this again.

"I'm really upset right now."

"Shhh, Sophie is starting again." I reached out for Maya's hand, but she pulled away from me.

Sophie caught her breath, picked another scroll, and called out

"S.P." I sat bolt upright. She had picked my scroll. I looked up at my father; he didn't seem to notice that Sophie was talking to me. I was very nervous about what she would have to say about my question. From what I had observed at Sophie's church, she spoke the hard truth to everyone and didn't soft-pedal anything. No subject eluded her ESP.

With Sophie, you took her gospel straight. "I am sorry, but ain't nothin' yew can do about this. Ain't nothin' here for yew to fix. So yew might as well stop tryin'. This all whole thing started long time before yew was even born. This is their troubles to work out. Each one has to go their own way. Your mama and your dad can no longer be together. They got their own work to do. Yew just go and do the best yew can. Like I said, this ain't have nothing to do with yew. This is their mess, yew need to find yur own way. And yew know what I'm talking about. I know this hurts, but that's the way it is. You'll be fine."

This was definitely not what I wanted to hear, but I knew it was the truth. On my piece of paper, I had asked Reverend Busch what I could do to make my parents happy and get along. Ever since that night in the kitchen during the Cuban missile crisis, nothing had been the same around the house or between my parents. Pop was busy running around with his voodoo friends, and Mom was hiding in the bedroom waiting for everything to return to normal. She had a hard time understanding that the man she married was busy standing on his head and chasing the devil. This was not the marriage she had signed on for.

I wanted everything to go back to normal, before meditation, before the incense, and before exorcisms replaced going to the movies and spending Sunday at the beach with a picnic lunch. I wasn't sure how to turn back the clock for all of us. Somehow I believed that if I could convince them to get back together, then we could be one big, happy, premacrobiotic family once again. But according to Reverend Busch, there was nothing I could do about it. The spirits had spoken. No matter how much I craved to live in a house with 2.5 children, a dishwasher, and remote control television, it wasn't going to happen, not in this lifetime. What Sophie said made me so sad, I wanted to cry.

There was a time that my parents had been so happy, so in love, and so destined for a wonderful life. It started in 1950 when fate moved its powerful hand, and my father found himself decorating my maternal grandmother's apartment in New York City. My mother could not help but notice this handsome middle-aged man tossing around bolts of brightly colored fabrics while proposing dramatic alterations in the existing decor. It was kismet—love fostered by the pursuit of beauty.

Falling in love with her mother's married decorator is probably not the wisest choice for any woman of any age. But it was particularly not a good idea for my mother. For her, Pop was a kind of creative Clark Gable, a heaven-sent relief from a house filled with four siblings and a single mother who had to scramble to feed and clothe them during the Depression. Mom's father, who occasionally bootlegged bathtub gin, died of a stroke when she was only seven. Life became unspeakably hard. My father represented freedom from settling down with Mr. Nobody and life as a secretary. At twenty-four years of age, she had already been fired from her factory job assembling glass trinkets because she was Jewish, and her secretarial job at some developer's office was going nowhere. No matter what it might be, Esther was ready for the next big thing in her life.

A glamour addict since she was a child, my mother lived in the movies, sitting through double, triple, and quadruple features again and again until she had memorized every line and nuance of the film. Taking her life cues from Hollywood, she imagined her days starting with "Lights! Camera! Action!" and ending with "Cut! That's a take!" Standing before her was a man who had once been in the movie business and had worked with Charlie Chaplin, and who now designed furniture and jewelry, painted city landscapes with a palette knife, wrote epic poetry (which he regularly submitted to the *Paris Review*), created photographs that had been shown in Steichen's New York gallery, and could make a New York City apartment look drop-dead gorgeous. Perhaps, she thought, there was an opportunity here for a little lights, camera, action in her own life. She sensed in this man the promise of a life of style, glamour, and society.

Still married to his first wife, two-timing Lewie embarked on a whirlwind courtship of Esther with poetry readings in Greenwich Village, modern-dance recitals, and walks through the Metropolitan Museum of Art as if he owned the place. They frequented jewelry workshops on Eighth Street, where they designed matching silver rings with a hidden ruby that glowed through an opaque moonstone the color of fresh milk. He seemed to know everything—and she was willing to let him be her guide.

Their love thing was too much to bear. Finally my father got a divorce from Mrs. Smith numero uno. Mom found work to pay the alimony, while Pop headed down Miami way as the advance scout to seek and claim new territory where they could share their lives. His brief stint in Hollywood had already taught him the year-round pleasure of living in sun-drenched heat. With no money to find food or shelter, the Miami beaches became his open-air bedroom. He survived for months on nothing but wild coconuts, drinking their milk and eating their hard white meat. As a midcentury Tarzan, he wrote passionate love letters to his Jane, begging her to come join him in his tropical jungle paradise. While it may seem romantic, it could not have been an easy life change for him at forty-seven.

Scrambling for money, he designed some exotic African-esque figurines that he was able to convince a man to cast for him out of plaster. At night he would paint them in empty parking lots illuminated by a few bare bulbs, and by day he went door to door. Eventually he scraped up enough cash to send for my mother. The starstruck lovers had a quick don't-tell-anyone marriage at city hall. The bride wore black, and it was done—for better or worse.

Just after the "I do's," Mom peered into the surrounding sun-bleached, flat, alien landscape and wondered what the hell she had gotten into. When Mom moved down, she was expecting lovers in paradise. The truth was that this was no kosher kitchen. With money and God an issue, the couple looked for shelter around upper Biscayne Boulevard, just past the Eazy Breeze trailer park. There a small white stucco two-story apartment building with rats, snakes, the occasional possum, and a broken stove became home. The eagle-eyed Baptist landlady took their money with no questions asked, no forms to be filled in, and no credit check.

Two days later Miss Baptist casually asked, "Hey, y'all ain't Jews, are ya?" Affirmative. The local sheriff was sent to free the property from the filthy Hebrew influence. Mom, unaware that being Jewish was a crime, fast-talked/sweet-talked that redneck with the blond peach fuzz on top. After a little back-and-forth, along with a stunning display of her intelligence, he tipped his hat and proclaimed, "Evenin', ma'am," calling it a day.

In this small hellhole hothouse of an apartment, Pop managed to look for work, paint portraits of local Haitian women, and began to create magnificent floating mobiles made from pieces of found scrap metal. Despite the economic hardship at the time, the abundant heat and sun were luxurious enough to fuel his creativity. Mom loved the idea of being married to this brilliant bohemian artist and living on the edge, contrary to everything she had ever known. Growing up in the Depression taught her to seek stability and security. But with my father, she was willing to throw all those goals out the window in exchange for a more interesting life.

It was a great love story. Unfortunately, "happily ever after" was not in the cards as it should have been.

Mine was the last question that Sophie answered that day. She looked tired. As she put my scroll back into the Peg-Board holder, she said, "God has spoken."

"That's right . . . Amen."

six

•

Meet the Preacher

The police car behind me came to a screeching halt. Maya turned around and said, "Uh-oh, I think they're after us."

"Just keep walking," I said. "We didn't do anything wrong." I heard the squad car's doors slam.

Maya and I were hanging out in the Grove, the overgrown, jungly portion of Miami that had become the secluded outpost for the bohemian rich, poor blacks, fabulous decorators who loved carpets with bold geometric patterns, and free-love hippies. We were on our way to the Head Shop on Oak Avenue.

Run by a visionary hippie—a skinny white boy with a big 'fro named Mike Lang, who would eventually go on to become one of the major driving forces behind the Woodstock music festival—the Head Shop was the gathering place for Miami's nascent hippie community. Mike had taken over a dilapidated wooden house that bordered on the black section and turned it into hippie headquarters. Inside the store was a small selection of trippy paraphernalia that I'm sure one day will show up at auction at Sotheby's: Day-Glo posters by Mouse Kelley advertising concerts at the Fillmore by Big Brother and the Holding Company or the Grateful Dead; brass pipes; Indian flutes decorated with pictures of Krishna; kaleidoscopes; and fluorescent colored plastic boxes for storing "stash." Anything that sparkled or was reflective ended up in the display case for Mike to sell to the local hippies. I would sit for hours on the store's steps. Throughout the day and night, people would congregate outside in small groups. God knows what critical information they were exchanging with one another. This was going to be Maya's first trip to hippie HQ.

I had to be careful. Introducing her to my father and Sophie Busch didn't work too well. Despite the magical otherwordliness of the Head Shop, where life passed in slo-mo, the people I hung out with there were a bunch of runaway underage kids who were nothing more than a pack of wild dogs. They slept on filthy mattresses in abandoned apartments with the windows smashed out and thought nothing of breaking into people's homes for money to buy food, drugs, and more drugs. We panhandled on Grand Avenue for spare change to buy cigarettes, sold the *Bulldog* and other underground newspapers that advocated revolution and "killing the pigs," and generally formed our own unit of antisocial delinquent outcasts. I'm surprised more of us didn't end up in jail.

Within seconds, another police car came to a screeching halt in front of us. We were pinned between the two cars. Six cops surrounded us.

"Hey, faggot, what's this, your mother's dirty rug?" The cop was tugging on my Mexican serape.

"Yeah, hippie shit, what's that filthy rag?" another cop spoke.

Then a huge cop stepped forward, his hand on his holster, and asked, "Where do you think you're off to, buying drugs? I'll bet you both are carrying some joints. Hey, Cecil, give this here girl—I mean guy—a patdown. Check out his woman friend as well."

Maya started crying. Two cops descended on her. They dumped

the contents of her purse on the road and used their feet to kick it around to see if there were any drugs. They picked up a bottle of Midol. One cop yelled, "Rick, got something!"

The big cop walked over and held up the bottle, looking at it carefully. Holding it between his thumb and forefinger, he shook it in Maya's face. It sounded like a pair of maracas. "Looky what we got here, young lady. I'd say you're looking at ten years, easy." With that, a second cop grabbed her hands and pulled them behind her back as if he was going to handcuff her. He flashed the big cop a huge grin like he had just caught the biggest kingfish out in the bay. "Yep, you sure got a problem here, missy. I knew you were a user just by lookin' at you. And I bet your little boyfriend's a dealer. Is he your pimp, too?" Both cops nearly doubled over in laughter.

The three cops that were guarding me found nothing in my pockets except a pair of house keys and nine single dollars. The big cop turned to me and said, "Son, you didn't answer my question, where are you off to?"

"We're going for a walk."

"Where are you walking to, your local stash house?"

"No, we're just out for a walk."

"Son, I'm going to ask you one more time, where you walking to?"

"We thought we'd get some ice cream."

"Ice cream? Now where do you get ice cream at this time of night and in this neighborhood?"

"That's why we're out for a walk, to find some ice cream."

With that, the big cop signaled one of the cops next to me with his chin. The cop kneed my groin and punched me in the stomach.

"Now, you still think you're out for some ice cream, or maybe something else? We can continue to refresh your memory as long as it's necessary."

"Uhhhhhhh," was the only answer I could utter.

"Huh? What'd you say? I couldn't hear you."

"Uhhhhhhh."

"Son, you just don't want to answer my question, do you?"

Wham! Another knee, another punch to my stomach.

Maya continued to cry. At that point, the big cop opened her Midol bottle, looked inside, and spilled them on the road. He then crunched them with his feet. "Cecil, you know, I think the best thing would be to just let these folks lead us to their home base. Let 'em go, and we'll follow them; they'll take us where we want to go. Oh, Bobby, if you want that fella's rag that he's wearin' to wipe your ass, go right ahead. It's yours." With that, the cop behind me named Bobby grabbed my serape, threw it into the backseat of the car, and let out a rodeo whoop. All the cops started yelling as they piled into the two squad cars and squealed off.

"Are you all right?" Maya came running over to me with tears in her eyes. "Oh my God, I was so scared, I thought they would kill us! Why did they do that to us?"

"For fun. They had nothing else to do."

"Do you think they'll follow us?"

"No, they'll find someone else to bother. I'll tell you what, instead of the Head Shop, let's go over to the Feedbag restaurant. They're having a screening of a Kenneth Anger movie and a Warhol film starting at midnight. I think you'll like them."

"What's a Warhol film?"

Maya and I weren't the only ones spending time in the Grove. In order to escape the imploding universe at home, Mom on weekends would attend a matinee at the Coconut Grove Playhouse. Afterward she and her friends would have lunch at the cozy Taurus Steak House, an old wooden shack nestled among the monster-sized banyan trees particular to the Grove.

One Saturday afternoon, as she sat down for lunch, she noticed Tennessee Williams sitting at the table next to hers. She leaned over and told him that she had seen *Summer and Smoke*.

"Well," Tennessee purred, "did you like it?"

"Like it? I was so depressed that I couldn't get out of bed for a week."

"Oh, good, it's supposed to be depressing." Tennessee smiled.

"Who the hell needs you? I can get depressed on my own." And with that, both parties returned to their lunch.

Pop also began to spend more time in the Grove. In the midst of this hippie heaven, there were a number of people interested in the supernatural. At times he would bring me to meetings held at the rambling pink Spanish Mediterranean bayfront estate of a former *Vogue* model from the fifties who was recently divorced from her husband, who had been a part of the military-industrial complex. The Vietnam War had been especially good to her and her gorgeous blond children. She was spreading her alimony wealth among freaks, flower children, and gurus.

The group usually consisted of a few stoned-out hippies who thought my father was a narc, a couple of massage therapists looking for a sugar daddy, and two or three librarian types seeking to free themselves from the earthly bonds of their dreary lives. Occasionally a medium would show up and produce astounding mind-reading demonstrations. Other times everyone held hands and tried to "feel each other's psychic energy." Or they might play a type of ESP parlor game where someone would write down a word or the name of a country, and they tried to "tune in to their being" and guess the answer. All together now: "ommmmmmmmmmm." After the meeting, "organic food"—the latest fad—was served. Brown rice balls with shredded carrots, pecans, and dates sprinkled with coconut were brought out on a tray by the Dominican butler along with a huge kettle of Mu tea— the drink of choice for committed macrobiotics.

Eventually my father moved on and discovered a more serious study group in South Miami. Each meeting started with a meditation followed by a different psychic experiment or discussion. Routinely, my father fell asleep as soon as the meditation began. He would sleep through the entire class, and then at the exact moment the class ended, he would wake up refreshed. It was a standing joke that before the meeting started, someone would inquire as to whether or not my father had taken his nap.

Marcia Flowers, the woman who ran the group, told me that on one specific occasion, my father woke up from his meditation nap and was suddenly a different person. Everyone in the room commented on his changed appearance. She described my father as now having a highly energized aura. It was her belief that during these naps he traveled to another dimension where higher beings were preparing him for his healing work.

At this particular meeting, my father rubbed his eyes after he woke up, got up without saying a word, and walked over to someone who was quite ill. He stood behind her and slowly placed his hands on her shoulders. As he stood there, he closed his eyes for about two minutes. When he opened his eyes, he removed his hands, and the woman commented that for the first time in days she felt a complete absence of symptoms. Without any explanation, my father had performed his first healing.

About a week after this incident, my father walked into a lecture by Arthur Ford, who headed the Spiritual Frontiers Fellowship (SFF), an organization of people interested in expanding the possibilities of human consciousness. This was in 1968. Arthur Ford was a world-famous medium who had spent much of the early twentieth century contacting the dead before large audiences throughout both Europe and the United States, including sold-out performances at Carnegie Hall. His messages from the other side were relayed to his clients by an entity known as "Fletcher," a spirit who took over Arthur's body as soon as he went into trance. Ford's clients and friends included Aldous Huxley, Upton Sinclair, Gloria Swanson, King George of Greece, astronaut Edgar D. Mitchell, and Mrs. Harry Houdini.

Ford's encounter with Mrs. Houdini sealed his worldwide reputation as a first-rate psychic with extraordinary powers. Harry Houdini spent much of his professional life exposing fraudulent psychics and mediums. However, in 1926 just before he died, he left a complicated ten-word secret coded message with his wife, Bess. No one but Houdini and his wife knew the exact words and their meaning contained in this code. Their understanding was that if a medium was able to deliver this message to Bess after Houdini died, then this was firm evidence that there is life after death. For many years Mrs. Houdini received thousands of letters from various psychics claiming that they had received the code. There was even a $10,000 reward offered to the person who could reveal the code. Unfortunately, none of them was correct.

During one of his trance sessions, Ford commented that Houdini's mother had come to him in a vision and appeared with the word *forgive*. This had been the exact word agreed upon between Houdini and his mother as a signal of communication from the great beyond. Once Ford was in psychic communication with Houdini's mother, it then opened the door for Houdini himself to begin communicating through Ford.

Over a period of weeks, Houdini would appear to Ford and give him a word here and there of his code. Then in one evening session, the entire code came through as "Rosabelle—Answer—Tell—Pray—Answer—Look—Tell—Answer—Answer—Tell."

As Ford reported in his autobiography, *Nothing So Strange,* this session was witnessed by a Mr. John W. Stafford, who was then the associate editor of *Scientific American* magazine, and his friend Francis Fast. These two then took the written code and delivered it to Mrs. Houdini, who proclaimed that the code was correct. Houdini had broken through the silence of death and delivered the code as agreed. However, this was just the first step in the cryptic communication between the dead Houdini and his living wife.

Mrs. Houdini then requested a session with Ford, which was witnessed by a number of observers, including a member of the United Press. During this trance, Houdini came through and delivered the same ten words. Only Houdini's wife knew that each word was a part of a carefully constructed code that once deciphered spelled out "Rosabelle Believe." This was Houdini's message from the afterlife. The press was notified in a written statement by Mrs. Houdini that, in fact, the great Houdini had come back from the dead. This astounding demonstration brought Ford global attention and solidified his reputation as one of the world's great psychics.

Arthur worked the celebrity circuit on both sides of the Atlantic with impressive results. He was shuttled from yachts to first-class hotels, ever ready to dispense precious psychic advice to heads of state and the needy rich.

Ford was a curious character. While gifted with extraordinary supernatural talents and a direct line to those who had passed on, he was reportedly plagued by obsessions that included fastidious skin care and the need to drink. His personal life was usually solitary, but occasionally it would be peopled by devoted companions of both sexes.

The topic of that Sunday's lecture by Ford was on mediumship and the afterlife. There were maybe fifteen people sitting on wooden folding chairs in a small church off North Miami Avenue. The audience was composed largely of single women, mainly in their fifties. At first glance, they could have been widowed or never quite got to the altar and were leading small, unnoticed lives. They were here for a last chance at hope and redemption.

Ford used his sonorous voice and profound intelligence to captivate his small audience, as he had done his whole life. Having briefly attended the Transylvania College for seminary studies, he learned his Bible and became a charismatic preacher. Unlike Pentecostal preachers who just scared the hell out of you, Arthur masterfully combined the Bible and religious history with a live feed from the hereafter. He was convincing to all present. As usual, my father taped this and many more of Ford's lectures. They are nothing short of captivating. At this lecture, Ford spoke about reincarnation, mixing strong biblical references with his own work as a clairvoyant.

Ford opened the lecture with the single most provocative question for humanity: "Where does the spirit go after physical death? You don't immediately go to heaven and play a harp. First you have to iron out your character when you are free of the body. You go where you choose to go; God doesn't send you there. You are the same person in the spirit world as you are here.

"Christianity started as a healing cult. It was taken over by the Roman emperor Constantine. Read in the New Testament from First

Corinthians 12:15, where Saint Paul lists all the spiritual and psychic gifts. He says you all have them, and you should use them for a purpose. In chapter thirteen he talks about love and says that before we can plunge into another dimension, we must get straightened out in this dimension, get rid of jealousy, greed, all those negative things that are often part of our lives. Develop positive love; make love your aim.

"Saint Paul gives you an account of what happens after you die. Go as far back as you like, and you will find that in the earliest written accounts, four thousand years before Jesus, people were aware of an invisible world. All religions grew out of the effort on the part of man to contact that world in some way. Jesus said, 'The things I do, you can do.' Paul knew there was a guiding force in the universe. Heal the sick. Raise the dead. Preach the gospel.

"Freud once said to me, 'If I had my life to live over again, I would be a psychical researcher.' The whole system of psychiatry and analysis as we know it today grew out of the work of a trance medium."

While Ford spoke, my father looked around for an empty seat. A woman sitting off to the side suddenly turned around and motioned my father to come over to her. He thought she was going to point him toward a seat. Instead she whispered, "I see in your aura that you are a healer. Please help me; I can't stop this terrible cough. Place your hands on my shoulders and send me your energy."

Puzzled by her request, my father reluctantly complied. While Arthur continued to speak, he touched her shoulders and began to feel a warm heat emanating from his hands. After about two minutes, he felt the heat subside and, without thinking, lifted his hands from the woman's shoulders.

"Thank you. You have healed me. I am better now." She turned back to listening to Ford at the podium as if nothing had happened.

Arthur continued: "We know that there is a cosmic force, and if you identify with that, you get results. We need to make healing legal again in the church. The medical profession is a fool's corporation. I don't think any spiritual healer who works honestly will get in trouble. They can do nothing to you if you work in a religious manner, especially if you don't prescribe. A spiritual healer doesn't need to diagnose or prescribe. The same power that heals a heart condition can heal a lung condition or a brain condition. There is no law against it unless you begin to practice medicine. You have all the power you need if you only learn to use it." With these few sentences, it was as if Ford was speaking directly to my father. Over the next several years, my father would be hounded continually by the authorities for "practicing medicine without a license."

Pop noticed that there was an empty seat a few rows up. He sat down and listened to the rest of the lecture. Arthur concluded with, "The only way for me to see God is to see Him in action through a person who does things through love. This is how God takes form."

When Arthur finished, people gathered to ask questions. Pop wanted to meet this man who spoke of healings and love. As he tried to make his way to Ford, he was stopped by a woman who delivered the same exact message he had heard earlier: "You are a healer, and I need your help. I have a heart condition." Without thinking or questioning, he walked to an empty seat, and after she sat down, he put one hand on top of her head and another on her shoulder. Once again he experienced a tremendous surge of heat in his hands, as if someone had suddenly plugged him into an electrical outlet. When the healing was complete, he felt the heat subside from his hands as if they were controlled thermostatically.

As he attempted one more time to make his way toward Arthur, he was stopped by a third woman who requested that he share his healing powers with her. "I was recently hospitalized with cancer," she said. "The doctor told me that I only have another month to live."

Worried that he would give this woman false hope, he said, "I'm so sorry, but there is nothing I can do for you."

"Yes, there is. You can heal me. I know you can. You have the energy that I need. Please give it to me. It will take only a minute, and it will make a huge difference in whether I live or die."

For the third time, my father performed a healing. When he lifted his hands, he looked around, and the church was now quiet and empty. He said good-bye to the woman and walked out to his car. There were only two cars remaining in the parking lot. As he put the key in the door, a man came up and introduced himself. "I am Arthur Ford, and I am supposed to meet you," he said.

"I enjoyed your lecture. Lately I've become very interested in healing."

"Yes, I know. You have a lot of work to do. You will be creating new methods of healing." My father didn't bother to ask how he knew. If anyone had access to psychic information about my father, it would have been Arthur. The two men instantly became best friends. While Ford was alive, they met constantly to discuss metaphysical matters. Arthur often introduced my father at his lectures as an "extraordinary healer."

While he was alive, Ford began contacting my father on a daily basis via psychic means with invaluable information on healing as well as answers to many of his problems. Even after Ford died, in 1971, he continued to "talk" to my father on a daily basis. One could think of this spirit communication as a regular "phone call" from a distant relative. Usually around four in the morning, my father would wake up and begin writing down the spirit dictation that Ford and others would implant in his brain. Over the years these messages grew to over five thousand pages of written communication from the unseen spirit world.

This ability to receive psychic dictation took some time for Pop to perfect. At first my father thought that he was imagining the words that came to him, and that they were his own creation rather than a direct link to the spirit world. Arthur reassured my father that the thoughts he was receiving were not his own. "You can't seem to let go of the thought that perhaps these words are yours and not mine. This questioning is good up to a point. The point is reached when your thought prevents my words from coming through. A telephone conversation would be interminably long if each few words are interrupted with the question 'Is this still you?' After you have confirmed that it is I, blank out your mind and let me come through."

As my father increased his ability to receive spirit communication, Arthur sent him a message instructing him to be more receptive. "We enter through a doorway which must be unobstructed, or our way is barred. This holds true with the mind and its thoughts. A cluttered mind cannot send forth clear thoughts. Unburden your mind and open the passage so that thoughts can flow and transform into words that your pen will solidify into permanence. Stand aside so that the channel is open and the flow is maintained, else you bar the way. The bounty is endless only if the way is clear. Receive without obstruction."

Pop had finally found the focus that he was looking for. The experiences that he had at Ford's lecture and at the meeting in South Miami were, for him, unmistakable signs that he was now a healer. Someone or something had suddenly flicked the switch and turned on his magic powers. Now, like a kid with a new toy, my father was eager to try his recently acquired abilities on anyone who was sick. It didn't matter if they had a cold or colitis, he loved to touch them, feel his hands heat up, and watch their symptoms disappear. It was as if he had waited his whole life to feel this surge of supernatural energy flowing through him doing good deeds for humankind.

Once again our house underwent a tangible transition due to my father's psychic interests. Seemingly overnight our isolated house became Lourdes central. People arrived in wheelchairs and on crutches, which they usually left behind. Bottles of medicine taken over the course of a lifetime were thrown in the garbage on their way out the door. Word quickly spread that my father could cure whatever ailed you. Pop was a bit like a teenager who had just received his driver's license but wasn't a really experienced driver. All he knew was that when he placed his hands near people, they felt better and they got better. Beyond this simple fact, he had no idea what was going on, how it was happening, or why. People arrived in beat-up old Fords and Rolls-Royces to see the miracle man. Often I would wait out in the backyard while Pop dissolved their tumors or healed their sore throat, so that I didn't have to interact with them.

Generally, Pop would have the patient sit in one of our white wicker chairs. Without saying a word, he would begin running his hands over the top of the person's head and then slowly over the front and back of his or her body as he intuitively searched for hot spots of disease that needed his healing energy. He looked like one of today's airport screeners "wanding" a passenger for metal items. Like a Geiger counter, his hands would suddenly react to a weak spot or a diseased area. It was at this particular spot that he would let his hands pause to pour forth the healing energy.

Eventually my father was able to instantly locate the specific areas needing his attention. One of his spirit guides—named Chander Sen, who had been a Tibetan monk in the fourteenth century—would shine a small pinpoint of white light that only my father could see, on the specific area where he needed to direct his energy.

Pop would stand stock-still, letting his healing energy pour into the person's body until this white light turned pink. This was the visible signal that the patient had received sufficient healing energy. During these healings, the house became very quiet. You could hear the dogs barking over on the next block. It was if the world had stopped while the mad scientist was at work. While all this transfer of healing energy was occurring, Mom would close herself off in the bedroom to read and smoke, waiting and hoping our lives would suddenly return to normal.

Oftentimes the patients would be spontaneously invited to join us for dinner, much to the surprise and dismay of my mother. These dinners served to celebrate a successful healing both for my father and for the patient. Though she never said a word, I could tell that my mother did not welcome these total strangers who captured my father's attention and intruded upon our family time. Her legendary social skills abruptly disappeared whenever a patient took center stage and left us off to the side of his attention. What was she supposed to do? Turn to a total stranger and say, "Tell me, Mrs. Wright, how did it feel when you discovered that you had a terminal diagnosis? Oh my, you must tell me all about it."

For me it was odd to witness this constant parade of outsiders who disappeared behind closed doors with my father and then an hour later emerged with a smile and an air of tranquillity to break bread as if we were all old friends. I sensed that these people were somehow not clean, but, rather, diseased and dirty; I didn't want them too close to me. My father, on the other hand, beamed when talking to his new-found friends/patients.

As his caseload increased, our lanai became an ad hoc waiting room. I would pretend not to look at the crowd of miracle-seeking, disease-ridden humanity as I passed them on my way to the living room.

Possibly in response to my father's miraculous helping of strangers, Mom became involved in Daytop Village, an early rehab center for addicts. She read everything she could on drug addiction, including medical studies, autobiographies, and hipster literature. Mom flew up to New York for a meeting with the Daytop Village brass. Most likely her subconscious goal was to open a local chapter in Miami, in case I needed to be treated. Mom would now talk excitedly about methadone and new protocols for getting people off of heroin and speed. LSD remained more problematic. Just as my father was curing physical disease, Mom was interested in curing the disease of addiction. Eventually the support promised her never materialized and the project collapsed.

One weekday morning in October, I slept through my alarm. When I finally opened my eyes, it seemed that it was still the middle of the night. The sky was an oppressive greenish charcoal black, the color of a still pond. This type of sky appeared only during major end-of-the-world storms—the torrential, awe-inspiring storms that shut Miami down for days. You knew the storm was bad when you heard the birds screeching frantically at one another to get the hell out of town. The typical aftermath of these storms left houses flooded, water wells backed up and undrinkable, cars unable to start, electricity out—and forget the phones; that would take another month. Downed power lines wove themselves across the road. Huge felled trees made many roads impassable. I felt as if I were in a surround-sound jungle

movie as the birds continued to talk about the storm. The air had that
heaviness to it that seemed to connote a lethal subelectrical charge
surging through the atmosphere. You could feel the pressure throughout your entire body. The only light came from enormous cracks of
lightning that appeared to rip open the sky.

I started to raise myself to turn around and look at the clock but
found that I couldn't move my body. I was paralyzed—my arms, my
legs, and my neck all felt completely numb, accompanied by a strange
electrical tingling.

I heard my father getting ready for work. I tried to call his name.
The best I could do was make a quiet whine: *"ehhhhhhhhh, ehhhh-*
hhh, ehhhh, ehhh." I was trying to push out the sound with my breath.
"Ehhhh, ehhhh, ehhh, ehhh, ehhh." I lay there with my eyes open, listening to the thunder. *"Ehhhh, ehhh, ehh."*

My father walked past my bedroom but didn't come in. He headed
for the kitchen. I could hear him turn on the blender. I tried sending
him telepathic thoughts that I needed help. "Pop, please come help
me! I can't move!" The only signal I got back was the *whirrrrr* of the
blender as he mixed up his usual morning breakfast. Then I heard the
front door slam and the car start. He must have been leaving early for
work. I couldn't believe he was going to drive in this storm. My only
hope was that my mother would eventually get up and find me.

Moments later the front door opened. Pop must have realized that
he had to wait out the storm. I was going to try to catch his attention
by making some noise, but I didn't have to. He came into my room,
looked at me, and asked, "Are you okay?"

"Uuhh, uhhh, uhhh, uhhhh," was my response.

He leaned over and put his hand on my forehead. "You're burning
up. Let's see what's going on." Pop sat down next to me and started
running his hands over my body. At first they felt hot, and then suddenly they turned wonderfully cool. Like a slow-motion windshield
wiper, he kept moving his hands back and forth, back and forth over
my entire body.

After he pulled his hands away, my head seemed unbelievably

heavy and fell to the side from its own weight. That was the first sign that I could move again. I wiggled the ends of my fingers. Whatever this paralysis was, it was slowly lifting. Pop looked at me and said, "You have nerve-gas poisoning. A lot of people are mysteriously getting sick, and no one knows what it is."

"Nerve gas!" I thought to myself. "What the hell is he talking about? How did I get that? I haven't been sniffing any nerve gas."

"I've got to remove this poisonous gas before it destroys your nervous system." He closed his eyes and said, "I remove all the toxic nerve gas from this body and send it to the sun for purification." With great regularity, my father used the blast furnace of the sun as a dumping ground for anything toxic. This included viruses, bad pharmaceuticals, and any kind of negative energy. Mentally, Pop would beam the offending items to the sun, where the intense heat would instantly obliterate the noxious substance, rendering it harmless. He always used this technique when he psychically removed cancerous cells and tumors from patients. Off the cancer went at the speed of light to be autoclaved by solar flares. I liked this idea and wondered if I couldn't use it to beam a couple kids from school to the sun for instantaneous incineration.

I vaguely remember watching a talk show at the time with Dick Cavett or David Susskind interviewing some genius think-tank type guy like Herman Kahn about how to dispose of nuclear waste. His solution was to put it on a rocket ship and send it to the sun for incineration. I told my father about the program, and he smiled and said, "Oh yes, we've been doing that for years with anything negative. It's a good idea."

As he placed his hands on my forearm, Pop began to explain how I had contracted this nerve gas. "Over the past few years, the government has been secretly dumping concrete containers filled with unused nerve gas off the coast of Florida. This was their way of burying this toxic waste that was left over from the government's chemical warfare program. Because of the movement of the ocean and, of course, this storm, some of those containers are cracking open, and the nerve gas is escaping. Somehow you were exposed."

"Ohhhhhkay," I thought to myself. "Last time I got sick it had something to do with my aura being out of alignment, which drained my energy from my etheric body, which resulted in my coming down with pneumonia. So now it's nerve gas coming up from the ocean floor. That sounds about right. I'll go with the nerve-gas explanation. Why not?" In situations like this, I felt that I had to humor my father a little bit, so I accepted each wacky new explanation with a straight face.

As cynical as I could be at times, I was also completely certain that my father knew things that no one else in the world knew. No matter how crazy they sounded, no matter how much I didn't want to believe him, no matter how everyone in the world would laugh at him, in the end, he was always right. The truth was that Pop could do things that no one else could do. Plus, after he ran his hands over my body, I could suddenly walk and talk again. Hard to argue with that.

Craaaaaack! Boooooom! Nature's soundtrack was deafening. The Miami End-of-the-World Thunder and Lightning Show had picked up again. The rain was coming down in hard, solid sheets, as if the monsoons had arrived. Visibility was two to three inches, if that. These intense tropical rains washed the air, and I hoped that they would wash away all the nerve gas that was making me sick.

Forgetting that I had been completely paralyzed just a few minutes earlier, I propped myself up in bed to talk to my father. Clearly, whatever he did was working; otherwise I couldn't have moved on my own. It was a quick journey from near-total paralysis to a casual father-son chat, which was cut short when he said, "I'm going to be late for a new client that's coming in from Switzerland to see me. I've got to go."

"But what about the storm? Do you think you should drive in this rain?"

"It'll be over within fifteen minutes."

Looking outside my window at the dense gray air, I couldn't imagine this storm ending before midnight. By the time I finally pulled myself out of bed, the sky had cleared as if the storm had never happened.

For years afterward, I completely forgot about my nerve-gas paralysis—until I came across a 2000 report titled "The Concept of Weapons of Mass Destruction: Chemical and Biological Weapons, Use in Warfare, Impact on Society and Environment," given at the Beijing Seminar on Arms Control. It confirmed that my father was correct about the dumping of nerve gas off the coast of Florida. The report stated: "During the 1950s, the U.S. conducted an ambitious nerve-gas program, manufacturing what would eventually total 400,000 M-55 rockets, each of which was capable of delivering a 5-kg payload of sarin. Many of those rockets had manufacturing defaults, their propellant breaking down in a manner that could lead to auto ignition. For this reason, in 1967 and 1968, 51,180 nerve-gas rockets were dropped 240 km off the coast of New York State in depths of from 1,950 to 2,190 meters, and off the coast of Florida."

A few days after I read this document, *The New York Times* reported on October 9, 2002, that "the Defense Department says it used chemical warfare and live biological agents during cold-war-era military exercises on American soil . . . according to previously secret documents cleared for release to Congress on Wednesday . . . The reports, which detail tests conducted from 1962 to 1971, reveal for the first time that the chemical warfare agents were used during exercises on American soil . . . and that a mild biological agent was used in Florida . . . Some milder substances did escape into the atmosphere . . . in an area of Florida . . ." Milder substances? Apparently my father was able to psychically access military secrets and activities almost thirty-five years earlier than *The New York Times*.

About a week after Pop neutralized the nerve gas in my body, I woke up in the middle of the night, hearing muffled voices. In my stupor, I thought I was at a séance and one of the spirits was trying to get through but had a bad connection. On several occasions I had actually seen this happen, where the guest entity (the dead person) could not quite align his or her vibrations with the host, and the message came out garbled, like a tape recorder playing something backward. This particular night, I wasn't fully awake and couldn't quite figure out where these voices were coming from. I wasn't sure if I was dreaming or not.

As a child with a hyperactive imagination, I frequently woke up in the middle of the night because of Technicolor nightmares with full Dolby sound. If only I had written them down, I could have sold them all as scripts for science-fiction B films and become the king of drive-in movies. At night I often heard possums walking on our roof. I thought these rapid little footsteps were aliens about to break into the house and kidnap me. Or I feared that there were unspeakable monsters gathering in my closet waiting to attack me. I would wake up terrified and cry for my father to come sleep with me, which he did. After some time, I would fall back asleep, feeling protected. Sleep was not my favorite activity as a child.

On good nights I dreamed repeatedly of flying enormous distances with great velocity. I not only flew around Miami proper but around the earth's upper atmosphere. Whenever I wanted to lift off, I just had to give a little jump, and I was quickly airborne. I did not have a cape like a superhero, just my own natural jet propulsion.

Even more disturbing than these nightmares was when I occasionally woke up to find myself actually floating about five feet above my bed. I would turn my head and look down, as if I were peering over a railing, and see my bed below me. During these events, the room was always illuminated with a kind of pulsing pinkish light with gold sparkles. Sometimes my body would rotate slowly as if on a gurney. Nothing much happened; I just hovered in midair for a few minutes and then would slowly descend until I landed softly back in my bed. It would take me another ten or fifteen minutes to relax and go back to sleep. I never told anyone about these occurrences, as I simply assumed that everyone woke up in the middle of the night floating five feet above his bed.

Many years later my father and I attended a lecture on astral travel. I learned that these experiences are known as out-of-body experiences. Among my father's friends, they were reverently referred to as OOBEs (pronounced "oh-bees") and were considered quite an accomplishment. Not everyone was able to have an OOBE. For some reason, I assumed they were pronounced *oooh-bees,* as in, "Oh boy, did I have a big oooh-bee last night" or "I'm exhausted because I was out all last night on my oooh-bee." Like participants at an AA meeting, his friends were always eager to share a report of an OOBE, especially if they could claim to have traveled to a distant planet or visited dead relatives who were now living and working on the other side. My father often spoke about leaving his body at night to travel to different dimensions where he would learn new healing methods. He was always met in his journey by knowledgeable spirit guides who took him to laboratories as well as other places of advanced healing. My father truly went to night school, only it wasn't on this planet.

That night in bed, I listened intently to the hushed voices, trying to make out what was being said. It sounded like code spoken in staccato tones, intense with emotion. As I became fully awake, I realized that the sounds were coming from my parents' room. They were having a discussion in the middle of the night. Something was wrong.

The truth is that something had been very wrong for the past year. Weeks went by when my mother moved into the living room and slept on the couch. She smoked and watched TV, and retreated to her own world, just as my father retreated to his. This was her form of protest, a sit-in against her crumbling marriage. Looking back, she badly needed someone to talk to about her pain and her loss of the joyful marriage that was once her dream come true. She was alone with her grief. No one was there to help her through this catastrophic crisis. Her SOS went unnoticed by the only two available witnesses: my father and me.

Glittering nights in Havana casinos, glamorous clients, and a stable, happy home—all the touchstones of her life—had vanished. There was nothing there to replace it. Bleak House had arrived. I was too young to know what questions to ask, to know how to listen, or to know how to even raise the topic, except anonymously with Sophie Busch. My father was overwhelmed by his new abilities and failed to notice that in the process, my mother and I had been displaced.

It appeared that at this point Pop was so busy with his new life that he didn't care what happened to any of us. Mom's courage and her determination not to appear weak or needy created a facade of stubbornness. In this standoff, she was not going to be the first person to raise the white flag. Unlike my father, she did not have a flying saucer parked outside waiting to whisk her away to a new life.

My parents were overwhelmed by their circumstances—one lost in thought, the other lost in space—and at times their mutual disinterest in each other could make me invisible. As a result, I had an unusual amount of independence. At any time of day or night I would jump on my bike and explore hidden areas of Miami, including vacant lots filled with poisonous plants, coral rock mansions, and abandoned shacks. Sometimes I would collect fallen mangoes and avocados that served as my lunch. If it was getting dark and approaching dinnertime, I would ride through the poorer neighborhoods and collect discarded soda bottles for the two-cent deposit. Eventually I filled my basket with enough bottles to buy a small box of Quickin' Chicken for dinner. During these long, thoughtful rides I always hoped that by the time I returned home, my parents would have finally sorted it all out.

One morning, to my great surprise, my father offered to drive me to school. I hadn't seen much of him for weeks because of his new schedule of working and running off to séances, yoga classes, and metaphysical lectures. For most of the trip, we rode in silence. Neither of us had really spoken to the other in a while, and we barely knew what to say. Finally I said, "You and Mom have to get a divorce. I can't take it anymore." He nodded his head. The following day he moved into the guesthouse next door, and my mother filed papers. Determined to make a clean start, she turned everything over to my father: the house, her jewelry, her car, her money. Everything except me.

At the time, divorce was really not that common. There was still the stigma of a "broken home" that hovered over my few friends at school whose parents had divorced. I thought it was cool and modern to have divorced parents and wore it like a badge of honor. However, society, along with banks and other financial institutions, did not look kindly on a forty-four-year-old woman with no income, no savings, no job—no nothing except a child to support. This was a time when banks did not issue credit cards to women directly in their name but rather as "Mrs. Robert S. Montgomery" or "Mrs. Lew Smith." Single women simply did not have credit cards.

Unfortunately, Mom had not really thought this thing through. The vivacious spontaneity that once made her the life of the party had backfired and resulted in disastrous decision making. Her great strength of uncompromising character now made her life difficult. Suddenly we had no money. There was no child support and no alimony. I don't know how my father imagined we were supposed to eat, but he rarely focused on such matters even during good times. Mom quickly found a job as a bookkeeper at the Bahama Steak House, where drugstore blondes sat at the bar on the off chance that they might be saved, at least for the evening, by some desperate stranger. Along with her miserly paycheck, Mom brought home the low-class perfume of cheap meat, overused cooking oil, and stale liquor on her clothes. Even the powerful aroma of night-blooming jasmine could not erase the bad smell of the Bahama Steak House.

My rare attempts at helpful advice were insensitive and painful. One night during dinner, I told my mother that she should go out and meet somebody. She dropped her head and cried silently. I don't know if the tears were for the lost love of my father or the difficult reality of her situation. I wish I could have understood better what she was going through. My mother did everything she could to hold herself and our house together. It was a tremendous burden, and I was not of much help. She had given everything to a marriage that left her with nothing.

In a futile effort to create the illusion of stability, I would occasionally cook a surprise meal. As the young chef of the house, I whipped up a brilliant medley of canned Green Giant vegetables mixed with freshly cooked soybeans, soy sauce, and seaweed. It was nothing short of depressing. Mom was stunned and paralyzed by her state of penniless freedom and suffered quietly. Meanwhile, Pop continued to live next door, bringing home new girlfriends and cohorts for a little late-night chanting.

I would commute between the two houses, pretending that my parents were still one unit just separated by a few yards of grass. After school or after dinner, I would usually walk next door to visit with my father. For some reason, I volunteered to do his laundry and would sneak pillowcases stuffed with his dirty clothes around the back of the house and into the laundry room. If my mother had ever found out, I would have been labeled a traitor and sent to the isolation ward.

Trained by my father that the spirits were always watching and ready to help, I waited for the smiling Hindu deity to magically appear and transport us on a magic carpet ride away from all of this sadness. With the wave of a wand, presto change-o, we would all be one happy family again. All the pain and grief would suddenly vanish. But no spaceship landed to take us to a distant planet where money grew on trees and all the little children skipped with happiness, surrounded by rainbows of divine light.

seven

•

Psychic Shopping

I had no idea whose car I was in. Someone was driving me home from a party that had occurred two or three days earlier in the Grove. I wasn't sure why I didn't have my car or how I had gotten to the party or how I had ended up in this guy's apartment or what happened over the past few days. As he drove, he kept calling me Michael. I didn't bother to correct him. He was rattling on about the police and how his ex-girlfriend became a stripper so that she could earn some money to go to Jamaica and then she married a guy she met at the gas station and moved to Arizona but that didn't work out so he thought maybe they should get together again but he thinks she had a baby with the other guy but wasn't sure so he tried to call her but someone else answered and hung up on him so now he's thinking of driving out to Arizona but wasn't sure of her address or if he could find her so maybe he would drive to L.A. and try to get a job but before he goes he would have to sell his furniture but that would take too much time and maybe he should just leave it but then he thought that maybe his current girlfriend would rent the apartment from him but if he left to go to Arizona maybe she would meet someone else and besides he met this guy that he really likes and now they're into free love but he really digs this girl but this guy is like someone different and it's different with a guy but when his girlfriend lost her dog then he—

"Make a left here and then go straight up Miller Road." The guy didn't notice when I interrupted him to give him directions to my house. "Okay, now make a right here, then to the end of the road, follow the curve, and it's that house on the right."

"Hey, I think I've been here before. I remember this place, although it looked different at night."

"No, um, I don't think so."

"Oh, yeah, this cool cat lives here, or maybe the next house up, I can't really remember. Older guy; I think his name is Lew. I was having bad flashbacks from acid, and it was weird, he kinda put me in a sorta trance and waved his hands over me. I mean, it was like really weird. I can't tell you what I felt, but I never felt that way before. Like this crazy electricity in my cells. This guy has powers. I mean, look at me; I'm totally back to normal."

"Yeah. Thanks for the ride."

"Hey, man, do you live here?"

"No, I'm just visiting."

It was getting to the point that my father was always around. I couldn't escape him. Either someone knew him, or through his psychic powers he knew where I was and what I was doing. It didn't matter if I was asleep, in the shower, or passed out at some party, he knew it.

Recently Pop had exponentially expanded his psychic capabilities with the discovery of a new tool called the pendulum, which was the magic key that opened a world of unlimited knowledge for him— past, present, and future. The pendulum, a small opalescent glass ball about the size of a pea attached to a short length of chain, allowed my father access to any type of information he required. Mainly he used the pendulum for medical diagnosis, but he could also determine for the police where the murder weapon was, which insurance agent he should use, if he should move to Kissimmee, what the distance between Luxembourg and Luxor is, the temperature on Mars, where his glasses were, where the missing person was, all in a matter of minutes. He put the FBI, CIA, and KGB to shame with his ability to almost instantly gather hidden data about anyone or anything in the world.

My father liked to say that he had a complete hospital in the pendulum. With the pendulum, he didn't need a stethoscope, a pathology lab, or an X-ray machine; he could diagnose quicker and more accurately than all the MDs and their fancy machines combined. He would astonish patients and doctors by describing to them in accurate detail the exact nature of their illness. Certain doctors who were open to my father's methodologies would often call him in secret and ask him to help them diagnose a problematic case that they could not solve. Their patient might be ill, but all their tests were coming up normal. My father could usually find the source of and the solution to their disease. Now, with the use of the pendulum, he was able to take a much more empirical approach to his healing work by diagnosing exactly the problem and directing his healing with pinpoint accuracy.

Up until this point, Pop would just open his hands and let the energy pour out without any control. He didn't have to diagnose, he just had to show up. While he was achieving remarkable results, this wasn't enough for him. He was after empirical results. He wanted to deliver healing energy in exact doses rather than just blasting a patient with cosmic rays.

The art of the pendulum is based on the arcane science of radiesthesia, which posits that everything in our material world is a collection of atoms vibrating at specific rates. Just like in physics, flowers vibrate at a different rate than rocks, plastic spoons, or lungs. According to the laws of radiesthesia, each of these vibrations can be measured—and in the case of an ailing body, manipulated and returned to optimal functioning.

Radiesthesia was reportedly known and used by the high priests and magicians of ancient Egypt. The modern father of radiesthesia was Abbé Mermet, a Swiss priest who in the 1920s began to use it for the purposes of medical diagnosis. Radiesthesia is a close relation to the art of dowsing—using forked tree branches to pick up the magnetic pull of an underground body of water. However, instead of tree branches, radiesthetists use pendulums—flexible metal wands made from wire, or even their fingers—to read the vibrations emanating from any object, person, or natural body.

Through radiesthesia my father was able to measure a physical malfunction both before and after a healing. In this way he could document the change that occurred from his healing. Using the pendulum, he could look into the body without an X-ray machine or into stellar space without a telescope. I never asked him if he could have picked stocks or horses and made a bundle. Most likely his answer would have been no, this was a God-given power to be used only for the highest good.

In an attempt to make his healing more scientific, Pop created a detailed chart that would allow him to diagnose every facet of his patients, from their psychological profile to the mineral content of their body, or if they had shingles or worms. In a matter of minutes, he could do a complete workup on a person whether they were sitting next to him, having dinner in Paris, or sleeping in Buenos Aires. This enabled Pop to document his diagnoses and healings in a way that would give him credibility and acceptance. His hope was that he would not be dismissed as a nut and as a result could work with doctors to teach them new methods of healing the body. He was tired of being harassed by the authorities and constantly having to prove himself over and over again. All he wanted was to be able to share his gift and alleviate people's suffering.

The pendulum functioned in a binary fashion similar to a computer's method of thinking—it could provide only a yes or no answer to a question. For example, you could not ask the pendulum, "What color shirt is Mark wearing today?" The pendulum would not respond. You needed to phrase the question as, "Is Mark wearing a red shirt today?" If the answer was no, the pendulum would swing in a counterclockwise circle. Next you would ask, "Is Mark wearing a blue shirt today?" If the answer was yes, the pendulum would then swing in a clockwise circle. My father developed a kind of shortcut in using the pendulum. If he received a negative answer, he would then mentally list all the colors he could think of, such as pink, gray, black, yellow, green, white, and so on, and wait until the pendulum began to spin in a positive clockwise direction.

A similar line of questioning could be used to diagnose any illness in the body, including hidden tumors that a doctor had failed to detect. A typical diagnostic session to locate a tumor in the body would go something like this:

"Is there a tumor in the body that the doctor did not diagnose?"

Yes.

"Is the tumor on the kidney?"

No.

"Is the tumor on the lung?"

Yes.

"Is it on the right lung?"

No.

"Is the tumor on the upper part of the left lung?"

No.

"Is the tumor on the inside of the left lung?"

Yes.

"Is the tumor on the upper right-hand section of the left lung?"

No.

"Is the tumor one centimeter in size?"

No.

"Is the tumor two centimeters in size?"

No.

"Is the tumor five centimeters in size?"

Yes.

"Will a psychic healing dissolve the tumor?"

Yes.

"Is the patient receptive to a psychic healing?"

No.

"Because the patient is not receptive, will the tumor return after a successful psychic healing?"

Yes.

"Can I alter the person's receptivity before the healing?"

Yes.

"If I alter the person's receptivity, will the healing be successful?"

Yes.

"Does the patient need additional medical intervention?"

No.

All these questions would be asked while holding the pendulum and watching it respond either yes or no. This procedure could be applied to diagnose all aspects of a person's health. Even the best doctor would have required hours, if not days, to hopefully deliver the same diagnosis after using blood tests, X-rays, scans, and even exploratory surgery.

In the way that we now use calculators, the Internet, and cell phones, Pop used the pendulum to verify anything and everything. There was no limit to the type or amount of information that was now available to him. Suddenly there was no guesswork left to his healing or his personal life. The pendulum made every decision for him with precision.

My father also used the pendulum for such practical tasks as grocery shopping, or to determine the nutritional content of a tomato or which apple had the least amount of pesticide residue. His shopping via radiesthesia was truly where the supernatural met suburbia in broad daylight.

Pop refused to put anything—and I mean anything—into his shopping cart without first checking it out with the pendulum. Whenever he asked me to go shopping with him, I tried to fabricate an excuse not to join him, as the outing always turned into a spectacle. I couldn't bear the openmouthed stares of the Cuban stock boys or the housewives as he whipped out his pendulum and held it over every purchase, waiting for the pendulum to indicate whether or not it was a buy. This habit of his had come from a message from Arthur Ford, who expressed his concern that my father was not vigilant about maintaining his vibrations at a high enough level. In the message, Arthur said, "You must check out each food you eat. Nothing should go into the body that is not of a certain vibration. Remember, my friend, you must keep your thoughts, actions, and body as pure as you can so you can be 'on call' at all times."

My worst nightmare was the produce department. Whenever possible, I tried to slip away as soon as we headed toward the fruits and vegetables. "Uh, Pop, I think we're running low on detergent. I'll get some and meet you by the checkout." As I scurried away, he would call out for me to wait for him so that he could run the pendulum over the bottles, as he didn't want to buy a detergent that might have too many phosphates, pollutants, or allergens. When I asked him why he would always use the pendulum to check the same brand of detergent he had bought last time, he told me that you never knew when they changed the formulation.

Acting as if he were completely alone in the store, Pop would hold the pendulum over a pile of cantaloupes and ask out loud, "Is this melon perfectly ripe, and will it provide optimum nutrition for my body?" He would then slowly scan the pendulum over the pile of melons, waiting for the pendulum to begin turning in a clockwise direction, indicating the perfect melon. Or he might ask, "Does this melon have the least amount of pesticides?" He would then wait until the pendulum gave him a positive response and nonchalantly place that melon in his basket. Sometimes I had to move twenty or thirty pieces of fruit until he found one that received a positive response from the pendulum.

Inevitably some widow would push her cart right in front of my father in an attempt to meet the man of her dreams. These ladies always assumed that he was really rich. After all, would a poor person have the nerve to hold a little crystal bead attached to a chain over a pile of fruit and ask out loud (too loud for me), "Does this bag of oranges contain the highest percentage of vitamin C?" They were always charmed by his eccentricity, and he immediately had another acolyte in the making. Pop had let his mustache grow into a professorial-looking goatee, which for some reason led perfect strangers to call him "doctor." Widows and divorcees really went for this look.

My father would nonchalantly tuck the small end of the pendulum through one of the buttonholes in his shirt so that it was always available. The pendulum was not exactly the French Legion of Honor, that small red thread that gentlemen of a certain status discreetly tucked into the buttonhole of their bespoke suit, but it gave my father that je ne sais quoi of extreme eccentricity.

As we walked down the aisles, testing everything from Saran Wrap to yogurt for toxicity and protein content, I could hear the curious whispers behind us. Occasionally I winced at the metallic crash of shopping carts as two disbelieving housewives collided with each other while watching my father dowse the zucchini. Before we reached the checkout counter, he would guess the total cost of the items in the basket and ask the pendulum to confirm. If it indicated a no, he would throw out another sum or two until he got a positive response. When we checked out, if the total differed from his number, he would tell the cashier that she had made a mistake. She would give him a nasty look, then cancel the order, check him out again, and inevitably find that his number was the correct amount.

In addition to food shopping, Pop rapidly found other applications, which included spying on me.

Adolescence requires a certain amount of rebellion, secrecy, and privacy. My father's psychic abilities preempted any of this. If I was trying to masturbate in the shower or sneak a cigarette, he knew. Since I wasn't supposed to be smoking, I went through an elaborate ritual before I would light the cigarette. First I would try to scramble and block my thoughts about smoking from being scanned by my father or his spirit friends by running algebraic equations or a list of phone numbers through my mind. I figured that would throw them off my mental trail. Only after I had cleansed my mind of the thought of smoking did I then look around to see if anybody was watching before I lit up. Even though I couldn't see anybody watching me, I always ended up getting caught. As soon as I walked back into the house, I was met with "Philip, you were smoking again, weren't you?"

I averted my eyes and responded calmly, "No. No, I wasn't." But there was no point in lying; it never worked and only made things worse.

"Philip, you are destroying your body. Your body is your temple. You don't own your body; it is a gift from God. Remember that the body never forgets an insult. You will pay the price for this later on. I don't want you smoking. You're killing yourself."

"But Mom smokes." I knew this was the wrong answer.

"Yes, and she's killing herself."

"No she's not. She's still alive." Being a smart aleck was not going to get him off my back.

"You know that I know when you're doing drugs or smoking cigarettes, so why do you make me lecture you like this? It would be easier if you would just take care of yourself."

"Yeah," I thought, "easier for him, but not for me."

Like most kids, I thought that smoking made me cool and adult. That's all I wanted, to be like the other kids and not the son of a psychic decorator who could read people's minds and cure cancer. What I really wanted was a father who mowed the lawn, drank beer, and fell asleep in front of the TV. But that's not the father I had. Instead I had Clark Kent, who at a moment's notice turned into Superman.

As my father became more proficient with the pendulum, he used it to check out my health, activities, and whereabouts at all times. No matter what I did, I was under surveillance twenty-four hours a day. There was no privacy. It didn't matter whether I was asleep, in class, or kissing my girlfriend—my father could, through the use of the pendulum, instantly flip the "on" switch to his private camera, tune in to me, and monitor my every move. At times I could feel it when he was mentally in the room with me. Sometimes it was like a breeze whooshing by me as he left the room. Other times when he was listening in, I could feel a little click in my brain, like when an operator checks the line or interrupts a call.

I remember one such incident that occurred around dusk as I was hiding some pharmaceuticals in a hole in the backyard for future use. They had not been directly prescribed for me. After carefully wrapping them in a plastic bag that I sealed with masking tape, I placed the bag into a plastic storage container that my mother used for leftovers. Behind a tree on the far side of the property, I dug a twelve-inch-deep hole and buried them. I placed a few heavy pieces of coral rock over the box so that I could find it easily when I dug it up. Artfully, I camouflaged the area with a natural-looking spread of leaves and twigs. While I was digging, I thought I kept seeing a gray shadowy figure moving around the periphery of my vision. I sensed it was watching me. But when I turned around, no one was there.

The next day I was in the mood for a few capsules and went over to my storage facility. I was pleased to see that none of the leaves or twigs had been disturbed by raccoons or other animals. The fresh dirt from the day before was easy to remove. After a few minutes of digging with my hands, I could feel the rocks at the bottom of the hole. I knew I was close. I cleaned out the remaining loose dirt, lifted out the rocks, and looked into the hole. There was no Tupperware filled with pharmaceuticals anywhere in sight. Even though the rocks were there, the plastic container was clearly missing. I started to dig down a bit deeper but couldn't go any farther because I had reached a bed of coral rock. Carefully, I sifted through the dirt to see if I had somehow missed the box. Nothing; no box, no pills. Finally I gave up and walked away. I didn't even bother to refill the hole.

That evening I went over to the guesthouse to visit with my father. We talked about my day at school and how he had just treated someone with schizophrenia. He then opened his desk drawer and pulled out my precious pills. He turned to me and said casually, "No medication is ever free of a side effect. Unfortunately, once you start with one pill, it sets up a reaction, and then you need another and another until you are taking so many pills, and all the chemicals are at war with your body, and you get sicker than you were at the beginning. I would prefer that you stay away from all prescription medication, especially if it wasn't prescribed to you." For emphasis, he picked up his pendulum to indicate that I had been under psychic observation. I felt a small jolt of electricity pass through my body and suddenly had trouble breathing, as if someone had just punched me in the chest. I didn't say a word. There was a deep silence after he had spoken. I didn't know how to respond. He had made his point loud and clear. I changed the subject and began talking cheerily about what happened in Latin class that day. Like everything else associated with my father's growing powers, I got used to it, the way that someone who has a chronic disease gets used to it; you wish it would go away, but it never will. It's just there, a fact of life.

Even though the pendulum had now become an indispensable diagnostic tool for my father the way a doctor uses X-rays, he would occasionally still perform healings the old-fashioned way in an emergency. With his gift, Pop felt it was his responsibility to help anyone he could at any time, especially if there wasn't a doctor around.

One late night in mid-May, we were driving home from an afternoon of visiting friends, and traffic was at a near standstill. As we crept along, I could see the revolving lights of the police cars flashing up ahead. There must have been about six cops on the scene attending to a three-car pileup. Two of the cars were intertwined, and the third had flipped over. Several bodies were lying on the ground. They appeared unconscious and were covered with blood. The rest of the passengers were pinned inside the cars. The ambulances had yet to arrive. As we passed the accident, my father quickly pulled his car off onto the shoulder of the road.

"Where are you going?" I asked. He didn't answer as he got out of the car. The police were too busy directing traffic and working their walkie-talkies to notice my father heading toward the accident scene. I watched as he stood there, looking at the bodies for a minute or two.

Just staring. He stepped over one of them to bend down and take a closer look at the other, a man dressed in a red T-shirt and shorts. With his eyes closed and arms outstretched, Pop started moving his palms in a circular motion over the person's head and then slowly up and down the length of his body. I noticed the person's left arm twitch like a fish that had just been caught. My father then placed his right hand about eight inches above the person's chest. While he did this, the person's head moved slightly from side to side.

I sat in the car thinking, "Great. We'll never get home now." I was hungry and wanted to call my girlfriend. Out of the blue, two cops came over, grabbed my father from behind, and pulled him away from the body. One of them screamed, *"What the hell d'ya think you're doin'?! Cain't you see this here's an accident scene?!"* He shook my father and yelled, *"What are you, Dracula?"* Then he said to the other cop, "Get this guy out of here. Book him." I couldn't believe what I was hearing.

"For what?" asked the other cop.

"I don't know. Interfering with a crime investigation, somethin' like that. I don't care, just get this jerk outta here."

The arresting cop quickly pulled my father's hands behind his back and said, "What do you think you were doin' over there? Huh? *Huh?*"

I didn't know whether to get out of the car and try to help or just sit there and keep listening. As usual, my father decided to tell the truth. "This man is about to die. I can save his life. Please let me get back to him."

At first the cop's eyes opened wide and nearly popped out of his head. Then a look of disbelief ran across his face before he broke out laughing. He called out to the first cop, "Hey, Sam, we got the Wizard of Oz over here! Claims he can save that dead guy over there." He started singing the theme song from *The Twilight Zone* in my father's face: "Doo doo doo doooooo, doo doo doo doooooo. Sam, you know, I think jail's the wrong place for this guy. Let's send him over to Jackson Memorial and get him in a straitjacket." They both laughed.

Overhearing this, I thought, "Uh-oh, now we're in for some serious humiliation from the cops. This time he's definitely playing with fire." I decided to get out of the car to see if I could help my father. It was one thing when my father argued with a doctor—there were few consequences other than bad feelings. But to argue with the cops, especially redneck Miami cops, was not a good idea. I thought my presence might let the cops reconsider their prejudice against my father—although with my shoulder-length curly hair and bell-bottoms, these cops would probably want to make it a double and throw me in jail as well. I noticed that the guy my father had been waving his hands over was slowly opening and closing his mouth as if trying to say something. By the time I reached the cops, they had my father handcuffed and were writing up a report. I said to the officer, "Excuse me, this is my father. My mom is probably worried, and we need to get home for dinner. Can we go now?" The guy ignored me. My father gave me a look that said, "Don't say anything. I'll handle this."

The cop walked a little closer to me, crossed his arms over his chest, and looked at me hard before he said, "Let me tell you somethin', son. Your daddy here is in a whole lot of trouble. He was messin' where he shouldn't a-been messin'. This here is police business. Now, I don't know *exaaaactly* what he was doin' over there with those people who are badly hurt, probably dead, but it's just no business of his. And we're going to make sure this don't happen again."

"But he was trying to help the guy. What are you going to do to him?"

"I didn't see your dad try to help nobody. Looked to me like he was trying to pick the guy's pocket or take his watch. We don't like that kind of stuff. I don't think no judge gonna like hearing what your daddy just did—foolin' with the dead folk. I don't think he's gonna like it one bit."

"The guy wouldn't be dead if you let him finish what he was doing. Besides, he wasn't picking anybody's pocket. That's ridiculous. Didn't you see that guy start to move? He probably saved the guy's life and could have done more if you hadn't stopped him."

This little speech made the cop angrier than he already was. Without looking up from the police report he was writing, he said, "Son, we didn't stop your dad from saving nobody's life. Is your dad a medical doctor?"

"No."

"Then how can he be helpin' that guy? *Huh?* That's the doctor's job. We only let medical personnel on the scene of an accident. Like I said, your daddy's goin' to jail for what he just done. I mean, it's a damn shame that people like your dad ain't got no respect for the dead."

"But the guy's alive! I saw him move. Why don't you go have a look? I know the guy's alive. My father helped him. You're making a mistake."

The cop laughed. "Son, we don't make no mistakes. Your daddy's the one who made the mistake. And quite frankly, if you don't shut your mouth, you'll be makin' a pretty big mistake yourself. How'd you like to spend the night over at the Krome Juvenile Detention Center?"

"Uh, no thanks."

"Huh? Didn't hear you, what'd you say?" The cop put his hand to his ear as if he were hard of hearing.

"Uh, no sir."

"Yup, that's what I thought you might say. So I suggest you just go on home now and leave us to do what we got to do here. This here is a bad accident, and we need to get it cleaned up mighty fast. And this here little diversion ain't helpin' us none. Hear?"

The cop was typical of the police at the time, who often made their own laws. Miami was just pulling out of deep segregation, and the cops still ruled the town as they saw fit. I knew if I provoked him, my father could disappear for a very long time on some trumped-up charge. I didn't know what to do and clearly wasn't being very helpful.

Pop looked over at the guy he had been working on, let out a deep sigh, and said to me, "He's not going to make it now. I don't think there is anything you can do. Take the car and go home. I'll be fine."

By the time I got home, it was already pretty late. I was tired and had no desire to even try to figure out what I was going to eat for dinner. My mother had the door closed and the lights turned off. I didn't want to wake her up to tell her that Pop had been taken away by the cops. I had no resources to help my father—no attorney, no money, no bondsman. At sixteen you feel powerless about most things, and this situation was just reinforcing those awful feelings. I figured I would deal with it by just going to bed and it would all be better in the morning.

I sat in the dark just thinking, my mind going round and round, wondering if I could have done anything different, was there anyone I could call. Finally I decided there was nothing I could do to help my father. Cynically, I figured, "This is the guy with the magic powers. Let him bend the jail bars with his psychic energy, make himself invisible, and fly out of jail. Let's see him get out of this one." After about an hour, I drifted off to sleep.

At some point in the middle of the night, I woke up hearing a car pull up in the driveway. The headlights were shining into my room. Though half awake, I heard my father's voice say, "Thanks for the ride." I thought I was dreaming. Then I heard a car door slam, and the car pulled out of the driveway. Briefly, I considered the possibility of getting out of bed to find out how he got out of this one. But I was so tired and not in the mood to hear how some spirit suddenly made the police sergeant tear up the police report and release my father. I rolled over and went back to sleep.

eight

•

Pink or Gray?

My father had just ruined my summer plans. I had rigorously scheduled every day of the week to sit mindlessly in Bayfront Park on my homemade tie-dyed blanket with incense posted at each of the four corners. Three fabulous months of watching girls in bikinis playing Frisbee with their dogs, filthy middle-aged men copping drug deals, runaways panhandling, and impromptu lectures by Buckminster Fuller and other cultural icons. It was a front-row seat to the most drugged-out scene in town.

Pop had other ideas as to how I should be spending my time. He asked me to come work for him at his design studio, where he could keep an eye on me. A summer job—just what I didn't want. Frankly, I would have much rather been out surfing and destroying my mind with drugs like every other sixteen-year-old white-trash teenager from my high school. But with my mother no longer showing up at the office, he needed a little extra help when he was busy with patients or clients. I was hired to move boxes, straighten up, and water the plants.

Pop's chic studio, located in the heart of the Miami Design District, was the former processing plant of what was once a large pineapple plantation. In the old days, the area was known as Lemon City because of its citrus crop. Downstairs, his showroom and conference area were decorated in early-sixties high modernism with a touch of classic Japanese minimalism. While the faux-Chinese look, with lots of red and black lacquer, was popular in the new condos springing up along Collins Avenue on Miami Beach, Pop favored the more serene Japanese Zen aesthetic. White angular desks that served as his sketching areas jutted out from the walls. The ceiling lights were filtered through gauzy fabric that looked a bit like rice paper, giving the entire office a modernist Eastern sensibility. Upstairs in the workrooms, a team of seamstresses fueled by thick black pots of Cuban espresso managed roaring industrial sewing machines to produce the bedspreads and draperies destined for Lew Smith–designed residences throughout the Caribbean.

Whatever project my father was working on usually gained a fair amount of attention. *Home Furnishings Daily, Florida Architecture,* and *House Beautiful* would give my father write-ups about his interiors and furniture designs. Or a small item would appear in the evening *Miami News* such as, "Those way-out colorful earrings that the girls on the *Gleason Show* are wearing were designed by Miami's bead-drapery king, Lew Smith."

Pop's impeccable attention to detail and original designs had caught the attention of such stellar local architects as Morris Lapidus and Alfred Browning Parker, who often collaborated with him on interiors for their residential commissions. Pop's office was ground zero for the rich and famous seeking whatever morsels of design that could be found in style-starved Miami. His roster of clients continued to grow and included *The Jackie Gleason Show,* Dean Martin needing beaded designs for his new restaurant, Walt Disney wanting some sparkling beaded draperies for one of the animation studios, beaded curtains for the Houston Astrodome, General Motors commissioning beaded curtains for its pavilion at the 1964 New York World's Fair, Jack Dempsey needing new furniture designs, the Cowles family wanting some beautiful draperies for Indian Creek, or some rich French folks desperate for a quick redo à la tropicale on a couple of Jamaican villas before Ian Fleming dropped by for lunch. It was not unusual to see a conga line of Rolls-Royces and their uniformed chauffeurs parked outside the office while their owners reviewed designs for their latest renovation with my father.

I was not exactly a brilliant addition to his design studio, as I slouched around all day in knee-high moccasin boots ringed with fringe and American flag shirts, acting aggressively bored. To fill the time, I ran a few errands and talked on the phone with Maya while my father met with clients in between psychic healings.

Despite this steady flow of glittering clientele, his office was slowly beginning to take on the look and feel of a free-needle clinic. Instead of a few chic ladies sauntering in with an armful of fabric swatches, lines of indigent-looking people formed in front of his office first thing in the morning, waiting to see my father for his magic touch. Word had spread that here was a man who could cure anyone of anything—for free. Pop never charged for these healings. He considered his ability a gift from God that money could not buy.

"Pardon ME!!!" the rich ladies would squawk, announcing their presence and demanding that the line of the dirty and infirm respectfully part to grant them entrance to my father's studio.

"I mean, reaaally, Lew, those people in front of your office are just too much. Wouldn't it be better to have some attractive-looking people sitting on your sidewalk? Can't you just give them some money, so they'll go somewhere else?"

"They're not here for money."

"Oh, reaaally! I suppose they are here to have their living rooms redone, or perhaps they are just dying for some of that faaabulous French silk you showed me last week to reupholster their sofas, ha, ha, ha."

"Actually, you're right, they *are* dying," my father would reply softly.

This remark was met with an alert silence.

"Those people out front are my patients."

"How *charming*! I didn't realize you were a doctor *and* a decorator. My, isn't that wonderful. Dr. Kildare and Sister Parish all rolled into one. Lew Smith, you certainly *are* remarkable. And where did you earn your medical degree? *Haaarvard?* That must be it. I would peg you as a Harvard man."

Pop would let them go on and on until they ran out of steam.

"I heal these people."

"Oh, you *dooo?* So you're like some sort of witch doctor? Ha, ha, ha."

"Not really. I use a power given to me by God to help whomever I can."

"Oh my, a religious man. You're not one of those nutty Christian Scientists who don't allow their children to get vaccinated, are you? Oh, I certainly hope not. Those people are just dreadful. They have one of those reading rooms in Palm Beach. How the Worth Avenue Association ever let those people rent office space is just beyond me. What were they ever thinking? These people should just give up and get themselves to a real doctor; we'd all be better off. I mean, it's all just too, too much. A good shot of penicillin never hurt anyone."

With the conversation headed toward a nonproductive show-down, my father would usually proceed to the business at hand. "Now, for the living room entranceway, what I suggest is that we move the wall and . . ." It was obvious, even to me, that the blue-bloods of Palm Beach and the illicit rich of the Caribbean did not enjoy waiting while my father healed someone's cataracts or heart condition. These people were used to getting their way whenever and however they wanted it. They did not find my father's newfound abilities terribly amusing.

Not only were the ladies disturbed by the sick and dying who competed for my father's attention, but they began to take umbrage at his changing staff. Mom had been the social butterfly who made all the matrons and decorators feel as if they were at a cocktail party as they went through the trauma of redecorating. Her departure dramatically altered the tenor of the office.

Long before it became federal law, Pop was always an equal opportunity employer. Back in the sixties, he hired blacks, homosexuals, Cubans, and the handicapped when no one else would. His multicultural staff adored him and enjoyed being part of the glamorous decorating business. But increasingly he was hiring newly acquired friends who were "on the spiritual path." His ever-changing staff from his personal Psychic Friends Network didn't even bother to pretend to have a sense of design or color. Instead they were hired on the basis of their questionable claims of being able to see auras and contact the dead on demand. Pop just liked being surrounded by people with whom he could share his newfound enthusiasm for anything metaphysical. As a result of this change in staffing, his studio became much less productive. The new employees may have known about psychic phenomena, but answering the phone or taking a simple message was far beyond their capabilities. While some of his clients were charmed by my father's eccentric staff, most were not. They tolerated pop's supernatural interests only because he was so well known, and they wanted his impeccable taste to grace their houses.

Eventually, even the *Miami Herald* had to alter its reporting on my father's innovative design work. "Decorator Enjoys Bonus Career as Spiritual Healer" was the headline of an article on my father's newfound talents. The reporter stated, "He says he's a spiritual healer— one who serves as a channel for the spirit to travel through and heal the sick. Sometimes his colleagues on Decorators' Row stop in during lunch hour for a quick healing of a headache or other problem." Toward the end of the article, my father mentioned his son, "who also shows signs of exceptional healing talent." Not the kind of publicity I was looking for.

One afternoon Mrs. Elizabeth Bennet from Palm Beach, a

longtime client, blew into the office wearing her signature Lilly Pulitzer pink dress ensemble and a head of expensively done hair. Perky and ultrarich, Mrs. Bennet was typical of Pop's socialite clients who did nothing but spend money all day long. As a result, she expected the world to stop the moment she walked into a room. Over the years, I had seen Mrs. Bennet request a new dining room, a new living room, a new maid's room, or anything else to give her a new project. When I was younger, Pop would take me as his assistant up to her enormous villa on Ocean Boulevard. My job was to hold the measuring tape as Mrs. Bennet found yet another part of the house that needed my father's attention.

Seeing my long hair and hippie beads, Mrs. Bennet shot me a look of imperial disdain. I'm sure that in her eyes I was a design error in my father's otherwise tastefully appointed office. She was the kind of shallow, materialistic consumer who was the target of my current hippie, anticapitalist hostility—even though she was providing the money that helped keep me in incense and bell-bottoms. So much for logic.

"Lew, *dahling,* we have a crisis going on." She emphasized the urgency of the matter by slamming her pink-gloved hands on her too-trim hips at the exact moment she uttered the word *crisis.* She stood with rigid posture in front of my father's desk. I could only imagine what the emergency was this time. In the past, I had seen her so distraught that she was begging to be institutionalized simply because someone's charity ball for the cancer league was scheduled on the same night as her charity function for the opera guild. Without missing a beat, she queried in an insistent tone, "Pink or gray?" After her pronouncement, she seemed to elongate her neck and peer down at my father, waiting for his inspired design decision. I had no idea what she was talking about. Mrs. Bennet and her other rich friends had this way of talking in a code that only they seemed to understand.

"Tell me, Lew, which is it? I must know immediately. Pink or gray?" She rapidly tapped her gloved hand on my father's desk as if demanding counter service at a luncheonette. "Mr. Maxwell wants to write up the house for *Palm Beach Illustrated,* so it has to be right. I don't know which will photograph better. The pink might be too bright, and the gray too dull. We can't afford any mistakes, because he has promised me the cover. We need to get this matter settled instantly." Like a general announcing the start of a military campaign, she banged her gloved fist on his desk for emphasis.

My father did not immediately respond to her emergency but instead tilted his head to the side like a dog hearing a distant whistle. He was distracted by something he had heard, and he looked back at her as she stood there ready for her marching orders. "Elizabeth, I hate to tell you this, but . . ." A pained expression came over her face, as if her name had been misspelled in the Social Register.

"Oh, for God's sake, Lew, don't tell me you can't get this done in time. I just can't impress upon you the urgency of this matter. Everything is riding on this—"

"You have a vaginal infection."

I don't know if it was the word *vaginal* or the word *infection,* but I watched Mrs. Bennet's military bearing melt, as if she had just received a shotgun blast to her pelvis. I waited for her to utter "pink or gray?" just one last time as she was going down. Instead, through clenched teeth and a tight smile, she said, "*Leeeew,* whatever are you talking about? I am in perfect health. Besides, this is not a doctor's office. I am here to talk about my carpet. Now, can we please get back to this pressing business? Robert is waiting in the car, and I have to get back to Palm Beach by two so that Mr. John can do my hair."

"Elizabeth, are your discharges painful?"

"Don't be silly." Turning her head to look away, Mrs. Bennett let out one of those polite little teatime laughs. "I have no idea what you're talking about." She waved her hand as if shooing a fly. "Now, if we use the pink carpet for . . ."

I thought to myself, "Of course she doesn't know what he's talking about." People like Mrs. Bennet simply did not admit to having vaginal infections or any other disease that was not socially acceptable. Instead they got tennis elbow, or gout from too much drinking, but never vaginal infections.

"This infection is causing itching and soreness and can lead to other more serious problems," my father explained. "I'm worried that this could spread and really turn into a major complication."

"Fine, Lew, I'll call my doctor in the morning. Will that make you happy?" Even though she was clearly rattled, she didn't move from her position in front of my father's desk. Her voice went up an octave and grew in volume. "Can we *please* get back to the carpet? Now, if you like the gray, do you think it should be one of those seagull grays that are so popular, or should we go with a deeper charcoal gray? Then again, the pink might be nice. *Lew Smith,* what *do* you think you're doing?"

Without saying a word, my father had reached out across the desk and placed both of his palms about three or four inches in front of her crotch. Mrs. Bennet probably thought he was trying to molest her, but I knew he was sending her healing vibrations to cure her infection. Pop was doing his laying-on-of-hands routine, to channel healing energy to her diseased area. God knows what this would have looked like if someone had walked into the office at that moment. I kept thinking this was one person he shouldn't have tried to heal. I was certain he was asking for trouble.

"*Ouch!* Stop that, you're hurting me!" I didn't know what she was complaining about. My father's hands were hovering inches away from her lower area. She was really resisting the healing. She should have considered herself lucky, as my father was saving her a trip to the doctor.

"I'm not touching you. See where my hands are? What you're feeling is the healing energy cleaning out the infection. I'm just guiding the energy to where it is needed. Stay still for another moment; we're almost done." For Pop, curing a vaginal infection was now as routine as applying a Band-Aid to a small cut. Mrs. Bennet wore an expression of disgust as my father proceeded to slowly move his hands over her pelvic area.

Based on what my father had told me in the past, his patients all felt a warm, tingly sensation when he performed his laying on of hands. I wondered when Mrs. Bennet would calm down and enjoy her warm, tingly moment. As far as Mrs. Bennet was concerned, my father was fine for picking carpet or wallpaper, but she certainly didn't want him to be physically close to her, especially down there. "*Really,* Lew. I don't know what you're doing, but I must ask you to stop. Now!"

With a sudden jerk, my father's hands flew away from her crotch as if it were a hot stove. I knew from watching previous healings that this meant that the session was over. Mrs. Bennet wiggled a bit as if adjusting herself and asked, "What was that snap I heard?" She quickly looked around the room with some alarm, as if the hook on her bra had just popped open. I was alarmed too—alarmed that she was going to hit him and start screaming for the police.

"Don't worry. That was the sound to signal you that the infection is leaving your body. It is now gone. You won't have any more problems. In case there is any residual infection, I want to give you some homeopathic tablets that will take care of it. Here . . ." Opening the drawer next to his desk, my father pulled out a small brown glass bottle of homeopathic medicine called Arsenicum album, which he had imported from England. He handed the bottle to Mrs. Bennet and said, "Put two of these under your tongue in the morning and before bed. This will prevent the infection from coming back. Do this for four days."

I noticed that Mrs. Bennet slipped the bottle into her purse. She got up to leave and said, "Call me tomorrow with your decision about the carpets. Don't forget we have a deadline to meet." Waving to me as she left, she called out, "Philip, nice to see you. Tell your father to keep his hands off the ladies." She giggled and disappeared into her waiting chauffeured Rolls.

When she was gone, I said pointedly to my father, "She didn't seem too happy with you touching her."

"But I never touched her."

"Yeah, but she thinks you did. I don't think she appreciated her healing. Maybe it would be better to ask someone if they want to be healed before you did it. This way they won't get so upset." I couldn't believe that I was giving my father advice, much less lecturing him. But I was both concerned that he had made an enemy of his client and that he was opening the door for serious problems.

"It really doesn't matter what she thinks. The important thing is that I removed the infection, and she won't have any more problems. The infection could have really spread throughout her body. I have a responsibility to heal whenever I can."

"Pop, I have nothing against you healing somebody. It's just that I don't want to see you get into trouble. You don't know who these people are. They could call the police and get you arrested. People don't seem to hesitate to call the cops on you."

"Spirit only sends people to me who are in need. I am always watched over and taken care of. Don't worry, nothing will ever happen to me."

"Okay."

Two days after Pop removed Mrs. Bennet's infection, a man in a bad dark suit walked into the office carrying a heavy briefcase. This was a man who went out of his way to let the world know that he had no taste and no style. I immediately thought to myself, "What's this guy doing here? He's not going to be buying any custom bedspreads or furniture."

"Can I speak to Lew Smith?" the guy said to my father. This was really unusual. Almost everybody who walked into the studio knew exactly who my father was from his pictures in the paper or his appearances at various charity functions. Even the cashier at Tang Too, the local Chinese restaurant, knew Pop from his picture in the society page of the paper.

My father got up from his desk and introduced himself. "I'm Lew. What can I do for you?" I could tell that my father was acting cautious by the way he kept his distance from this man. Usually Pop was very effusive when he greeted people. I wasn't the only one who didn't like this guy.

"Ray White, FDA. A complaint has been filed against you."

"Complaint? For what?" My father had a look of shock on his face. He and Mr. White stared at each other like two gunfighters. Neither one of them was going to be the first to back down. They were oblivious to my presence.

Mr. White recited from memory, "Distributing unapproved pharmaceuticals, practicing medicine without a license, endangering the health and welfare of a U.S. citizen."

"Doing what?" Pop acted like he hadn't heard the man properly. His mouth dropped open in disbelief.

Mr. White repeated the charges. "The person who filed the complaint claimed you dispensed pills that gave them stomach cramps and induced hallucinations. They said that they had to be hospitalized. It is our responsibility to investigate these claims in order to protect the health and welfare of American citizens. We understand that you distributed some medication by the name of Arsenicum album. We don't show any such medication in our registry. Where did you get this Arsenicum album?"

As soon as I heard this, I knew that bitch Mrs. Bennet had done this to get back at my father because he had embarrassed her. I wished my father had listened to me and asked her permission before he began to heal her or just let her suffer with her infection. Meanwhile, he had probably saved her life—or at least a trip to the doctor. God knows what her millionaire husband would have thought about her unmentionable infection.

Not realizing that he should have an attorney present, my father began to hand the FDA just what it wanted. "I don't quite understand your charges, because Arsenicum is a homeopathic remedy made by pulverizing, refining, and distilling various substances such as arsenic until only the healing essence of those substances remains," he said. "It triggers the body's own healing mechanisms to produce well-being. Because there is no traceable medication in homeopathic tablets, it is impossible that Arsenicum could have induced hallucinations or any other disease." My father assumed the matter was now closed and extended his hand to bid Mr. White good day.

"Excuse me, Mr. Smith, but you said you are dispensing arsenic? Are you aware that arsenic is a poison?"

"Arsenicum album works like a charm, especially on ambitious, demanding people. It seems to reorient their disposition; rebalances the body so that all the systems align harmoniously."

"Arsenic is a poison." Mr. White was very upset.

"Well, maybe it could be used as a poison, but in a homeopathic dose there is no poison, just the healing vibration. Do you understand the basic concept of homeopathy, known as 'like cures like'? Look, a lot of medicines originate from poisons; take digitalis, for example. So when you compound something homeopathically . . ." Pop was talking way too much.

"I'd like to see the bottle of this Arsenicum." Mr. White pushed aside some colored-pencil renderings on my father's desk and opened his attaché case. He raised his eyebrows as he removed a Polaroid camera and a ream of official-looking documents with my father's name on them. I sensed that Mr. White thought that he was in the presence of a major criminal and that arresting Pop was going to make his career.

Pop opened a desk drawer filled with various bottles of homeopathic tablets, copies of esoteric prayers and anatomy charts, and strange devices made from copper wire and magnets. Rummaging around his alternative medicine cabinet, he produced a brown glass bottle, which looked the same as the one he had given to Mrs. Bennet.

Mr. White, excited by the easy cooperation of his prey, grabbed the bottle from my father's hand and began examining it. I couldn't understand why he was making such a big deal over this one bottle. Since I was a kid, my father had given me homeopathic tablets whenever I was sick. I never had any side effects because side effects from homeopathic medicines are impossible.

"You see, Mr. White, unlike the medicine the doctor gives you, these pills have no negative effects and will never harm you."

"No side effects?"

"None. As I told you, there is no medication of any kind in these tablets. Just the essence and vibration of the healing substance."

"No medication?"

"No. Nothing."

"So these are nothing more than sugar pills?"

"Not exactly. They are sugar pills that contain a specific healing energy but no specific medication."

"Mr. Smith, this is more serious than I imagined. Not only are you prescribing and distributing unauthorized and poisonous medications, you are peddling fraudulent medications. This is a matter we will have to bring before the attorney general."

My father blinked in astonishment. He couldn't believe what he was hearing, and neither could I. The gravity of the situation—a situation I felt was about to spiral out of control—was finally beginning to hit him. Pop had always talked to me about the evil FDA and how it was in the hands of the moneyed pharmaceutical profession. I vividly recalled his countless stories of doctors being jailed by the FDA for trying to cure cancer through strange methods that included magnets and laetrile, a supposedly natural anticancer agent made from the pits of apricots. A lot of those doctors fled to Mexico and set up alternative cancer clinics to avoid persecution. Suddenly all those stories about the FDA were hitting home. I could just imagine my father being hauled away in handcuffs. They were definitely out to get him. I realized there was no way for him to retract his earlier statements. For the first time I could ever remember, Pop looked very nervous. I wanted to help in some way but just didn't know what to do.

Mr. White closed his attaché case, laid the bottle on its surface, and began to load his Polaroid with film.

"What are you doing?" My father's voice had gotten smaller.

"Evidence," Mr. White said with a "gotcha!" smile.

I was surprised that my father, with all his psychic powers, couldn't make Mr. White simply disappear into thin air. Usually he would say a prayer or contact a spirit guide who could make his problems vanish as suddenly as they had appeared. Just then Pop looked startled, as if he had heard something break. He began to swat at his neck like a mosquito was buzzing him. "Mr. White, would you excuse me for a moment?" he said. "There is a matter I need to attend to in the back. I'll return as soon as it is taken care of." The FDA agent didn't bother to look up from his camera. He was busy trying to get the best angle of the bottle, as if he were shooting a jewelry catalog for Christie's.

I quickly followed my father into the back workroom. "Pop, what are you going to do? I don't want you to go to jail."

"Don't worry, I have no intention of going to jail. The spirits won't let me. I am here to do good, and these idiots won't stop me." Along with improving his psychic abilities, my father was increasingly contacting his spirit guides for advice just as one would pick up the phone to ask a question of a lawyer or a good friend. I had no idea where or how he "met" these spirits. There was no formal process of introduction that I was aware of; they just seemed to appear and be on call at all times. Most of the time, he used their supernatural expertise for assistance with his healings, but at times like these, he used them to rearrange reality when necessary.

"Crystal. I'm glad you contacted me," I heard him say under his breath, "I urgently need your help." Crystal was one of the first spirit guides to work with my father. He told me that Crystal was a small black woman who had died in a fire around 1860. Apparently Sophie Busch knew her well and was able to describe her physically to my father. Crystal was summoned for emergency cases, which were her specialty. Whenever she wanted to let my father know that she was present, she would tickle the back of his neck, which is why he had been swatting at the invisible mosquito a few minutes earlier. Clearly, she had been observing the exchange with Mr. White and signaled my father to the back room so they could strategize. Speaking to Crystal in an exaggerated whisper, Pop said, "Don't let him photograph the bottle. If he does, they'll have the evidence to put me in jail. What can I do? Tell me."

As I watched him talk to himself, I was actually relieved. Finally, I thought to myself, the reinforcements have arrived. I wasn't sure if Crystal was up to the job. I could never hear when the spirits talked back to him, so I was unaware of what advice Crystal had given him. All I knew was that when he was done with his conversation, he calmly walked back into the front office.

By then the FDA agent had taken six Polaroids of the Arsenicum bottle, which were laid out on the desk. Mr. White was looking at his watch, waiting for the photographs to develop. He peeled the black paper backing from the first photograph and, without really looking at it, placed it back on the desk. As he peeled off the backing from the second photograph, he did a double take. His eyes squinted, his brow furrowed, and his mouth was slightly open. He turned the photograph this way and that in the light, looking at it from different angles.

Together my father and I leaned over the front of the desk to look at the photographs. The Polaroid technology was still relatively new and considered quite miraculous. Whenever my father photographed one of his interiors, I loved watching him peel off the black paper backing, wave the photograph in the air to dry it, and then take a chemical-smelling, pink fiber squeegee that came with every pack of film and wipe it across the front of the photograph to "fix it."

Mr. White's photos were in perfect focus. I could see the attaché case and the desk clearly, but for some reason, the bottle of homeopathic tablets appeared as a white blur. It looked as if a cloud had blown across the photograph. Something had gone terribly wrong when he took the picture.

I watched Mr. White peel the backing off the remaining photographs. None of them showed the bottle in focus. "Must have moved the camera," he said to himself. "I'm going to try it over here by the window." Some of the bite had gone out of his bark because of this mysterious technical problem with the photographs. My father let out a deep sigh of relief. I could see the color return to his face. He started to whistle a tune and calmly went back to working on the rendering that was on his desk when Mr. White walked in. I could tell by his mood that somehow everything was going to be okay. This made me feel a little better about the situation, although I still couldn't understand how my father was going to get out of this mess.

This time Mr. White placed his attaché case on the floor and firmly put the bottle on top of the case. He had good light from the window. Kneeling down, he propped his elbow against his knee to avoid shaking the camera. He was taking every precaution possible to make sure the photographs weren't blurred again. Mr. White inhaled and held his breath as he slowly pressed the shutter button.

With each picture, he repositioned the bottle, and he took shots from various angles to cover all his bases. After he finished shooting, his cockiness returned. Once again, he picked up the pictures, laid them on my father's desk, timed the photographs, peeled away the backing paper, and set them out to dry. As before, everything was in perfect focus except the bottle. There was still a white blur where the bottle should have been. "I don't understand what's going on here," he said. "The camera was working perfectly yesterday. Maybe the film's bad."

My father, a former newspaper photographer, glanced at the photos and said with just a bit of condescension in his voice, "How can the film be bad when your briefcase is in perfect focus?"

"Then it must be the lens."

Pointing with his Prismacolor pencil at the clarity of the photograph, my father said, "No, it looks like the lens is working perfectly. Look how sharp everything is."

Mr. White was getting angry. He shook the photograph in my father's face and said, "Then how do you explain *this*?!"

"I don't know, maybe the bottle was never there to begin with and this is all in your imagination." I couldn't believe that my father was taunting this guy. He should have left well enough alone. I didn't know whether or not FDA guys carried guns, but if they did, he was certainly going to start shooting at my father.

"Are you crazy?" Mr. White screamed. *"Yes, that's it, you're crazy!"* His face was now a bright crimson. *"I'm going to speak to my supervisor! Believe me, you will be hearing from us! We'll have you in jail so fast you won't know what happened to you!"* With that, Mr. White packed up his camera, ripped up the photographs, and threw them on my father's desk. Then he opened the bottle of Arsenicum and emptied the pills all over the desk and stormed out. I watched as the little sugar pills scattered everywhere and then landed on the floor.

My father started laughing at Mr. White's sudden departure. I was still shaking from the incident and didn't find it at all funny. Out loud he said, "Thank you, Crystal," as if talking to someone sitting across from him. He turned to me and with great confidence said, "I don't think he'll be back."

"But the guy said he would be back, and I'm sure he's going to be back," I said. "He was really mad. Maybe you should call the police and report him."

"Philip, he *is* the police. The police are on his side."

"Then maybe you should call a lawyer. You could go to jail."

"Why should I call a lawyer? Crystal was my advocate."

"What did she do?"

"I don't know exactly what she did. All I know is that I asked her not to let him photograph the bottle, and that's exactly what happened. You saw it yourself. With spirit, you always get what you ask for. You need to be very specific. The briefcase was in perfect focus because I didn't say anything to Crystal about it. I only asked that the bottle not be photographed, and that's what she did. Those blurred photographs were her doing."

"I thought it was the camera."

"How could it have been the camera? Didn't you look at the pictures? Everything was in focus. It was Crystal who blurred the photographs. This is how things work when you know how to tap into a higher power. As long as you work within the light, you are protected."

"Pop, I still wish you would take precautions and not put yourself in these dangerous situations."

With some annoyance he said, "Philip, you continue to see things only on the material plane. If you would only make the effort to see things from a metaphysical point of view, you would understand what I'm talking about. You don't ever have to be afraid, because you can control everything that happens to you. There are a lot of forces and energies available to help you in whatever you seek to accomplish. They are there for the asking."

nine

•

Dios Mio, Dr. Siegel

As the summer progressed, I watched my father perform even more remarkable healings on a daily basis. Summers were usually slow in his business, but the healings kept the office humming. Patients now outnumbered clients three to one.

One day Zvi, the young man who ran the custom carpet design studio next door, stopped in to ask my father a question. I liked Zvi and always enjoyed talking to him. He was a kind of hip wise-cracking guy from New York's East Side whose brother was a professional flamenco dancer. As a result, Zvi understood "creative types." On the side, when business was slow, he would create large geometric acrylic paintings à la Frank Stella in pastel tropical colors. He was selling about three a week, as they were all the rage with the decorators who had no idea what to do with those big blank walls in the new condos. I would bring in articles about New York pop artists from my underground newspapers, and we would argue about their merit. Zvi made me feel like an adult.

"Lew, tell me, did they switch the days for the garbage pickup?" Zvi asked. "I thought it was Wednesdays and Fridays, but when I put out the garbage last week, they left it, so I'm wondering if—"

Pop interrupted Zvi and asked, "What's wrong with your eyes?" At first Zvi didn't know what he was talking about and remained silent. Then it dawned on him. "Oh yeah, I've been having trouble seeing out of my right eye. Things look blurry. The doctors don't know what it is. I think they're going to give me some sort of special glasses, but if that doesn't work, there's not a lot they can do. They gave me some drops, which stung my eyes and were totally useless. Anyway, what I came by to ask was what are the new days for garbage pickup? Is it still—"

My father asked Zvi to sit down for a minute and close his eyes. Pop stood up, went behind him, and placed his right hand over Zvi's eyes and his left hand on top of his head. Within seconds Zvi mentioned that his eye felt very pleasant.

"Lew, what's going on?" he asked.

"Just give me one more minute." When my father took his hands away, he asked Zvi to look around the room. He did.

"Wow, they're like normal again. Did you just do that?"

"Yes. You just needed a little rebalancing. You'll be fine. Garbage is picked up out back on Thursdays."

Thirty years after this incident, I ran into Zvi at a small Portuguese restaurant in New York's Greenwich Village. I asked him if in all the years he was my father's neighbor he had ever witnessed or experienced my father's healing ability. "No, not really, just I was losing my eyesight in one eye, and your father put his hand over it, and after that I could see perfectly. Nothing really out of the ordinary for your father." With that, Zvi gave me a hug and a huge smile. To this day, he still does not wear glasses.

In the midst of the ever-changing freak show of patients and psychic employees at the office, there was one constant: elegant Christina. For years she worked quietly, pretending to ignore the increasing paranormal activity around the office.

Christina, who must have been in her late thirties, had left behind an empire of sugar plantations, houses, and servants when she fled Castro. Every day she showed up to work with immaculately styled frosted hair and makeup so perfect that she could pass for Sophia Loren's sister. Christina's eyebrows were drawn in big mocha-colored arches, and she had long, long nails painted the color red you only see now in an Almodóvar movie. Her dresses were always formal, but in a tropical sort of way. They were all made of exquisite fabrics styled with an Oriental flair. It was the kind of dress you might imagine Madame Nhu wearing as she descended the stairs of a Pan Am flight, posing for photographers while waving to the oppressed masses. Very often, both Christina's and Madame Nhu's dresses had a long slit far enough up one side to reveal just enough knee and leg.

Christina started her day with "Good morning, Mister Smith. Good morning, Felipe." And those were the last words she spoke until she said, "Good evening, Mister Smith. Good evening, Felipe." The truth was that Christina had decided not to speak much English for political reasons, in order to show solidarity with her native country now under occupation. She believed it was her job to keep the mother tongue alive—not that it was in any danger of disappearing in Miami.

Before she began work every day, she performed her ritual morning meditation: a spritz of perfume behind each ear, the slow slathering of hand cream applied with scientific precision, and a gentle patting of her hair so that it was just so. With that, she let out a long but quiet sigh and went to work. I think she spent most of her day obsessing about the loss she suffered because of Fidel. Here she was in a foreign country, without her cook, her maids, her driver, or her acres of sugar, while her dashing husband, Roberto, now bagged groceries at the A&P.

Every once in a while, she would quietly ask me after lunch to drive her somewhere "very important." We would sneak out of the office and hope to return before my father noticed. As soon as we got into my little blue Fiat, Christina insisted on the top down, no matter how hot it was. She grabbed small moments of glamour whenever and wherever she could. Before we took off, she quickly tied a scarf over her head, slipped on her oversized Jackie Kennedy sunglasses, and directed me to the nearest department store, where she would quickly drop a bundle of cash that probably exceeded her weekly salary on a few small jars of essential cosmetics. Like my father, Christina lived in her own little world—except instead of talking to the dead, she pretended she was still the mambo queen of the sugar plantation.

One day the remote, gorgeous, and ethereal Christina appeared for work with her makeup running and clutching her breast as if she were having a heart attack. Her cool, impenetrable facade had cracked. *"Ay Dios mio!"* she cried as she walked in. I was surprised to see her in such a state. Alarmed, my father immediately sprang into action. "Christina, what happened, what's wrong?"

"Ay Dios mio. Dios mio . . ."

My father turned to me and said, "Philip, get Christina some water and find that bottle of homeopathic Pulsatilla pills in the drawer next to my desk." Turning back to Christina, he implored, "Christina, Christina, tell me."

Christina's English suddenly became completely proficient. *"Mi madre*—my mother—last night she had stomach pain at dinner." Christina grabbed her stomach and sobbed. *"Ay Dios mio.* They take her to the hospital and say she has the cancer. Today they are going to take out her stomach." Christina collapsed into a chair, screaming and crying uncontrollably. *"Mi madre, pobrecita, ayyyyy . . ."*

With his arm around her shoulder, my father said, "Don't worry, we'll take care of this." Christina probably thought this meant that my father was going to pay for the operation. Instead of taking out his checkbook, he went to his desk and took out a small pendulum and a chart filled with diagrams. In his left hand, he held a paper clip that had been straightened into a kind of pointer, which he slowly moved down an anatomy chart. With his right hand, he held the pendulum, which alternately swung clockwise and counterclockwise. Using Christina as a direct conduit to her mother, he psychically examined her mother's medical condition.

After a few minutes of probing questions, the pendulum indicated to my father that Christina's mother had been misdiagnosed and did not have cancer. According to his psychic examination, an impaction in the colon was creating the shadow on the X-ray that had led the doctor to diagnose cancer. To Christina, my father's ritual was all perfectly normal. She saw him do this every single day and probably assumed this was what American decorators did as part of their job.

"Christina, your mother does not have cancer."

"What? *Ay Dios mio!* How can this be?"

"She has an impacted colon. No cancer."

"Oh, Mister Smith, thank you so much." With that, Christina assumed that my father had taken care of everything and proceeded to prepare for work, starting with her perfume spritz and hand lotion application. As she opened the jar of hand lotion, Christina said to me, "Oh, Felipe, your father is so nice. Thank you very much."

"Christina, you need to call the hospital and tell them not to operate; otherwise there will be a big problem," said my father.

"Ohh, noooo. No, I can't do that. I can't talk to the doctor." As she spoke, she waved her pointer finger in a tick-tock motion like a metronome. "No. He won't listen to me. No." Pointing at my father with that finely honed milelong bright red nail, she said, "You talk to the doctor. Okay?"

"Okay. I'll do it. What is her doctor's name?"

"I don't know."

"What hospital is she in?"

"I don't know. The ambulance just took her . . ." With this, Christina waved her hand with big nails in the direction of "away." The gold bracelets she had on when she left Havana tinkled like wind chimes.

"But how did you know she had cancer?"

"Oh, yes; the doctor called." Christina nodded, raised her mocha eyebrows toward the heavens, and with a sidelong glance, added authoritatively, "The doctor told me." She gave her head a little side-to-side shake as if to imply that she was so important that the doctor had called her directly.

Most ordinary humans would start calling the hospitals to see if Christina's mother was registered. Instead Pop opened the yellow pages while holding his paper-clip pointer in his left hand and his pendulum in his right. With the pointer, he slowly went down the list of hospitals in the Miami area. When his pendulum began to rotate in a clockwise direction, he looked to see what it was reacting to. It was St. Francis Hospital. After a bit more investigation with his pendulum, he located Christina's mother in room 708.

Pop got on the phone and discovered that her mother's doctor was already in the operating room preparing for the surgery. He turned to me and said, "We need to get over to the hospital as quickly as possible to stop this operation before it's too late." While I was happy to help out Christina, I wasn't looking forward to a big confrontation with the doctor. I knew that no doctor was going to listen to my father.

We all jumped into my father's car and started speeding up Biscayne Boulevard like Batman and Robin on an urgent mission, with Christina in the backseat crying uncontrollably. As soon as we arrived at the hospital, my father ran to the nurses' station. "What room is Mrs. Cortez in? We need to see her right away." The nurse smiled at the three of us. Looking official, she paused and checked her chart. "Sir, I'm sorry, but Mrs. Cortez is scheduled for surgery and is on her way to the OR. Perhaps you'd like to have a seat and wait?"

"I need to see her right away. This is an emergency. She is not to be operated on. You must stop the operation."

This seemed to wake up the nurse a bit. She said, "And who are you?"

"Lew Smith."

"I see. Did I understand you correctly in saying that the surgery must be stopped? And are you her doctor? Because according to the chart, Dr. Siegel is Mrs. Cortez's doctor." With that pronouncement, the nurse promptly returned to her duties of smiling and staring at the peach-colored wall in front of her. Case closed.

At that very moment, Mrs. Cortez was wheeled out of her room by the orderlies. We saw her as they brought the bed down the hall toward the OR. She had been prepped and anesthetized. My father grabbed the bed and said, "You are making a mistake. She does not need surgery."

"Uh-oh," I thought, "here we go again." I hated it when my father confronted authority. Normally he was a shy man who avoided any type of argument. But when it came to his healing activities, he was absolutely convinced that God was on his side, and there was no stopping him. I was waiting for the "look." Sure enough, the orderlies gave him that unmistakable look that said, "You are out of your mind, you crazy old man." That look was usually quickly followed by a look at me that said, "Can't you do something about this?" During moments like these, I wished I could wave my magic wand, say the secret words, and presto—a door would suddenly appear that would allow me to walk right out of this situation. Why couldn't my father just be like everyone else? As far as I was concerned, I would rather have Christina's mother be operated on than watch my father being made fun of by the doctors and nurses.

The orderlies, determined not to give up their turf, started yanking on the bed to force my father to let go. At sixty-four years old, he was no match for these two young, husky guys. However, he was determined that Mrs. Cortez should not have her colon cut out unnecessarily. A tug-of-war ensued. Fortunately, the elder Mrs. Cortez was in dreamland as her hospital bed was pushed and pulled backward and forward. The orderlies screamed at the head nurse to call security.

Two even bigger guys quickly showed up, pulled my father away from the bed, and then subdued him with an arm lock. The chief of security said, "Mister, get away from that patient. This is a hospital, not a wrestling arena. If you're not gone in thirty seconds, I'm calling the police." My father, while twisted into a pretzel by the two guys, attempted to convince security, as if they would understand, that he was there to save Mrs. Cortez's life. Little did they realize that they were talking to Merlin the Magician, Mother Teresa, and Superman all rolled into one. My father stated calmly, although slightly out of breath, "A misdiagnosis has been made. Mrs. Cortez should not be operated on. You are making a terrible mistake. Talk to her daughter; she's standing right there. She'll tell you."

With this cue, Christina promptly forgot her English and started waving her manicured hands in the air while talking rapid-fire Spanish. I had never heard Christina speak this quickly before. She always spoke perfectly articulated Spanish, as if she were the queen of Spain. Now no one understood a word of what she was saying. The guards gave her the same "Are you crazy or what?" look they had given my father. Her performance made the scene even more surreal. By the end of her monologue, Christina finally got with the program and began singing *"Dios mio!"* operatically at the top of her lungs. She threw herself on top of her mother, screaming and waving her hands as they wheeled her toward the OR. Despite the heavy security presence, this mini sit-in, perhaps the first ever staged at a Miami hospital, worked brilliantly. Dr. Siegel was called from surgery for a powwow with my father, the nutcase.

"Mr. Smith, you are interfering with this woman's surgery and critical care. How did they even let you into my hospital? I've never seen behavior like this before. Do you understand what you are doing? Your behavior is criminal. Are you aware of the serious nature of this matter? You must be out of your mind." The doctor stood about six-three and glared down at my father with an imperious air. Calmly and with authority, my father explained to Dr. Siegel that Mrs. Cortez had an impaction, not cancer, and that the operation was not necessary.

"How do you know this? Who told you this?"

"I get my information cosmically by tuning in to Mrs. Cortez's body."

"You what? From where?" Dr. Siegel stared at my father with visible contempt.

Calmly, my father began to explain the mysteries of the universe to Dr. Siegel. "Everything in the universe vibrates at a certain rate. By using these vibrations, I was able to tune in to Mrs. Cortez's body and find that she does not have cancer. I could not find cancer anywhere in her body."

Dr. Siegel assumed that tone that certain doctors assume when they want to dismiss ignorant mortals. "And when did you perform this exploratory surgery? We have no record of this diagnosis."

"I used my pendulum just about an hour ago and found there was no cancer. She has an impaction, which can be easily eliminated by some citrate of magnesium. If you don't mind me asking, Doctor, how did *you* determine the diagnosis of cancer?"

Dr. Siegel cleared his throat before he answered. "Well, we, uh . . . we saw a shadow on the X-ray."

"A shadow? You're cutting her open based on a shadow? And you think *I'm* nuts?"

"Well, once we perform the exploratory surgery, we'll know better. What am I doing even talking to you? You're not even a doctor!" With sheer annoyance, Dr. Siegel dismissed my father's metaphysical diagnosis. "There is no blockage. This woman has cancer, and her life is at stake unless we operate. Why am I even wasting my time talking to you?" The doctor turned abruptly and started to walk away.

"Are you sure?" This simple question stopped the doctor in his tracks. "What if she doesn't have cancer? What if you open her up, take out her colon, put her on a colostomy bag for the rest of her life, and you made a mistake? Isn't it worth postponing the surgery for just one day?" My father smiled at the doctor.

"There is no need to postpone surgery. It must be done. Are you questioning my diagnosis?"

"No, not at all. I am providing you with more accurate information than a shadow on an X-ray."

"You think that you can tell me that Mrs. Cortez does not have cancer psychically? Perhaps it is you who should be hospitalized—over at Jackson Memorial, in the psych ward." Dr. Siegel was practically spitting his words at my father.

At this point Christina began screaming while clutching her mother, "No! No! No! *Mi madre* is coming home. Mister Smith promised me. She comes home." All of Christina's expensive makeup was running down her face. This was a nice dramatic touch that really increased her credibility. It was as if she had been rehearsing her whole life for this moment. If she had wanted a second career as an actress on the Spanish *telenovelas,* this would have been her showstopping audition.

While Christina continued to cry, a nurse came over and whispered something in Dr. Siegel's ear. He then turned to my father and said, "You know what, I'll put Mrs. Cortez back in her room. We will reevaluate the case. But if in the meantime she dies, we will have you arrested for manslaughter. And I'm not kidding."

"That is fantastic. Thank you, Doctor." My father was beaming. He had prevented an unnecessary operation and saved Mrs. Cortez from painful and potentially life-threatening surgery.

All of us went back to Mrs. Cortez's room for a few minutes. Christina bent over and kissed her mother, who was still under anesthesia and oblivious to the current crisis. She then said a little prayer in Spanish and crossed herself when she was finished. We left the hospital confident that everything was going to be okay.

By the time we reached the parking lot, the orderlies had secretly wheeled Mrs. Cortez back into the operating room, and the surgery began. The doctor had cleverly placated my father. When the doctor opened her up, they found no cancer but instead an impaction in the colon, exactly as my father had diagnosed. Since they already had her open, they proceeded to remove a large portion of her colon as a "precaution" and closed her back up. Those were the days when doctors had no accountability, and malpractice suits were rarely, if ever, filed.

The next morning Christina came into the office again in tears.

My father was surprised and expected her to be overjoyed. Just like the day before, my father asked, "Christina, what's wrong? Tell me."

"*Mi madre.* They make another operation, and now she has no stomach."

"*What?* But I thought—" My father immediately picked up the phone and called the hospital. "Dr. Siegel, please . . . he's in surgery? Please have him call Lew Smith. Yes, Plaza 8-7552. Yes, oh yes, he'll know who I am."

What my father didn't know and didn't bother to check was that Dr. Siegel was at that moment back in surgery operating on Mrs. Cortez *again*. Overnight her colon had become infected, and the infection was spreading through her body. They now opened her up to remove even more of her colon. My father turned to Christina, who was still crying, and said, "We'll take care of this. I'll find out what's going on."

With that, my father took out his pendulum and began watching it spin in response to his questions. It was making large counterclockwise circles. After about a minute, he looked up and said to no one in particular, "Something is really wrong." His eyes darted around the room as if he were searching for an answer. He looked back down to the pendulum and watched it spin again. This time it spun to the right in ever widening circles. Pop closed his eyes. His lips started moving. About a minute later, he opened his eyes and said to Christina, "This is very strange. I think they are operating again on your mother, and I'm not sure why. Nothing was wrong with her to begin with. I'm getting that she has an infection. I don't quite understand this. Why would she have an infection when all she has is an impacted colon?" Pop had it correct; it's just that his logic was getting in the way of the information that was coming through.

My father picked up the phone and called the hospital again. Dr. Siegel was still in surgery. "Christina, let's go over to the hospital and find out what's going on." All of us got in the car and drove back to the hospital. When we got there, Christina's mother was in Intensive Care, and my father asked the nurse at the front desk to page Dr. Siegel. They waited about a half hour, and still no doctor. My father went back to the nurses' station and explained the urgency of speaking with Dr. Siegel.

"I'm sorry, but Dr. Siegel is not available. I've put the page in and let him know that you are waiting to speak with him. I believe he is still in surgery."

"We need to know the status of Mrs. Cortez and why she was operated on again. There was no need for any of this."

The nurse stopped listening and answered the phone. "Fourth floor ICU . . ."

The day passed. Finally, around three in the afternoon, I spotted Dr. Siegel coming down the hall, speaking with several other doctors. I nudged my father, who got up and started walking toward him. The doctor saw my father and kept walking.

Pop ran after him. "Dr. Siegel, it is important that I speak with you." There was no way that the doctor did not hear my father, but he picked up his pace and tried to avoid him. My father caught up to him and said, "I need to know what has happened with Mrs. Cortez."

"You're asking me? I thought you were psychic and had all the answers; why don't you look it up with that magic pendulum of yours?" With that, the doctor began to walk away.

"I do know what happened, and I already consulted my pendulum. I know exactly what is going on."

"Okay, genius, you tell me, since I'm only the doctor."

"It's very simple. You made a mistake, a terrible mistake. You performed unnecessary surgery on Mrs. Cortez. You didn't want to listen to me because you think you know better. As a result, you took out half her colon when you didn't have to, and now she'll have problems the rest of her life. Plus, a serious infection set in, causing you to go back in. There was no cancer, just like I told you. And now it's too late. There's nothing you can do. But Mrs. Cortez was the sacrificial lamb to your big overblown ego."

At first the doctor blanched, his eyes opening wider and wider. He couldn't believe what he was hearing. Apparently no one had ever spoken to him like this. Pointing his finger right between my father's eyes, the doctor tried to control himself as he said, "You, my friend, are deranged and psychotic. How dare you speak to me this way! I saved Mrs. Cortez's life. Had I listened to you, she would have been dead. Do you hear me? I saved her life. Now, if you'll excuse me, I have people that need me." The doctor spun on his heels and headed down the corridor.

My father walked back to Christina, who looked at him with the face of a broken person. "I am so sorry. I did everything I could," he said. "Your mother should not have been operated on. It wasn't necessary. They lied to me. But she'll be okay." Christina held my father's hand and cried quietly. I looked away.

As soon as we got to the office the next morning, my father called the hospital to check on Mrs. Cortez's condition. She was still in Intensive Care. My father asked to speak with Dr. Siegel. Once again, he was in surgery. He asked the nurse why Mrs. Cortez was still in the ICU; she should have been in her room recovering. "Well, she's recovering from surgery."

"But that was yesterday."

"No, she had surgery last night."

"I think you have someone else's chart. I want to know about Mrs. Cortez. Mrs. Sonia Cortez. She had surgery yesterday."

"Sir, I *am* looking at the chart. It says she had surgery last night."

"That's impossible. There was no reason for this."

"You need to call Dr. Siegel's office; I'm sure they can tell you more." *Click.*

Pop called the doctor's office and asked the receptionist to speak with the doctor. The receptionist gave her standard answer: "I'm sorry, Dr. Siegel is in surgery today. He can return your call this evening. Who's calling, please?"

"I'm calling about Mrs. Cortez. The hospital just told me she was operated on last night, and we did not know about this. I need to know what is going on."

"Are you her husband?"

"No, I'm a friend."

"I'm sorry, but I can't release any information except to family members."

"Her daughter is standing next to me but does not speak English." My father motioned for Christina to come stand next to him.

"Well, I can't give you any information."

"Let me put her daughter on the phone. You talk to her in English, and I'll listen in on the extension." Pop covered the receiver and said, "Christina, pick up the phone on the other desk and say hello."

Warily, as if in a Hitchcock movie, Christina lifted the phone and shook her hair out of the way before she put it to her ear. "Hello?"

"This is Dr. Siegel's secretary, Amanda. Are you Mrs. Cortez's daughter?"

"Yes . . ."

"Well, Dr. Siegel is in surgery, and I will tell him to call you later this evening and let you know what is going on. Thank you. Bye."

Before my father could intervene, Amanda hung up. Christina looked at my father, waiting for her next cue. With great resignation in his voice, he said, "We need to go to the hospital, but first let me see what I can find out."

My father grabbed his ruler and pulled out the pendulum from his shirt pocket. With the pendulum in his right hand, he slowly moved it up the ruler. His hand stopped at the five-inch mark, and the pendulum swung in a clockwise direction. He wrote down something on a pad, then pulled out a copy of *Gray's Anatomy*. In his left hand, he pointed with the straightened paper clip to the various organs in the body. He looked over at the pendulum, which again swung clockwise. Finally he pulled out a list of medical conditions, which he scanned with the paper clip. The whole process took about three minutes. He looked up at Christina and said, "Your mother has peritonitis." Christina's eyes widened in fear. "When the surgeons operated again, they made more mistakes, and your mother's abdominal cavity became infected. This is terrible. It's too late to do anything. None of this should have happened."

Having watched this drama for a couple of days, I was finally waking up to its seriousness. "Is she going to die?" Not the question I should have asked in front of Christina, who began weeping. The last few days were taking their toll on her.

"Christina, Christina, she's not going to die. She will get through this; it will take awhile. I can't repair what they've done. They've taken out too much of her colon. I can do whatever is possible to help her heal quicker so that she doesn't have any more infections. I think we need to go down to the hospital and find out what's going on."

Back we went to the hospital. My father asked for Mrs. Cortez. The nurse didn't respond but first checked her records. "I see that Mrs. Cortez is still in ICU."

"Okay, thank you." My father took Christina's hand and headed toward the swinging silver doors of the ICU.

"Excuse me! Excuse me! Sir, sir, sir, stop! You can't go in there. Stop!" The nurse got up from her station and started running after my father. *"Stop. No visitors. You can't go in there."*

My father turned around and said, "We're going to see Mrs. Cortez. I need to see how she's doing."

"No, no, you can't. No visitors. I'm sorry."

"But we need to see Mrs. Cortez. This is her daughter. She wants to see her mother."

"No. Not now. You'll have to wait until she's moved to her room."

"When?" My father really wanted to get in that room and see what was going on.

"I don't know. Why don't you call us this afternoon, and we'll let you know."

"Can't you just let her daughter in for a few minutes to see her mother?"

"No. Not right now."

"Can we call Dr. Siegel? I'd like to speak with him."

"I'm sorry, but Dr. Siegel isn't here today; he's off on Fridays."

"So who is looking after his patients?"

"One of his associates."

"May I speak to him?"

"Let's see. I think Dr. Falk is covering for him today. I need to go back to my desk and try and page him."

Christina and my father followed the nurse. She paged the doctor. My father reached over and held Christina's hand. Within a few minutes, a chipper Dr. Falk appeared. He was the opposite of the imperious Dr. Siegel. Warm, friendly, open. He approached my father with a smile and an open hand. "Hello. I'm Dr. Falk. How can I help you?"

My father introduced himself and Christina. "I'm inquiring about Mrs. Cortez. This is her daughter. We're very concerned about her. This is now her third operation, and I'm wondering where it's going to end. It seems things are getting worse."

"No, not at all, she's doing quite well." Dr. Falk punctuated his statement with a big smile.

"Doing well?" my father asked.

"Uh-oh," I thought, "here it comes."

"Dr. Falk, Mrs. Cortez was fine when she walked in here. She had a simple impaction that could have easily been remedied. Instead she had dangerous and unnecessary surgery. As a result, she became infected, and now she has peritonitis. She's lost much of her colon, all because she was misdiagnosed."

"Misdiagnosed? I'm sorry, I don't understand. I'm not that familiar with this case, but I doubt that she was misdiagnosed. Mrs. Cortez had cancer that needed to be removed. I'm not sure if we're talking about the same patient."

"Did they actually find any cancer during the procedure?"

"I wasn't there, but I'm sure they did. Otherwise, why would they have operated?"

"I can tell you they didn't find any cancer, because there never was any cancer to begin with."

"Mr. Smith, I can understand that this is very upsetting, but let me assure you that everything—"

"How would you feel if they took out most of your colon for no reason?"

"Well, I doubt that they would have—"

"Look, it's too late to fix this. When can we see Mrs. Cortez?"

I was relieved that he didn't start going into the whole psychic-pendulum-diagnostic-doctors-don't-know-anything routine. Let's just find out where Mrs. Cortez is and go home, was my attitude.

"Well, uh, I, uh, let me check. I believe she is recovering in the ICU, and it may not be until tomorrow that she will be able to return to her room, but let me make sure. I'll be right with you."

Dr. Falk went behind the nurses' desk and started looking through charts. He appeared to be slightly flustered by my father. Looking up, he said, "Yes, here it is. Mrs. Cortez should be back in her room tomorrow. She's heavily sedated, as this last surgery took over three hours, and—"

"Three hours? What were you doing to her for three hours?"

"Well, um, she had some complications, and we were able to correct them, and now she's fine." Dr. Falk worked hard at forcing a smile.

"Dr. Falk, is there any way we can get in to see Mrs. Cortez for just a few minutes? We won't disturb her. I think I may be able to help her, if I could just get in there for a moment or two."

"Help her? In what way? Are you a physician?"

"No, but I think I can speed her recovery and eliminate the recurrent infections that she is experiencing due to the unnecessary surgery."

"Oh. Well, I think that she's doing quite well."

"Doctor, if she has one more surgery, she won't survive. You will have killed her."

"Well, but Mr. Smith, we are not killing her, and she is doing fine, and she will be in her room tomorrow, and if you'll excuse me, I have some patients I need to see. I'm sorry, but I think tomorrow would be better for you to visit."

Once the doctor left, my father turned to the nurse and asked if we could get into the ICU for just five minutes.

"I'm sorry, no one is allowed into the ICU—visiting hours are over." She went back to reviewing her charts.

My father looked at Christina and said, "Let's go. I'll do what I can for your mother from the office."

As soon as they got back to the office, my father sat down at his desk and pulled out his diagnostic charts. For the next half hour, he used his pendulum, his paper clip, and a variety of medical texts to further diagnose and send healing energy to Mrs. Cortez. While my father worked, Christina went into the back and put up a pot of strong black espresso. Its thick, roasted aroma filled the office. Growing up around *los exiliados,* I started drinking Cuban coffee at a very young age, while all the other kids were still sucking on their bottles of Yoohoo. As I sipped my *cafécito,* I picked up the phone and started gossiping with friends.

About a half hour later, my father stood up from his desk and said out loud, "Okay." He went to the bathroom, washed his hands to remove whatever negative vibration had accumulated, and headed to the back workroom looking for Christina, who was calmly applying nail polish with intense concentration. My father said to her, "Christina, listen, I've lifted your mother's fever. That's why they didn't want to let us in to see her; the infection was taking over her body. These doctors have made a total mess of this. I wish I could have stopped them from operating. I couldn't. I think I need to have a lawyer on retainer just to threaten all the doctors who won't listen to me. But the good news is that her fever is gone. I brought her temperature back down and removed the infection. You will be able to see your mother tomorrow. Don't get upset when you see her; she won't look good, she's been through a lot. I'll keep working on her so that we can get her home in two or three days. She is going to have a colostomy bag. With what they did to her, she might never have a normal bowel movement. She will constantly autotoxify and will always be sick for the rest of her life. However, after she's home for a few weeks, and the body has had time to rest, I may be able to fix her colon, and within six months she'll be functioning normally. Please be patient with me, and I'll do everything I can for her."

Christina had had enough excitement for the day. She remained focused on her nails, admiring them and applying more polish as my father spoke. Without looking up, she said, "Thank you. Thank you, Mister Smith."

The next day, Mrs. Cortez was back in her room, although she was in and out of consciousness. My father and Christina drove over and spent several hours at the hospital. Mrs. Cortez had indeed been running a dangerously high fever, which was now gone. She needed to rest.

Just as my father predicted, Mrs. Cortez was released and sent home two days later. Her recovery was slow. For the longest time, it appeared that she would never regain her health—a fact that Christina was quickly accepting. But after two months, Mrs. Cortez was up, moving around, and able to sit outside to take the fresh air for about an hour a day. She gradually began to eat normal food instead of baby food, and her spirits grew stronger. Daily, my father monitored her progress and sent her healing energy. About four months after the operations, Mrs. Cortez was back eating *moros, sofrito, vaca frita,* and other staples of Cuban cuisine. In short, she was her old self again.

It was around this time that a man and woman walked into my father's office late one afternoon looking for beaded draperies for their bedroom. They discussed the particular look they were after, and my father began making suggestions. Suddenly my father turned to the man and asked, "What do you do? Are you a doctor?"

The man said, "Yes, a radiologist."

My father loved having doctors as clients because he could pick their brains and learn firsthand about medicine. "Doctor, if you don't mind, I have a question. Can you tell if someone has cancer from an X-ray?"

"No, not really. What you can see is a shadow on the X-ray, and that might indicate cancer, but no, you cannot see cancer on an X-ray."

"So, if someone had an X-ray that showed a shadow in their colon area, a doctor might think that they had colon cancer?"

"Probably yes. But that does not mean that they have cancer."

"Do you have a card? I like to keep the business cards of my clients."

"Sure." The doctor took out his business card and handed it to my father.

After studying the card, my father said, "Oh, I see you work at St. Francis."

"That's right, I'm the staff radiologist there."

"By any chance, would you be familiar with Mrs. Sonia Cortez? She was recently operated on in your hospital."

"Oh, yes, I know the case well. I reviewed the X-rays."

"So, you looked at the X-rays and determined that she had cancer?"

"Well, like I said, she had a shadow, and it was determined that she was at risk, and the best option was to perform a procedure."

"But couldn't that shadow have also been an impacted colon?"

"Yes, it could have been, and if I remember—it was a while ago—I think that was in fact what she had."

"So the surgery was unnecessary, and if she had been given an enema or a laxative, she would not have needed surgery?"

The doctor began to shift in his seat. He had clearly said too much already. "No, surgery was absolutely necessary because we wouldn't have known otherwise. We needed to take precautions."

"Precautions?"

"Yes, if the surgery had not been done, then the cancer could have spread."

"But she didn't have cancer."

"That's correct."

"Then how could it have spread?"

"Mr. Smith, I was not the surgeon on the case. I only read the X-ray."

"But it was based on your recommendations that the surgery was performed."

"Why are you so interested in this case? What has this got to do with you?" The doctor was becoming aggressive.

"Let's just say I'm an interested bystander. I knew that Mrs. Cortez didn't have cancer, and I tried to stop them from operating when they didn't have to. As a result, she ended up having three operations that almost killed her and nearly destroyed her life."

"Well, I don't think they had any choice. If they had simply ignored the shadow, and it was cancer, she would have died. Even though there were difficulties, she's alive. The doctors did a good job."

"But they didn't have to operate."

The doctor shrugged his shoulders. "How did you know that Mrs. Cortez didn't have cancer? Sounds like you are guessing after the fact."

"Speak with Dr. Siegel. I'm sure he'll remember me as the man who tried to stop him from operating, but he went ahead anyway after I told him not to."

"But how did you know?"

"I'm psychic. Not all of the time, but much of the time."

"What do you mean, psychic? I don't understand what you're trying to say."

"I can look into people's bodies, give them a diagnosis, and heal their illness without surgery or medication."

The doctor started laughing. "You mean like science fiction?" He continued to laugh and slapped his knee good-naturedly. "You can look inside someone's body—that's a good one."

"Well, at the moment, I can tell you that you have been plagued by a bad back for the last seven years. You've tried medication, and there was some minor surgery, but that didn't work. This condition affects your ability to stand at work."

The doctor just looked at my father. He didn't say a word.

My father continued, "If you want, I can get rid of your backache right now, and you'll never have a problem again." The doctor continued to just stare at my father. Without waiting for him to respond, my father suggested, "Okay. Let's try something. I believe that you are in some discomfort at the moment. Right now it feels like a cross between a pinch and a needle sticking you. Give me a minute, and I will remove that pain. Do you think that is possible?"

"No," replied the doctor. He gave my father a look of annoyance. Now his wife was staring at my father as well. She gave her husband a look that said, "Let's get out of here; the hell with the beaded curtains."

My father said reassuringly, "You don't have to do a thing. Just sit there. Please relax and let the healing take place." With that, my father stood up and walked behind the doctor's chair. He took three deep, noisy breaths, closed his eyes, and held his hands straight out in front of him. Starting at the doctor's head, my father moved his hands slowly up and down the back of the chair. He paused briefly at the doctor's lower back. When he was finished, my father walked around the desk and sat back down in his chair. He looked at the doctor and said, "Stand up and tell me if the pain is still there."

Slowly the doctor got up, stretched, and walked around the room. Next he bent down and quickly touched his toes. He didn't say a word until he sat down, then he marveled, "This is the first time in years that I could move without pain. How'd you do that?"

"You're not really interested in how I did it. Let's just say that this is what I do."

The doctor's wife suddenly chimed in, "Maybe you can help me. I've had arthritis in my left hand for the past year, and nothing is making it go away. I can hardly hold my golf club. In fact, it's only getting worse, even with all the injections they are giving me."

"Of course, just relax. You hand will be good as new in just a minute or two."

She placed her hand on the desk and pointed to the knuckle at the base of her thumb. "Here is where it hurts the most, right at this joint."

My father closed his eyes and placed his open hand above hers. He let it hover there for about a minute and then started rotating it clockwise. After he took his hand away, he opened his eyes and said, "That's it, the pain should be gone. You won't have any more problems with that hand."

The woman flexed her hand a few times, flicked her thumb back and forth, and slowly said, "Yes . . . yes, I think the pain *is* gone." She let out a little laugh and looked over at her husband. Without saying a word, they both stood up and walked out of the office and never returned.

ten

•

In Shock

"That's correct. It's the left eye. Yes, it's a bit cloudy."

I thought I overheard my father talking to someone on the phone and didn't want to interrupt. When I walked by his study, I noticed that he was at his desk, holding the pendulum in his right hand over an anatomy chart. "How long?" he asked. "Three days? Complete remission? Yes, it already seems a bit clearer. Okay, thank you, Dr. Han." No one else was in the room, and the phone was on the hook. My father was talking to himself.

I poked my head in. "Hi, Pop. I wanted to ask you—"

"Just a minute." Holding up his left hand, he signaled me to stop talking. He then turned his attention back to the chart. "Okay, yes, I'll look for that. Could you please check with me in three days? Thank you again for your help."

"Who were you talking to?" I was certain that my father had lost his mind since I last saw him an hour earlier.

"Who? Oh, that was Dr. Han. He dropped by to check on my eye. It's been hurting, and I couldn't see so well."

"Who's Dr. Han?"

"My eye surgeon."

"Oh."

Over the last year, my father had been busy making tons of new friends—invisible friends. His relationship with the spirit Crystal had just been the start of his social networking with the invisible souls. All of a sudden he was on the A-list party circuit for the deceased. Doctors, physicians, Indian chiefs, and Tibetan monks were constantly dropping by to say hi. Each one would introduce my father to a buddy who specialized in a particular technique that he needed in his healing practice. One guy was a virologist, another an orthopedic surgeon, another was an enlightened master willing to instill cosmic consciousness in my father. At any given moment, Pop would be having a yakfest with someone on the other side who would be diagnosing one of his patients or training him in some new form of healing. Thank God that long distance to the dead was free, or he would have had some monster phone bill. As my father became more acquainted with their personalities, the dead became like relatives of an ever-expanding family. Sometimes they made him laugh, or they would annoy him with their constant prodding or their impatience over his inability to learn a new healing method. He interacted with them no differently than he did with anyone alive. To him there was no separation between the living and the dead.

Daily, various spirits would check in with my father and dictate long, detailed messages on everything from new forms of advanced healing, to other medical issues, to personal matters of finance and love. Over the years, my father accumulated thousands of these messages from ethereal beings. Everyone including Sir William Osler, William James, and Dr. Edward Bach would drop in for a chat. Usually Pop would wake up around four in the morning to begin receiving his daily dictation. He would sit with a pen in one hand and his pendulum in the other. Slowly he would write down the words in a spiral notebook as they were being dictated or implanted in his mind by the communicating spirit. However, whenever there was an emergency, no matter what time of day, the spirits made their presence known and provided immediate diagnostic information. Each spirit had his or her own individual calling card—a specific signal to alert my father that he or she was present. Some tickled him on the back of his neck or tapped at the corner of his eye.

While surrounded by spirits at home, I spent my days surrounded by normal high school kids whose concerns were limited to going steady and getting a new car. At their houses, they had to deal only with family members that they could actually see. They had no knowledge of the distant galaxies my father traveled to or the strange universe that I inhabited once I left school and went home.

At the time, many of the girls in my high school class were getting nose jobs. They all went from those nice, thick, real-looking noses to those ridiculous noses that taper into a little ski jump on the end. I don't know what they were thinking, but they all went to the same doctor one after another, especially around Christmastime. While they were busy changing their appearance, I wanted a complete brain job that would remake my life free of the supernatural influence. I was hoping that there was some sort of magic pill that could suddenly turn me into a normal kid, something I simply did not know how to be. As much as I tried to mimic my classmates in their speech, dress, and interests, it never quite worked. The strangeness of my daily home life prevented me from ever being one of them. How do you talk to another kid at recess and ask, "So, what spirits is your father talking to?" Or, "Yeah, last night after dinner, my dad dissolved a lung carcinoma; what is your dad's success rate?" Unlike the other kids, I had no road map or guidance for growing up, such as joining the football team, dating a cheerleader, acing the SATs, or getting into law school. I needed a bit of help, and I didn't want it to come from a dead person.

Not knowing what else to do, I thought it might be a good idea to see a psychiatrist in the hope that he could cure me from my haunted life. Perhaps someone could make sense of everything for me and point me in the right direction. While I had no idea what I thought a psychiatrist might actually do for me, the thought of seeing somebody who supposedly had the tools to create normalcy provided a certain amount of relief—something along the lines of a lobotomy, but without all the cutting and drilling.

I remembered a girl at school, Betty, telling me that her father was a psychiatrist. Everyone made fun of her. She was dumpy and ugly and seemed in deeper psychological trouble than I would ever be. But it was my only lead. I gave her father a call, explained who I was, and made an appointment. One day after school, I rode my bike over to his office with about six months' of pocket money to pay for the session. His air conditioner was broken, so he suggested we meet in the garden. Only in Miami can you do analysis and get a tan at the same time.

The good doctor leaned forward and with a warm smile said, "So what brought you here?"

All my determination and nerve instantly vanished. I was terrified to tell him about what really went on at home, for fear that he might have both my father and me committed. No one, especially a psychiatrist, was going to believe stories about instantaneous healings, talking spirits, and alien communication. The previous night's séance at the house had involved my father talking to a spirit who advised him on how to clear up kidney infections using boiled leaves from the backyard. I knew it was suicide to tell the shrink about this. I started to sweat. Coming here was not a good idea. In a panic, I mentioned the first thing that came to mind.

"Um, I have this girlfriend, and I'm having a lot of sex, like, all the time . . ."

"Well, that sounds normal. I assume you are using protection."

"Um, yeah. But then I sleep with other people too."

"And how does she feel about that?"

"She thinks it's funny."

"Funny?"

"Yeah. She loves to hear about it."

"That's interesting. What does she say when you tell her about your other activities?"

"She laughs."

"I would think most girls would be upset if their boyfriend was dating other girls."

"Well, this is kind of different." I knew we were getting way off track from my original intention. This type of questioning was all new to me, so I just followed his lead.

"How so?"

"Well, it's not always other girls. Sometimes it is and sometimes it isn't. It depends."

"I don't understand. So if it isn't other girls . . . Please don't tell me you are having sex with animals."

"How do you have sex with animals?"

"Could you please answer the question?" I could see that the doctor was getting upset.

"I thought I did. I still don't understand how you can have sex with animals."

"That's not what I asked."

"Sorry, so what are you asking?"

"Who are you having sex with besides other girls?"

"Well, see, sometimes I'm at these parties, and there are a lot of other hippies, and there might be three or four people having sex together, so it can be a couple girls with a guy or a few guys—kinda mix 'n' match. So, if I'm at these parties, sometimes I join in if I like the people, and sometimes I don't."

His face grew red, and his jaw tightened. "You are having sex with another man?"

"Well, kinda all together. Not really just with a man, but, like, a bunch of us fooling around." This didn't seem so unusual to me, having grown up around my father's interior decorator colleagues, who were always sleeping with anybody and anything. I had developed a very open approach to sexuality, especially as part of my hippie free-

love ethos, but I could tell that the doctor thought I had violated the
most basic laws of humanity.

His voice grew firm. "Let me tell you something, young man"—
and here he stood up and began to scream at me—"*A penis is meant for
a vagina. Anything else is dangerous and abnormal. You are in crisis and in
need of emergency care!*"

For a few more moments, the doctor stood there, snorting deep,
hard breaths. The veins in his forehead were throbbing. After a long
silence, during which he just glowered at me, he fell back into his
chair. He gripped its arms, and his eyes nervously looked around the
garden. He refused to look at me, as if I were some kind of leper. His
reaction terrified me.

I figured that since he was the doctor, he knew more than I did. "I
must be really sick," I thought. "He'll probably put me on something
like Nembutal, Miltown, or Thorazine, and maybe I'll be institutionalized for a bit." Part of my perverse teenage-rebellion phase was that
I would rather take the advice of a medical doctor, no matter how
outrageous or ill-founded, than that of my intuitive, powers-by-God
father.

I had never considered that what I was doing was immoral, un-
ethical, or against nature. I hadn't realized that having sex with a
woman and a man was bad. In fact, I thought it was normal; it seemed
very open and loving. But after listening to this psychiatrist's warning,
I was terrified that I had done irreversible damage to my karma. And,
boy, was I going to catch hell in the next life.

As he regained his composure, he said with a forced calm, "Fortunately, I have someone who treats people like *you*. It is urgent that you
see him at least three times a week. He's very busy, but I will get you in
on an emergency basis."

Emergency basis? I knew it: things were really bad, much worse
than I anticipated. My few times in bed with a bunch of hippies
had led to a crisis of epic proportions. My concerns of living in a
spook-filled house were quickly forgotten. Thank God I came to be
diagnosed just in time! Now I needed to be cured of this horrible

psychiatric problem. I was definitely a case. This might even be one for the medical journals.

I had imagined our session to be something more along the lines of slow, deep hypnotic conversation in which every word and every sentence revealed profound truths. When I was ten, my mom had taken me to see a black-and-white movie about Freud with startling close-ups, which had permanently formed my image of psychiatrists. Mom loved anything having to do with the drama of tortured psychology.

"This is going to be tough and a lot of work, but we will get you on the right track," the psychiatrist promised. "As soon as you leave, I will call the other doctor and make the appointment for you. Now, what else is on your mind?"

"Um, I guess we've covered just about everything for today." I thought this was an appropriate closing statement for my first session with this doctor. As I left his office, I realized I had used up all my savings on this one visit, and I couldn't figure out how I was going to pay for two doctors. I was in a state of shock at what a mess I was. Needing to see two psychiatrists simultaneously five days a week sounded pretty bad to me.

Because of the severity of my illness and my compromised financial status, I had no choice but to talk to my father about seeing the psychiatrists. How else could I continue my very necessary mental health treatments? I was now concerned that if I didn't go through with treatment, I might end up emotionally damaged for life. Even though I knew Pop wanted the best for me, I was positive that he would veto any further visits to the shrinks. There was no way the son of a psychic was going to be lying on the couch when the spirits could do a better job for free. However, because of my critical psychiatric situation, I felt that I needed urgent intervention that was beyond the scope of the spirits. I wanted to try something really unusual—like professional medical care.

That night, after dinner with my mother, I went next door to speak with my father about the seriousness of my condition. He was upstairs in the loft bedroom, sitting at his desk. I climbed the circular staircase and sat on the couch behind him. Using what little courage I had, I blurted, "Pop, I need to see a psychiatrist."

He didn't seem the least surprised by my statement. But then again, why should he? Most likely someone or something had already informed him that I had seen a shrink. Still, he asked, "Why? What's wrong?"

"I can't tell you. But I have to go. It's very important. If I don't, I'll go crazy." As soon as the words "I can't tell you" left my mouth, I realized I had made a huge mistake. There was no point in not telling my father anything, since he already knew or could easily find out. One way or another, I was going to have to come clean with the whole story. But before my father could even respond, the lamp above his desk blinked rapidly three times as if the bulb was about to burn out. "Uh-oh, here we go," I thought. This was the signal to my father that his friend Arthur Ford was trying to contact him with an important message.

When Arthur was alive—and even after he died—he would communicate with my father via psychic means. Instead of ringing my father up on the phone, Arthur would blink the lights to initiate the communication. Sometimes we would be having lunch in a restaurant, and the lights in the room would stutter three times. Startled, people would look up from their meal, look at each other, shrug, and go back to eating, unaware that my father was receiving a psychic message. It didn't matter if we were driving on the highway or in a movie theater, Arthur found a way to blink a light and let my father know that he wanted to talk to him. Arthur always checked in when he had some timely comment or urgent lifesaving information about one of Pop's patients. Sometimes Arthur would blink the lights when my father was in midsentence in order to help clarify what my father was saying. Like a good secretary, my father would then take out a pen and patiently write down Arthur's message on a napkin or any other handy piece of paper.

In one of his communiqués, Arthur explained the blinking lights this way: "I discovered that the energy force I was able to tap into was more powerful than the power used for lighting, and that if I directed this power to the light source, it interrupted the flow and cut it off momentarily and caused a blinking effect. I merely use it as my calling card and a means of alerting you that I am with you."

The instant the lights blinked above his desk, my father casually announced, "Oh, Arthur's here; he has a message for me." He began to write down Arthur's words on a yellow legal pad as if taking dictation. The timing of the blinking lights made it obvious to me that somehow Arthur had been listening in on our entire conversation. Now he was going to disclose every detail about my sex life and my visit to the psychiatrist to my father. This was extremely embarrassing. Arthur's presence made me realize that there were probably spirits in the room as well, also listening and watching. I hated this intrusion into my personal life. Why couldn't I just talk to my father in private without eavesdropping spirits? Why was Arthur sticking his nose into my affairs at this very uncomfortable moment? My father remained hunched over the desk and filled pages of his pad with this very long message.

For the first time since I had known Arthur, I became really angry at his presence. Didn't this guy ever sleep or go spook other people besides my father and me? While Pop continued to write, I said under my breath, "Stupid know-it-all assholes, get the fuck out of here." I didn't care who heard me. I felt cornered and betrayed, as if someone I trusted was tattling on me.

Minutes later, my father swiveled around in his chair to face me with several pages of notes, as if he had hot news right off the teletype. Without any introduction, he began to read what Arthur had dictated. "On his own, Philip went to see a psychiatrist because he is worried about the interference of spirits in his life. He doesn't realize how fortunate he is to have them watching out for him so he can avoid the problems usually confronted by other mortals. However, they understand his desire for independence and will respect that. Because of this visit, Philip now incorrectly thinks that he has a psychiatric problem because he is experimenting sexually. This is normal and nothing to be concerned with. He thinks seeing a psychiatrist will help. It won't. In fact, it may make things worse. I wish he would reconsider. However, he should make his own decisions. The doctor has recommended that he see another psychiatrist named Dr. Edwin. His office is located at 1945 Twin Lakes Drive, phone 983-1407. I do not approve of this doctor or his methods. Only Philip can decide what it is that he wants to do. As always, he has free will . . ."

"Free will?" I thought to myself. "Since when do I have free will, with every damn spook and psychic in the universe poking his nose into my business?" It was not surprising that Arthur knew not only Dr. Edwin's name and address but his phone number as well. Plus, now my father knew the latest installment of my sex life. All I wanted was the money to see this psychiatrist. I couldn't wait to get on that couch and complain about these fucking spooks hovering all around, bugging my mind and telling my father my every secret. I wanted them to go away and leave me alone, but I knew there was no escape from these guys.

Pop continued to read the rest of the message, which went on in detail about my various "problems" for several pages. After he was done reading, Pop said, "Well, you heard what Arthur said. What do you want to do?" My father and I were allowing this dead person to participate in the decision making regarding my psychological well-being as if he were a psychiatrist himself.

"I want to go to the psychiatrist," I said somewhat petulantly. Anything seemed better than dealing with these busybody mind-readers. I didn't care what it cost or how much work was involved. I was desperate for someone to hear me out, to take me seriously and not laugh at this situation that was driving me nuts. Besides, the doctor made it seem as if I was on the verge of a nervous breakdown (which was in vogue at the time—usually suffered by rich house-wives). As much as I appreciated alternative lifestyles and creative personalities, I did not want to become a mental ward of the state.

"You don't have to go."

"Yes I do."

"Maybe you should think it over for a day or two."

"No. I know that I need to go. I have to."

"But if you gave me a few minutes, we could get to the bottom of what's bothering you, and we could finally fix it. You don't have to go through all of this—*primitive*—psychiatry, which really doesn't work anyway. It's very easy, if you'd just let us—"

I wanted no part of my father and his friends in my head. "No. I think it's better if I go to the doctor; this is all kind of complicated." I was looking forward to finally saying to a sympathetic ear, "How would you feel if you were having sex with your girlfriend and felt your father or one of his invisible buddies watching you?"

Not only was I genuinely concerned for my mental well-being, but I also thought that going to a psychiatrist was very sophisticated—even though the one I had chosen was an idiot. He was, nonetheless, a psychiatrist. I couldn't wait to say to Maya in conversation, "My psychiatrist said . . ."

Despite Arthur's warning, my father reluctantly agreed to pay for the doctors. A day before my first visit, Dr. Edwin called to confirm the appointment. My rabid desire to see a psychiatrist was cooling down. Now I was not so sure that my supernatural problem would be understood by anyone. My whole situation was not something that was easy to explain in a forty-five-minute session. The longer I stayed away from the psychiatrist, the less disturbed I felt. Before he hung up, Dr. Edwin said, "I'd like you to look through magazines and cut out pictures of men you find attractive."

I wasn't quite sure what the point of this was, but it sounded like some sort of art project, so I agreed. "Oh, okay. Any pictures?"

"Just pictures that you like. Maybe you want to paste them on a board."

"Yeah, I can do that."

That evening I had Maya come over to help. She seemed excited that I was going to a psychiatrist. "My psychiatrist wants me to tear out pictures of good-looking men," I explained. Something about saying "my psychiatrist" made us both feel very grown up.

"What for? Don't you think that is a little strange? What does this have to do with you and your father?"

"I don't know, maybe this is like a Rorschach test or something."

"That makes sense. Okay, let's get started." Maya opened *Newsweek* to a picture of a gray-haired gentleman drinking scotch. "What about this one?" she asked.

"Nah, I don't know; something's not right there. He looks kinda old to me. Let me get my *Playboys* down from the closet. I'll bet there might be some in there." I kept my treasure trove of *Playboys* carefully hidden. For the next several hours, we cut and pasted pictures of men from shaving ads, hosiery ads, and English Leather cologne ads. By the end of the evening, we had about sixteen guys nicely mounted on pieces of colored cardboard.

"This looks like enough," I said as we flipped through the pictures.

"I still think you should have gone with that skinny guy in the jeans ad."

"I don't know, he just didn't do anything for me. This whole thing is sort of stupid."

"Yeah, but going to a psychiatrist might be helpful."

"I guess so. Now I'm not so sure that this is going to do any good; it's just too weird."

"You're used to weird."

Dr. Edwin was an average-looking guy in his mid-forties. Despite his apparent blandness, I sensed something shadowy about him. In the barely lit room, I could hardly make out his features. He reminded me of Dr. No—dark, manipulative, and evil. The office had no windows, dim lights, and the thermostat was set at a chilly sixty-five degrees. The place had the feel of a cave.

On my first visit, I sat across a large desk from the doctor, and we exchanged brief pleasantries for a few minutes. I was waiting to show him my handiwork and ask for an explanation as to what we were going to do with these images. He didn't say a word about the pictures. Instead he motioned to a large, black, and somewhat ominous leather recliner at the far end of the room and asked me to take a seat. I was swallowed up by this anonymous La-Z-Boy. Without any warning, he quickly strapped me down and then fastened electrodes to each of my forearms with Velcro straps. With the touch of a button, the lights were lowered almost to complete darkness. It all happened so fast that I didn't even have a chance to ask what was going on.

Taking the chair next to me, Dr. Edwin held up the first of my pictures. It was a guy from a Chevrolet ad. In a flat, mechanical voice, Dr. Edwin said, "Imagine having sex with him." Just because I had a couple of encounters with a group of women and men, Dr. Edwin assumed that I wanted to have sex with men from magazine ads. No matter how hard I tried, I couldn't get excited looking at pictures of guys combing Brylcreem through their hair or smoking a True Blue cigarette.

Now that I was strapped down, I thought that this was my opportunity to talk about what Arthur said last night in a message to my father. I figured I had nothing left to lose. As I was getting ready to speak, Dr. Edwin insisted, "Imagine having sex with him." Clearly, it must have been showing on my face that I wasn't trying hard enough. I was beginning to think that these psychiatrists were a lot stranger than my father.

Next to the doctor was a small black metal box with two dials and wires leading from the back directly to my arms. Seconds later, while I was supposed to be deep in sexual fantasy, Dr. Edwin pushed and held a small red button on the face of the metal box.

This unleashed a cascade of electric shocks through my body. Just as in the Frankenstein movies, where the monster receives massive dosages of electricity, I bucked as the voltage surged through me. My mouth flew open, my eyes rolled backward, and my mind went numb. On cue, I made a low guttural sound of controlled pain: *"Ahhhhhhhhhhhhhhh."* He must have forgotten that there was a skinny kid attached to the end of those wires as he kept his finger on the button for what felt like hours. After running through all the images (that's a lot of sexual partners in forty-five minutes, more than even I could handle), I was unhooked, unstrapped, and told, "See you Thursday."

On the way home, I felt both oddly optimistic and extremely nauseous. Maybe those jolts of electricity could burn away the demons, and I would be spook free. I imagined that the electricity would somehow destroy the circuits in my brain that allowed the spirits to eavesdrop on my life. I decided to let Dr. Edwin continue his aversion therapy. I needed something, anything, to help me make sense of my life. So far the drugs and the sex had not really worked. As crazy as Dr. Edwin's methods seemed, I wanted to believe some good would come of it. Besides, at that point, I didn't see much difference between a doctor using electricity to cure my demons and my father harnessing invisible energy to cure disease. This just seemed like a more modern way to go about it.

It seemed pointless to discuss this first session with my father, since most likely his spirit spies were in the doctor's office with me and had already filed their report. I also decided that it was best not to tell my mother. I didn't know how she would react, and it was just too long a story to have to tell her. Frankly, I did not feel like explaining why I was getting hooked up to a machine to get shocked while looking at ads of men smoking cigarettes. Anything I would have said to her would have been analyzed by her crystalline logic, making the whole enterprise seem ridiculous, so I kept the entire experience to myself. Besides, I was already a professional secret keeper; what was one more item tucked away from public scrutiny?

There was just one problem with keeping my latest secret. The next day my forearms were covered with raised red circular welts where the electrodes had burned into my skin. These burns made me look like a junkie or a botched suicide case. I immediately went out and bought some long-sleeved shirts—a rarity in Miami—which I wore in the 94-degree heat. Maya assumed that I was shooting drugs. At the time, any kind of addiction was considered extremely cool, so I never had to explain the red sores on my arms when we were naked.

After a few weeks, I dropped Betty's father. No matter how many times I tried to steer the session toward discussing my father and his healings, the doctor would start screaming at me about my disgusting sexual perversion. Since I was already getting shocked for my disgusting sexual perversion, I figured I didn't need to spend more money to hear it in stereo. The aversion shocks were a sufficiently bizarre therapy that I convinced myself that it was somehow reorienting the circuits in my brain and making me immune to the supernatural influence.

I stayed with Dr. Edwin for another two months until I realized that the whole exercise was pointless, just as my father and Arthur had warned me. I was tired of the welts on my arm, the nausea, and feeling like a trained dog. The magic cure-all for an undiagnosed illness was not forthcoming. Drugs, sex, and shocks had all failed to create a desired state of blissful unenlightenment. I was running out of ideas as to how to self-medicate or self-analyze myself into a nonsupernatural existence.

eleven

·

Futurama

While buying a pack of cigarettes in Super X Drugs, I noticed a small pile of tickets left on the windowsill by the door for a free lecture offering "a release from all problems through the science of Dianetics."

"Wow," I thought, "I could certainly use a release from all problems through anything available, especially something legal." Hopefully it didn't involve jolts of electricity.

Whatever Dianetics was, it seemed to be what I was looking for to set me free. I put the ticket in my pocket and knew with absolute certainty that I was ready to convert to Scientology. Just the name, Scientology, sounded like the future to me. I imagined high priests guarded by men in black rubber space suits with ray guns. Somehow I sensed that the premise of Scientology was instant erasure of who you are, followed by an instant creation of who you would like to be. My father's spirits seemed so ancient and creaky compared to the futuristic appeal of Scientology. Yep, this was it. I was going to become a Scientologist. Good-bye hocus-pocus, good-bye séances, and good-bye nosy spirits. Hello futurama.

When I got to the church, a run-down storefront operation conveniently located around the corner from my father's design studio, I took one look around and had to quickly recalculate my expectations. There were no futuristic sentries guarding the holy laser beam that contained all universal truths. Instead there were a few pieces of abandoned office furniture, a rickety pine bookshelf loaded with paperback copies of *Dianetics* featuring an exploding volcano on the cover, and a massively overweight woman wearing an Indian block-print muumuu sitting behind a gray metal desk. To my surprise, style was not a huge consideration in this religion of the future. The woman automatically smiled at me with one of those big and insincere stewardess smiles that discourage any real interaction. It was just me and her smile one-on-one in the holy church. There were no masses of worshippers engaged in scientifically induced religious ecstasy. No one was storming the gates of Scientology looking for the next great thing—except me.

I wasn't quite sure what to do as I stood there in my paisley print shirt, square-toed boots, and hip-hugger bell-bottoms made out of mattress ticking, so I picked up a pamphlet describing the philosophy of Scientology. I then walked over to the desk and handed the woman my ticket. "Um, hi. I'm here for the free lecture on Dianetics."

"Great!!!!"

"This is kinda my first time here."

"Great!!!!"

"Okay."

"Great!!!!"

"Uh . . ."

"Hi, I'm Toni!!!! Who are you?"

"Philip."

"Great!!!!! Well, Philip, we don't have any clears in the Org today, and none of the auditors showed up, so . . ."

"Huh?" I was used to space talk and speaking in tongues, but this Scientologyspeak was something new. The truth was, I kind of liked it. It all sounded so "yes sir, right away, sir." I would eventually learn this new vocabulary, in which "clears" were enlightened individuals and "auditors" disseminated Scientology. *"Maybe you could come back tomorrow?"*

"Yeah, I guess tomorrow is okay." But I was more than a little disappointed. I wanted my new life to start right then and there. I didn't want to leave until I had some real idea of how I was going to fit into Scientology's grand scheme of advanced global human evolution. The least Toni could have done was give me a tour of the church. But that offer was not forthcoming. I turned to go.

"Hey, Philip, I have a great idea. Why don't you hand out some tickets for our free daily lecture? Brian would really like that."

"Who's Brian?"

"Oh, Brian is our best auditor. He's from England and knows Ron."

"Ron?" This place seemed like one big, happy family. Maybe Scientology would become my new home after all.

"Ron." Toni just kept smiling as she said the name. She was so dazzled by saying his name that she seemed incapable of explaining to me that Ron was L. Ron Hubbard, a former science-fiction author and founder of the church. L. Ron, or just plain Ron, was revered by devoted Scientologists throughout the universe. He had taken a few tenets of basic psychology, added "e-meters" (which function as a kind of lie detector to psych out sensitive emotional problems), mixed in a bit of his own science-fiction language, and *presto!*—a religion that enjoyed tax-free status from the IRS.

"Um, okay, I'll do the ticket thing," I decided. Toni handed me a stack of about two hundred tickets—just like the one that I had brought in. "Where should I go?"

"Anywhere . . . everywhere . . ." She spoke these two words with a smile and a far-off look. Her tone seemed to imply that by this humble act of handing out free Dianetics lecture tickets, I would be taking my first step to becoming a Scientologist extraordinaire.

Miami was just not the kind of place where you saw people walking on the sidewalk, so handing out tickets was not going to be an easy job. Everyone, except the extreme poor, drove everywhere or stayed home. However, in my quest for enlightenment I was willing to give it a try, so I left the church, turned right, and walked down Biscayne Boulevard. After three blocks, I finally saw a guy coming toward me. "Hi, free ticket for lecture at Scientology . . ." He passed right by me without even looking up. "Please join us at the Church of Scientology for an important lecture . . . Hi, here's a free ticket for a lecture!" I shouted after him, giving it my best.

Another block later was the bus stop in front of Denny's on Thirty-sixth Street. A group of about six black women was waiting. As I approached, half of them feigned a strong disinterest while checking me out with careful sideward glances, and the other half stared at me with outright hostility.

"Um, free tickets."

They didn't even look at what I was offering. As I turned to go, I noticed an elderly Bahamian woman wearing thick black-framed glasses and a straw hat with a wilted rose sticking out of the side holding up two copies of *The Watchtower*. A Jehovah's Witness. She looked at me over the rims of her glasses with passing interest. I don't know if she thought I was competition or just some nutty white boy in the wrong part of town.

This wasn't working. I turned around, and as I walked by the church's large picture windows, I quickly stuffed my stack of undistributed tickets under my shirt so Toni would not see my failure. She was sitting behind her desk, staring out the window, and didn't seem to recognize me as I walked toward my car in the parking lot. I needed to try some other part of town.

Perhaps Coconut Grove, with its large bohemian population, would be a good location. I certainly felt a lot more at home there.

After I parked the car behind the 7-Eleven, I walked up and down Main Highway, circling through Commodore Plaza and ending up on Oak Avenue. My free tickets were a hit with every stoned hippie I encountered. "Hi, free ticket to Scientology lecture" was consistently met with either an understated "wow" or a tepid "far out." I quickly unloaded about half my tickets. The rest I left on a ledge in front of the Oak Feed Store, the only health food store in Miami that sold bulk foods. The place had that "Ye Olde Country Store" feel and was one of the few locations where you could see a large group of unwashed people all wearing tie-dyed T-shirts and harem pants breast-feeding their natural children while they occupied the stools at the juice bar for the entire day.

Having done such a good job, I was looking forward to reporting to duty the next day at the church, or as Toni had called it, the "Org." When I walked in on Sunday morning, she was still wearing the same Indian print muumuu and sitting behind the desk, smiling. I didn't know if Toni spent the night behind the desk or if she had gone home and not changed her clothes. I was betting on the former. She smiled but did not seem to recognize me.

"Hi!!! Welcome to Scientology!!! I'm Toni."

"Uh, Toni. I was here yesterday."

"Great!!!"

"I'm Philip. Remember?"

"Great!!!"

"I handed out all the tickets."

"Great!!!"

"Is Brian here?"

"Brian?"

"Yeah. To give the lecture."

"Lecture?"

"Yeah. Free Dianetics lecture."

"Oh!!! Free Dianetics Lecture!!!"

"Yeah. Free Dianetics lecture."

"There's no lecture today. Brian is busy auditing."

"I thought the ticket said free Dianetics lecture seven days a week at one o'clock."

"Hey, I have a great idea. Our communications class starts in half an hour. Why don't you take that?"

"Communications class?"

"Yeah. It's great. You need to take it anyway."

"I do?"

"Yeah!!! You want to communicate, don't you? Clear communication between beings is the first step in practicing Scientology. It helps reduce the power of the reactive mind. Fifteen dollars."

"Huh?"

"Fifteen dollars. For the communications class."

It never occurred to me that Scientology actually cost money or that there was a detailed price list attached to the different levels of enlightenment. All I had was $3 and change in my pocket. I asked Toni if I could owe her the rest.

"Great!!! Hey, I have a better idea. Why don't you come work at the Org? This way you would be around a lot of clears, and it would help pay for your auditing. So why don't you come in around ten tomorrow morning?"

"Um, I go to school."

"Why? That's a real waste. You should come here. We'll teach you everything you need to know. I dropped out of school, moved to San Francisco, and became a Scientologist. Now my life is great!!! I used to live with this black guy, and we sold drugs and balled all the time, and then he got busted, so now I'm here, and, wow, it's really great. Just great!!!"

"Oh."

"So come after school; say, four to ten? Weekends are good too. Okay? See you tomorrow."

At this point, my knowledge of Scientology was limited to what I had read in the pamphlet I'd picked up the day before, but now that I would be working at the Org, I guess I was a Scientologist. When I walked into the house, I announced, "Hey, Mom, I got a job."

"Oh really?" She was totally surprised; suddenly her layabout hippie son was appearing to be responsible.

"Yeah. I'm working at the Org."

"What exactly is your job?"

"I forgot to ask."

"Well, then, how do you know you have a job?"

"They asked me to come in and work." I hated when my mother asked realistic questions like this. She was the opposite of my father; she had too much reality, he had none. What did she know? Of course I had a job.

"Who's they?"

"The Scientology lady, Toni. It will pay for my auditing."

"Who's Toni?"

"The Scientology lady."

"Scientology? Is this like a medical place?"

"No. Forget it. I'm going next door to talk to Pop." It was too hard to explain to my mother about my spectacular new future at the Org. I went next door to see my father. He was sitting at his desk, holding a pendulum over a map of Canada.

"Hi, Pop. What are you doing?"

"I'm looking for someone."

"Who?"

"I think his name is Mark . . ."

"So how can you look for him if you don't know his name?"

"Oh, that's easy. I just tune in to his vibration. He's lost somewhere around here in the mountains. His wife called me today and asked me to find him. She called the Canadian Mounties, but they haven't turned up anything. It's been over a week."

"He may not be alive. That's a long time to be lost in the mountains."

"He's definitely alive. The pendulum told me. I've tuned in to him now. I'll find him in a few minutes. He'll be okay. What's up?"

"I just got a job."

"Hey, that's great, congratulations." Pop continued to dowse the map as he spoke to me. "So where are you working?"

"Over at the Org on Biscayne Boulevard."

"What are you going to be doing?"

"I don't know."

All of a sudden the pendulum began spinning rapidly. "Got him."

"Huh?"

"Here. He's right here." My father was tapping on the map with the straightened paper clip that he used as a pointer. "Okay. I'll be right with you. I have to call Margaret."

"Who's Margaret?"

"The wife."

My father dialed the phone. While he waited for Margaret to answer, he wrote down in a notebook the longitude and latitude where he found the missing man. "Hello. Is this Margaret? Yes, this is Lew Smith. Lew Smith. Yes, you called me about ten minutes ago about your missing husband. I understand. Of course. Well, let me give you the exact location. It's a place called Castle Mountain in Alberta, and on a map the coordinates are approximately 51 degrees north and 115 degrees west. Uh-huh. No, I have no idea how he got there, but he's there. Yes, I'm sure. He's okay. He seems to be in a state of shock and really dehydrated, but he'll be okay after a couple days at home. Sure, yes, I think you should call and tell them where to look. They may not see him from a helicopter; there are a lot of trees. I don't know, tell them whatever you want. They may hang up on you if you tell them a psychic in Miami found him. Why don't you tell them that it came to you in a dream? You're right—they're not going to believe that either. But they're certainly not going to believe you if you tell them that a stranger in Florida found him. Look, just call them now, don't waste any more time. Just tell them that's where he is, and they need to go get him right away. That's it, don't answer any more questions. Once he's settled in, would you please give me a call and let me know that everything's okay? I'll manage his care from here. No, nothing's

broken. It seems that night came, and he lost his way. He's very scared
and needs to be kept wrapped in blankets for a few days. What's his
name? Something with an *M*? Mark? Michael? Mark. Okay. Good.
Okay. No, you don't owe me any money. I'm happy to help. You're
welcome. Bye." My father turned to me and asked, "So who are these
people you are working for?"

"The Scientologists. I think it's kind of interesting. Maybe you
would like it. It's all about one's potential. Their goal is to make you
a clear. You should come by the Org sometime. They do this thing
called 'assist'; it's like your healing. When someone has a cold or something, they put their hands near the person and send energy just like
you do." I thought this would convince my father that Scientology was
a good thing. It also made me feel a bit comfortable in that I was doing
something that was similar to but different from what he was doing.
"They also have a way of explaining how the spirit survives death, sort
of like reincarnation. It's kinda what you do."

"Let's see . . ." My father picked up his pendulum and watched it
for a minute. It swung in a counterclockwise direction. He looked at
me. "No good."

"What?"

"This is not the place for you. There are a lot of people with
negative vibrations at this place. They don't know what they're doing.
Unintentionally, they hurt a lot of people. They open them up psy-
chologically, get in there, and fool around, promising them something
they can't deliver. Also, certain people there are on a power trip and
use that to control some of the newer people. I'm not saying that's true
of the entire organization, but this particular place is really low. Some
of the people in charge have dark forces in them."

"You sure? I kind of liked it over there."

"Well, you haven't met everybody yet, have you? Go. It's up to
you. You may spend a few months there, but that's it. There's nothing there for you. There are other places for you to learn. Besides, it's
going to cost you a lot of money that you don't have."

"No it won't," I said smugly.

"Why?"

"Because I'm going to work there, and all my lessons will be free."

"Well, maybe that's what they told you."

"Pop, I really think I should do this. It'll be my own thing."

"I understand. Just be careful; there are some strange, unhappy people over there."

Of course, I had no interest in listening to my father. I was determined that Scientology would set me free.

While other kids at school spent their weekends hanging out at the beach or just driving around getting into trouble, I went to work at the Org. At seventeen, I was the youngest person in the place. My duties included basic filing, answering phones, handing out free lecture tickets, and straightening up the *Dianetics* books. Occasionally I would complain to Toni that I wanted more important work. She always convinced me that I was making an invaluable contribution to the Org—that I was part of a larger mission to propel humanity into the future and as far away from 1969 as possible. Toni reassured me that my being around the Org and all the clears was what was really important for my growth. I usually got home from work about eleven at night, grabbed some cold soybeans from the fridge for dinner, and went to bed.

It was extremely difficult to balance school and a full-time job. My grades were slipping. I was now averaging Ds in most classes. The guidance counselor had warned me that I was no longer college material and that I should consider attending a trade school. After weeks of research into suitable careers for me, she suggested that plumbing might be an ideal choice, since I was good with my hands.

As a Scientologist, I considered her advice and the rest of my schooling irrelevant. After all, I was on the path to the ultimate truth. I envisioned myself at the Org for the rest of my life, eventually becoming best friends with Ron, hanging out with him on his yacht, known as *Sea Org,* and bringing his science-based enlightenment to the world. Toward this goal, I had quickly developed an ongoing correspondence with L. Ron Hubbard, sharing my various thoughts about making the Miami Org more visible and spreading the gospel of Scientology worldwide. He would write back and encourage me to disseminate my ideas throughout the organization.

Toni was not interested in hearing about my correspondence with Ron. She was too busy telling me about her traumatic romances ("Oooh, he's so fine" and "Boo-hoo-hoo, he beat me last night") while asking me to marry her. This was a huge compliment because Toni had a well-known policy of dating any black man who even looked at her. She drove an aging Volkswagen bug and lived deep in Liberty City, the poorest black section in Miami. The one time I went to visit her, I could not help but notice that the presence of a 350-pound white woman wearing Indian print muumuus created some hostility among her single black women neighbors. They loudly accused her of bringing nothing but trouble to an already troubled neighborhood and trying to steal their men. Back then a black man having sex with a white woman was, if not punishable by law, certainly considered grounds for an arrest and a beating by the Miami cops.

Toni's talk of marriage abruptly ended with the arrival of Florence, a clear and an auditor from England. I think Florence was sent over by headquarters to get the Miami Org in shape. Possibly my letters to Ron had set off alarm bells at Scientology HQ. Obviously my father wasn't the only one who felt the place was less than top-notch.

A petite woman with a Mia Farrow haircut, Florence emulated the Scientology fashion code of white turtleneck, blue blazer, and beige Sansabelt trousers for men and women. She spent her days barking orders and screaming at me. Her favorite refrain was, "Philip, pull yourself up by your bootstraps and get back to work." My previously flawless filing was suddenly deemed inferior, I never handed out enough tickets, and my phone manner was less than satisfactory. After about a week of Florence's nonstop abuse, I asked her when I was going to be audited. I was anxious to get on the road to becoming clear.

Florence responded icily, "What are you talking about?"

"I started working here to pay for my auditing. I've been working almost every evening for the last several months, and I thought—"

"I don't know anything about that. For this to happen, I would have had to authorize it, and I didn't, so let's just forget about it."

"Um, I think Toni authorized it."

"*Ton-eee?*" she exclaimed with real disdain. "What business does Toni have making such authorization? I'll have to have words with her. Toni has had only a few hours of auditing. She has a long way to go before she even thinks of going clear. This is ridiculous. Now get back to work." With that, Florence walked away to attend to more important business. I was more concerned about having gotten Toni in trouble than not getting my auditing. As instructed, I pulled myself up by my bootstraps and returned to work.

Eventually I was able to convince Florence that it was in the best interest of the Org that I be audited. In this way I could describe the process to others and encourage them to sign up for this enlightening experience. Once she understood the potential business opportunity I presented her, she consented. Finally I was taken to the holy of holies, the tiny room at the top of the stairs, for my session. There, sitting atop one of those folding bridge tables, was the fabled e-meter, just waiting to free me from the tyranny of my reactive mind loaded with "engrams," or painful memories. Sitting across from me was a very tall and extremely thin man who displayed a permanent smile and whose eyes were wide open, as if his sight had just been miraculously restored. The session consisted of the thin man asking me a few seemingly innocuous questions, consulting the e-meter after each answer, and writing something down. It was all over in about fifteen minutes and seemed to be a teaser introductory session to get me hooked on auditing. At least I had gotten a chance to hold the tin cans just like the clears, and it was a lot less painful than getting shocked.

Several months later I asked Florence when my next auditing session was. She looked at me with extreme condescension and said, "When you can pay for it." With that, she turned on her heels and walked away from me.

I was now fully prepared to buy my way into salvation. There was no doubt in my mind that Scientology would not only release me from the restraints of my confusing life but confer on me supernatural powers that rivaled my father's. The first auditing package would run around $1,500, an unimaginable sum in those days. I'm sure Toni lived on much less for an entire year. I suggested to Toni that we create a savings plan at work where I would donate $50 a week from my savings while also working to pay for my auditing. This proposal was immediately accepted, and I happily went about contributing to my auditing fund and cleaning the floors. The truth was that no one was tracking my working hours, and I was going to pay, in full, for my auditing.

When I had contributed over $500, I thought this was sufficient to start the pay-as-you-go auditing process. I mentioned this to Florence, who pretended not to hear a word I said and simply walked away. Another month went by, and I again requested to begin my auditing. No response.

Maya had begun to wonder when I was going to have my auditing. She was eager to hear about this latest adventure in my search to become enlightened. "They have a lot of money of yours—they should start auditing you or give you your money back. I don't like these people." Maya especially didn't like Scientology, since she never saw me anymore.

I couldn't sleep that entire week, worrying how I would get my auditing. It seemed hopeless. Maya was right; something was wrong. I wasn't getting anywhere near becoming a clear, much less my lower-grade auditing. On the next Saturday morning when I reported for duty, I told Toni I wanted my money back. Without looking at me, she said, "I wouldn't do that. Just go home and forget it."

"But I never got my auditing, and that's a lot of money, and nothing is happening."

"I don't think this is a good idea. Just forget it; go do something else. I wouldn't ask for your money back if I were you."

"Why not?"

"It can get serious."

"What do you mean, 'serious'?"

"Go away!" With that, Toni picked up the phone and began to dial. I noticed that she was dialing the recorded time-weather report—371-1111. She pretended to talk into the phone at the recorded message. "Hello, Martin, *hiiiiiii,* it's Toni down at the Org. Yes, that's why I'm calling . . ." I continued to stand there until she shot me a mean look that let me know she was going to hit me if I didn't get out of there.

I left work without saying anything to anyone. When I got home, I called Maya and told her what happened. "I have a really bad feeling. When I told Toni I wanted my money back, she got all weird and told me that something bad would happen. I don't know what to do. I've sort of heard stories about people in Scientology suddenly disappearing. Now I'm kinda scared."

Maya always looked out for my better interest. "I think you need to get out of there. For whatever reason, they don't want to audit you. Maybe you should ask your father what to do."

"No, I have to deal with this on my own. He warned me against going there in the first place. So what should I do? I don't think they're going to give me my money back."

"It's a lot of money, and they didn't give you anything for it."

"Yeah, but I'm scared."

"You know, you should ask that guy Jerry on the football team to go with you. He's crazy enough to punch someone in the face if they give him any lip. He gets into fights all the time. Tell him you'll give him twenty dollars if he gets your money back."

"Do you think he'll do it?"

"Jerry will do a lot of things for twenty dollars, and this looks easy. Don't forget, he's really big and completely nuts."

"Okay."

On Wednesday afternoon, Jerry, who weighed close to two

hundred pounds, squeezed into my little Fiat and came with me to the Org. When we walked in, Toni looked away from me. I asked to speak to Florence.

A few minutes later, Florence appeared and in a condescending tone asked, "Where have you been? We need the PC reports filed. Now."

"Florence, I never got my auditing, and I want my money back."

"What money? You never paid for your auditing."

"Yes I did. I paid five hundred fifty dollars so far, plus all the hours I worked, and I never got any real auditing after that introductory session. So I want my money back."

"I think you should get back to work. Immediately!"

"Yeah, but I want my money back."

"We'll talk about that later." Florence turned to walk away.

Jerry spoke up. " 'Scuse me." Florence kept walking and headed toward the stairs to go up to the auditing room. " 'Scuse me!" Jerry ran and stood in front of her, blocking her way. The clock was on, and he began to earn his fee. In his best threatening tone, he said, "My friend came here to get his money back. Give it to him, and we'll go."

"I don't know what you're talking about. We don't have any of his money."

Florence had a point. I contributed to my weekly auditing layaway plan in cash, and to my knowledge, no record was ever kept.

She continued coolly, "Besides, Philip isn't ready for auditing yet. As a PC"—preclear—"he still has a lot of class work to complete. He'll be audited when I say he'll be audited, and that will be quite a long time from now."

Jerry looked at me, slightly confused. I could tell he had no idea what Florence was talking about. He temporarily lost his focus until he asked, "Hey Phil, how much money do they owe you?"

"Five hundred fifty dollars."

Jerry repeated the number to Florence. "Five hundred fifty for my friend here, and we go home. Otherwise, it's not me you're messing with but my dad, who is a big litigator for the city."

Florence was not impressed. "Excuse me. I have work to do." She pushed Jerry aside and went upstairs.

Jerry looked at me as if to ask, "Now what?"

I figured the party was over and turned to leave. Toni sat at her desk, looking down at some flower-power doodle that she pretended to be engrossed in.

The next thing I heard was yelling. I turned around and could not see Jerry but heard his voice from upstairs. The staffers looked startled. But no one moved. I ran up the stairs and saw Jerry banging his fist on the wall next to Florence's head. "Gimme the money now!"

Florence screamed back, *"No!"* When she saw me coming up the stairs, she started yelling at me, "You will be excommunicated for this and will never be able to set foot in any Org in the world! We will have to rout you out!"

Jerry, who went to some sort of after-school Christian football meetings, put his face in front of Florence and screamed, "This ain't no fuckin' church, lady! You're full of shit! Only the pope can excommunicate, not you! Now give me that goddamn money!" He picked up a heavy metal stapler off the desk and was about to whack Florence on the head. It was immediately clear to everyone that if Jerry let loose the stapler, Florence would not be auditing anyone again, ever.

"Okay, okay. Toni, come up here immediately!" Florence was bent over and panting. Her eyes were wildly searching for a way out of the room.

I heard the stairs groan as Toni pulled herself up them.

"So cut the shit, let's go, where's the money?" Jerry was still "on purpose," as they say in Scientologyspeak.

"It's coming."

I went downstairs. As I walked by Toni, she said without looking up, "You're fucked. Really fucked. This goes all the way to Special Command."

I heard Jerry upstairs losing his patience. "The money *now,* bitch, or I let loose. You and this place won't be standing by the time I'm done."

Those were the magic words.

Florence came down the stairs, went into the back, and returned with five one-hundred-dollar bills.

I let Jerry take the money. He counted it and said, "I think we need another fifty."

Florence went into her purse and handed him two twenties and ten ones. She was silent. As we started to leave, she regained her composure and said, "Philip, this will be communicated directly to Ron. I know he was interested in you. He will be disappointed. We will be forced to do an ethics review."

I surprised myself by responding, "Don't bother, I'll write Ron myself. He'll be happy to hear from me about how badly you run the Org."

On the way to the car, Jerry was hootin' and hollerin' like he had just won a major game. Jerry handed me the money. I gave him one of the hundred-dollar bills. "What's this for? My fee is twenty dollars."

"You earned it." I was sad. My dream of a lifelong affiliation with Scientology had ended badly. I had really wanted to find a home at the Org, become enlightened in a scientific way, and have a unique understanding of a new kind of truth, just as my father had discovered new kinds of powers. I felt anxious and in a bit of a free fall.

When I got home, I called Maya.

"I know I'm not supposed to laugh," she said, "but it's very funny. I wish I had been there. I knew Jerry could do it. What are you going to do with the money?"

"I was thinking that you and I should go to Europe for our summer vacation. You know, backpack, sleep on the beach, youth hostels. Just for a month or two. Let's get out of here. I have enough money. We can go on one of those European planes; it's only a couple hundred dollars. Let's go to Greece and Paris. This is a better way to spend the money than on auditing."

"When?"

"As soon as we can get tickets. I'll call tomorrow."

"Okay, I'll talk to my mom and dad."

Maya's parents were dead set against the idea. Her father was convinced that she'd be raped by village peasants while I was roasting on an open-air spit. My mother thought I was little young to be on my own in Europe but knew better than to say no, since it wouldn't do any good. Deep down inside she loved the idea of me running off to Europe to become a sophisticated world traveler. Maya and I quickly planned our dream itinerary: Paris, Italy, Spain, and Greece. The day after school let out for the summer, we were at the airport with backpacks and sleeping bags, boarding some hippie airbus that originated out of Iceland.

Our first stop was to be Paris, but at the last minute, and for no particular reason, we changed our minds and jumped a train to Spain. Maya spoke the language, and it seemed as good a place as any to start our adventure. In Madrid we found a small pension and took a wonderful turn-of-the-century room. Tall ceilings, faded green velvet curtains almost in shreds, blue and white tile work in the bathroom. The neighbors' wash was hanging in the courtyard, and the heavy smell of olive oil infused the air. Neither of us had seen anything like it, and we were overcome by the romance of the place. The owner had the maid bring us a morning coffee.

As I started to unpack, I suddenly felt as if all the blood had completely drained from my body, leaving nothing but a hollow core. This was immediately followed by a pervasive tingling, crawling sensation all over my skin. I started sweating and shivering, and collapsed onto the bed. After about twenty minutes of being completely immobile, I became delirious with fever. Maya later told me that I began to speak some nonsense language and was thrashing violently about in bed. Panicked, she ran to get the lady of the house, who took one look at me, cried, *"Dios mio!"* and ran off in search of the local doctor.

Maya went downstairs and asked the woman in the kitchen to prepare some manzanilla tea for me, which was her mother's favorite herbal cure-all. When the housekeeper brought the tea, I was completely frozen in a fetal position and shaking violently. I was unable to even raise my head or open my mouth to drink the tea.

When the owner of the house finally returned with the doctor, I was lost in a haze of fever, chills, aches, and sweat. He looked me over quickly and told Maya there was nothing he could do until the next morning, when he would be able to get someone to draw my blood. He thought it might be malaria or typhoid, and told Maya, "Put cold compresses on his head—and pray." He crossed himself as he left the room. Maya was terrified that if I died, she wouldn't know what to do with the body or what to say to my parents. After all, we were only seventeen and very far away from home for the first time.

For the next half hour, Maya washed me down with cold towels, when suddenly my fever completely broke. I opened my eyes and asked calmly, "Why am I all wet?"

Maya started to cry. "Oh my God, I thought you were going to die! I never saw anybody so sick. I just didn't know what to do. I can't believe the fever is gone. It just suddenly vanished. Thank God you're okay."

The next morning, with this incident behind us, we resumed our travels. After our first stop in Madrid, we completely abandoned our original itinerary and traveled to cities and countries based on spontaneous decisions. Never before had we felt so free. We slept on the beaches in Greece, ate grilled octopus, and visited the great works of Italian art that I had seen only in books as a kid. Late-night Paris cafés and long train rides through the Spanish countryside filled with miles of sunflowers.

Two months later, when I returned home, I called my father from the airport to let him know I had returned. "Hi, Pop, I just got back. We had a great time."

"I'm so relieved you're home safely. I'm really sorry about what happened in Spain. I just couldn't get to you quickly enough."

"Huh? What are you talking about? What happened in Spain?"

"Don't you remember? You were really sick with a serious infection."

I must have blocked the incident, because I had no idea what he was talking about. "Pop, I honestly don't remember anything like that. Anyway, I've got to tell you about Florence. You would love Florence, especially the churches. The architecture is amazing; to think that they created these buildings so long ago. You know, now that you mention it, I do remember something happening in Spain. Maya told me that I had a fever or something. And then it was gone. So what were you saying about how you couldn't get to me?"

"I had been tracking you based on the itinerary that you left for me. You were supposed to be in Paris, but when I looked, you weren't there. My connection with you had been severed. At the time, I felt that everything was okay and that I would look for you in the morning. So I went to bed. In the middle of the night, I heard an alarm clock ringing. You know that I don't have an alarm clock, so I knew that it was spirit waking me for a reason. That's when I realized that something was wrong with you, but I wasn't sure where you were. So I got out a map, and with my pendulum, I started to look for you. I kept checking Paris, but the pendulum indicated that you weren't there. I looked in England and Italy and still couldn't find you. Spain was the last place I looked because that was going to be the end of your trip. But I found you in Madrid. I can't remember the street name, but I have it written down somewhere. Once I found you, I instantly began checking out your vital signs."

"Sounds like you were up all night looking for me."

"No, not really. I think it took about twelve to fifteen minutes to locate you once I started the search. My real concern was that your vibrations had dropped dramatically, and I felt that you were in danger of dying."

"This is when I had the fever?"

"Yes, so I did a quick scan on you and started raising your vibrations and tried to stabilize you. Once you were stabilized, I could track down the problem and get your systems working. There were a lot of other problems going on. If they hadn't woken me up, I don't know if you'd still be alive."

"Oh, thanks," I said with some irritation. I was not aware that I had been at death's door. I thought to myself, "So what if I had a fever? I would have gotten over it anyway. Just let me have my fever without always watching over me. I'm old enough to take care of myself." At that point, I would have gladly traded a week of fevers to have a father who didn't know where I was and wasn't in the room with me and my girlfriend while we were in Spain—or any other country, for that matter. If he was in Spain with me, did that mean he was with me in Paris, Rome, and Athens? Yes, it did.

"Next time I'll know that I should check on your whereabouts several times a day and not rely on your itinerary."

Despite my annoyance with my father's psychic snooping, I was impressed with his ability to locate and heal me while I was somewhere in Europe. For the first time, I began to think that just maybe I should actually start paying attention to this weirdo father of mine.

twelve

•

Into the Etheric

It was a brilliant Saturday morning in December. Clear, cloudless skies, seventy degrees, no humidity, and the birds were busy singing the weather report to the world. I was expecting a call from my friend Mark. Since I was no longer spending all my time at the Org, I started to hang out on Saturdays with a few of the more eccentric kids from school. Maya hated surfing, so Mark and I had planned to go with Cindy and Davida. He was waiting for his father to come home so that he could use the car. Mark's family had recently moved down from New York so that his father, a painter, could teach art at the University of Miami. On his first day in school, Mark looked a bit like Chad Stuart, the lead singer in the British folk-pop group Chad and Jeremy, with his wavy chestnut hair, square tortoiseshell glasses, and denim work shirt. He was sitting alone in the cafeteria emanating Bob Dylan cool, dressed in clothes from the Army-Navy store. We took one look at each other and immediately bonded. It was clear that we were both young members of the avant-garde.

Davida and I both loved the singer Laura Nyro and spent hours discussing who in our pop-cultural pantheon was shooting heroin. With her long hippie hair and gauzy blouses with subtle embroidery, Davida had a kind of haunted angelic quality that appeared in her endless obsessive self-portraits that she drew in her black leather-bound sketchbooks with her scratchy Rapidograph pen. Davida thought and acted like a full-fledged drug addict without actually being one. Cindy, on the other hand, was just a sweet, goofy girl who loved to take acid and listen to the same Grateful Dead song over and over and over and over again.

Unlike California or Hawaii, Florida surf never amounted to much. The water was too tranquil, except during a hurricane, when surfers risked their lives to catch good waves. The best we could man-age was to paddle out and slowly ride a sleepy wave in to shore. While neither Mark nor the girls were paragons of normalcy (how could they be if they were hanging out with me?), their company helped me for-get that I was the son of *My Favorite Martian*.

Several months earlier, I had found a little surf shop in Miami Beach, down on Ocean and Second. It was a storefront next to a bagel shop, where we would rent boards along with a cake of wax for five dollars and eat fresh, warm bagels. We were the surf shop's only customers that day if not the entire weekend. At the time, this part of Miami Beach was exceedingly uncool. The area was largely shuttered and abandoned except for the kosher butcher and bakery on Washington Avenue. It was the large population of elderly Jews that encouraged people to disparage the area as "God's waiting room." Davida and Cindy would pack a picnic lunch, which we would eat in the shadows of the abandoned, rusting dog track that was once part of Miami Beach's high-roller circuit. Eventually the track would be torn down and become the epicenter of the glamorous high-rise Miami Beach known as South of Fifth.

That morning I had been dressed and ready to go since eight-thirty, but by ten o'clock Mark still hadn't called. He told me under no circumstances to call his house, because his sister was sick, and he didn't want me waking her. I told him that I was going to spend the morning hanging out with my father and to call me over at his house. Waiting for Mark's call, I sat on the back porch, where I could hear the phone ring, and leafed through my latest copy of *Eye,* a short-lived, glossy counterculture magazine that featured fashion spreads of long-haired kids in bell-bottoms and multihued striped shirts. Every month the magazine ran interviews with underground heroes such as Rudi Gernreich, Timothy Leary, Twiggy, Yoko Ono, Andy Warhol, and Peter Max. *Eye* was my window onto another world that seemed even more exotic than the supernatural one at home.

Finally the phone rang. I jumped up and ran to the kitchen to get it before my father did. I knew it was Mark calling. "Hello?" There was a slight hiss and crackle on the other end. It sounded like long distance.

"Hello. This is Mrs. Stanley Moore. May I speak with Mr. Lew Smith?"

"Just a minute, please." I put my hand over the mouthpiece and yelled out, "Pop, it's for you!" so he could pick up the phone on the other line. "Stupid woman," I thought to myself. "Why did she have to call? Now my father will be on the phone forever, and Mark will never be able to reach me." This was decades before call-waiting. Mark would probably call, get a busy signal, pick up the girls, and go surfing without me. Just my luck. I was furious. Rather than hang up the phone, I decided to listen in, so I would know when he was finished with his conversation.

"Hello?" my father answered.

"Mr. Smith, my name is Nancy Moore. I'm calling from California. I was given your name and number by a woman named Linda Davis."

When she announced herself, I heard the *click* of my father turning on the tape recorder. This meant it was going to be a long call. He had started taping all of his conversations as records of his healing activity. "Oh yes, how is Linda?"

Linda Davis was a well-known writer who specialized in popular books on nutrition, an esoteric subject at the time that interested only little old ladies from Pasadena. Linda lived in L.A. and had been friends with my father for some time. Over the past several months, despite all her nutritional knowledge, she had found herself increasingly ill with some mysterious disease that no doctor could diagnose or treat. She began to bleed spontaneously not only from her nose, but also her eyes and at times from the palms of her hands. She had seen oncologists, cardiologists, internists, and endocrinologists, with no success. Finally she called my father. In the space of a few minutes, Pop diagnosed her illness as a case of possession.

It seems that Linda had a lady friend who had recently moved in with her. This woman, according to the information my father received from his spirit guides, was generating a lot of negative energy. From the minute the bad-vibe lady arrived, she had begun to take over Linda's life: controlling her finances, her social calendar, and her professional life. Linda was exhausted and frightened. In a few minutes over the phone, Pop removed the possessing entity using a series of antipossession prayers along with his pendulum. He restored Linda's vibrations and her equilibrium. When he told Linda that she had to get this woman out of the house immediately, Linda responded that she was afraid and didn't know how. My father said, "Well, then I will." With a few more rounds of the pendulum, he told Linda to leave the house for the day. When she returned in the evening, the woman would be gone. She did, and she was. Linda's bleeding stopped immediately.

"She's quite well," reported Mrs. Moore. "Her health has improved dramatically. She had such a strange condition; I had never seen anything like it. However, I'm afraid that my mother isn't doing too well, which is the reason I'm calling. It seems that she has a blood clot on her brain. She's in the hospital. The doctors do not want to operate because she has a heart condition and she's diabetic. They're afraid that if they operate, she'll end up a vegetable because of her weak heart. There's nothing they can do. So Linda suggested I call you and that you could help my mother."

"How old is she?"

"Eighty-three."

"Well, let's see what we can do."

I thought to myself, "Why couldn't her mother just have a cold or a bad back? That wouldn't take so long. But a blood clot on the brain—this will take at least an hour."

"Mrs. Moore, I'm going to ask you to help me here. I need to use you as an intercessory to send healing energy to your mother."

"You mean we don't need to fly out and see you?"

My father laughed. "No. I can do it all over the phone. It doesn't matter where in the world your mother is. I can still read every organ in her body and send her whatever medication she needs, all through thought. There is no time or distance limitation on how I work. We are all just energy. The idea of doctors and medicine is antithetical to the true nature of the body, which is pure spirit manifested in a physical form."

"Well, okay," Mrs. Moore responded somewhat weakly. Her patrician voice led me to believe that she was not a fan of anything alternative, and I could tell by her tone that she was a little sorry she had made this call. I'm sure that she, like so many others, had called my father because everything else had failed, and he was her last resort. "Now, what is it that I have to do to help you?" she asked.

"Not much. Just think of your mother. Keep a picture of her in your mind. See her in perfect health, surrounded by a white light. Feel as much love for her as you can."

"Well, we've never been that close and—"

"I know that. That's why I want you to really feel that love for her. She needs to feel it, and so do you."

"Okay. I'll do the best I can."

"Do you want your mother to be healed?"

"Of course I do!"

"Then you'll have to do better than that. I want you to really love her. It will make my job a lot easier."

"Okay."

My father cradled the phone on his shoulder as he used two hands to begin dowsing the mother's health status. "Level of acceptance?"

"Excuse me?"

"I'm just checking your mother's level of acceptance—her willingness to be healed." My father was now holding his pendulum over one of his charts as he scanned the mother's various energy bodies and determined their vibrational status. "I have now been given permission to heal her. Fortunately, she is very open to this."

"How do you know that?"

"I'm scanning your mother's emotional and soul characteristics as we speak. I need to find out whether the cause of her clot is physical, emotional, or karmic. That will tell me where to work. But first I need to raise your vibrations so I can send the energy through you. Visualize her."

"I see my mother in my mind now."

"Good. Okay, I've raised your vibrations to the cosmic level. Here we go . . . First I'll check out her heart. I see I need to normalize her heartbeat. Good. Now, I'm sending through you a particular healing energy. What did you just feel?"

"I felt something in my head, as if my brain were made of feathers. It feels so light."

"I just sent you something that dissolves blood clots. It went to the head right away to dissolve that clot in her brain."

"Well, that's what I felt. Something in my head just opened up."

"Now let's work on the diabetes. Wait just a minute. Okay. I've stabilized her blood sugar. I don't think she'll need her insulin shots anymore. That will go a long way toward her feeling better and having more energy. Let me do one more thing. I've just developed a new medicine made from the thought-form of venom."

"You mean like venom from snakes?"

"Yes. I call it Pro-Ven, and it repairs the immune system. It's very dangerous to work with. Doctors are now using cobra venom in a new medicine, but it has a lot of side effects. I've distilled the healing essence of the venom and placed it into a thought-form."

"Ohhhh . . ."

"Just a minute, I need to do something else. Good. Hold on. I just selected four bottles of cell salts that I put on my sender board that will direct the specific healing energy that your mother needs. I'm also sending her Pro-Ven through you. What did you feel?"

"I felt something in my stomach, something like a change in my stomach. Strange. I can't quite explain it."

"Okay. I also want to send her some color energy that will help repair the functioning of her brain." I heard my father let out a deep exhalation. "By the way, I just checked your mother, and I see no signs of cancer, so we don't have to worry about that. She's clear. Okay, now I'm going to send more cell salts to her so the body can rejuvenate. I'm sending her enough surplus cells so the body can pick and choose what it needs. I think we've covered everything. She looks to be in good shape. Now, when are you going to speak to your mother again?"

"Probably sometime tonight."

"Well, then, give me a call tomorrow and let me know what happened. I'm sure you're going to have a good report."

"Thank you so much for your time. I can't believe what has just happened. I will definitely call you tomorrow. What do I owe you?"

My father laughed. "Nothing. I don't accept payment for doing God's work."

"This is incredible. Thank you so much. I really appreciate it. Good-bye."

"Don't forget to call me; I want to hear how she's doing. Good-bye."

I was relieved that she had finally hung up. The call didn't take as long as I thought it would. Pop wrapped it up in less than fifteen minutes. It was now almost ten-thirty, and I hadn't heard from Mark.

Either he tried to reach me and couldn't get through, or his father didn't come home from work. Now it was getting too late to get over to the beach.

My father called from his study, "Philip, would you come in here for a minute?" Probably I was going to get stuck with some chore. I found him still at his desk with all his healing charts and diagrams laid out. They looked like celestial navigation charts for travel to distant planets.

Pop worked at a long, slightly trapezoidal white desk that was suspended from the wall. On the desk were cardboard boxes that once held other products and had been cut down to size in order to hold small glass vials containing various homeopathic medicines, Bach Flower Remedies, dried leaves, and flowers, as well as mixtures of exotic oils that had been compounded based on recipes given to him by his spirit guides. There were no labels on any of these bottles. Instead, on the top of each bottle was a number and a letter code indicating what each remedy was used for. This way he could simply grab a bottle of dried periwinkle leaves or Allium cepa without having to look at the label. He never physically dispensed this medicine. Either the patient would hold the bottle in his left hand to absorb the energy of the remedy, or, for absent healings anywhere in the world, my father would place the bottle of medicine on what he called his "sender board," which propelled the healing energy to the patient. This sender board looked like a very small turbine engine built out of wood with a large copper coil in the middle, a flat area of copper screen mesh, and a large tubular magnet.

Pop's study was always an oasis of tangible serenity. Whenever I stood there by myself, I could always sense a subtle high-frequency electricity that permeated the room. It felt as if all the whizzing atoms that invisibly surround us slowed down to create this thickened high-energy atmosphere. You could almost feel these particles knocking into you as you moved around the room. If you listened carefully, you could hear a slight background hum that sounded like zzzzzzzzzzzzzzz. I had no idea where that sound came from, but to me it sounded like a swarm of slowly hovering bees. Or possibly it was the sound that flying saucers made as they were waiting to lift off for extragalaxy travel.

Over his desk were shelves containing many of the reference books you might find in a doctor's office, such as the *PDR, Merck Manual,* and numerous anatomy books. Using his pendulum, Pop would consult these books in order to describe in medical terms to a patient the exact nature of his or her condition. Other times he would simply open a book at random, and waiting there was the correct description and treatment protocol for the disease in question.

He also used his pendulum to dowse the anatomy books in order to determine the exact location of the disease. He would then jot down this information for his patients to give to their doctors who had been unable to accurately diagnose their disease. Watching over all of this activity were pictures of his patron saints Arthur Ford and Chander Sen, along with a small collection of various types of crucifixes. Ford's and Chander Sen's pictures gave you the sensation of one of those haunted houses in the movies where the eyes of people in the paintings follow you around the room.

In addition to the pendulum, his other main diagnostic tool was a rectangular card that he called his "finder chart." On the front was a series of concentric circles that contained numbers and words and looked a bit like a diagram for a physics experiment. To the side of the circles were various lists of diseases, their possible causes and remedies.

Pop would hold his pendulum over this chart to determine whether an illness was caused by a virus, bacteria, poison, allergy, hormonal imbalance, or psychiatric condition. Let's say the disease originated as a psychological problem. Next, he would investigate if there was subconscious resentment in either this life or a past life, and who caused it. He would describe to the patient in exacting detail what caused the illness, when it happened, and why it happened. More often than not he would also provide the exact date and time of the incident that set off the emotional trauma that eventually manifested as disease.

The chart also indicated the various treatments, such as cell salts, Bach Flower Remedies, or other healing methods.

The most intriguing aspect of this finder chart was that it allowed my father to also diagnose the invisible energy bodies that he claimed surrounded our main physical body. Each of these energy bodies functions at a unique vibration and serves a specific purpose in maintaining our physical body. On his chart each of these energy bodies—etheric, astral, mental, and emotional—is represented by a separate concentric ring.

As his healing methods became more exacting, he discovered that disease does not always originate in the physical body. Many times it can begin in any one of the other bodies and eventually materialize in our physical body. For example, if there is a problem in our emotional or mental body due to discord with a family member, it might ultimately appear in our physical body as a heart attack or brain tumor. According to my father, one day our cells don't suddenly start mutating all by themselves for no reason. The disease originates from disharmony in one of our energy bodies and then eventually becomes a physical problem.

I often heard Pop tell me that "someone can appear perfectly healthy and yet when I check the etheric body, I find that he is riddled with cancer. While this cancer may not have manifested in the physical body, it eventually will. It is much easier for me to remove cancer from the etheric body than to wait until it enters the physical. This is the beauty of being able to diagnose the full spectrum of our various bodies—you can catch a disease before it starts to do lethal damage.

"Unfortunately, doctors don't know that we have multiple, interconnected bodies that affect our health. At this point, their medical knowledge is not sufficiently advanced to acknowledge the existence of these other bodies. However, they will one day understand this concept of the interconnectedness of all our different bodies. This is one reason that many people who are treated by doctors never seem to get better. They are treating the symptoms of an illness that may have originated outside of the physical body, in either the etheric or astral. As a result, they never eliminate the real cause of the illness." My father believed that you could never heal any illness until you discovered its actual cause and then eradicated it.

Just the week before, my father had told me an amazing story about how these various energy bodies of ours actually function. "One of the main problems with Western medicine is that doctors only look at a symptom and then treat that specific symptom. A person will never get better this way. They may temporarily experience a relief of symptoms, but the underlying problem is still there and will eventually manifest itself in another way in another part of the body at another time. If they don't find the true cause of the illness, they will never cure the problem.

"Last week a lady called and told me she was in the hospital with her nephew, who was a young, very active, athletic kid. Without any explanation, he had suddenly become extremely weak and could hardly get out of bed," he said. "After several days of tests, the doctors discovered that his liver was failing. They didn't know why, just that it was not working. Even though he was only eighteen years old, the doctors didn't have much hope for his survival. So she asked me what I could do for him. I told her I would check him out and give him a healing. I scanned him, did a complete workup, raised his vibrations, repaired his liver, and adjusted his thyroid, which was also very weak. I gave him what I thought was a full treatment and told her that he would heal rapidly.

"A couple days later, the woman called and said that his test results were not improving, and the doctors felt that her nephew would be dead in a few days. What was strange was that even though the test results showed his liver was in failure, the kid was actually feeling much better. He was walking a bit and seemed to have more energy. No one could explain what was going on. She wanted to bring him over to meet me and asked the doctors if she could take her nephew home for a few hours. They had no objection, as there was nothing they could do to save the boy. He came over to the house and told me that he was feeling almost normal. When he had first gone to the hospital, he was so tired he couldn't even walk across the room. While he was in the hospital, his doctor told him to eat as much sugar and drink as much Coke as he could."

I interrupted his story and said, "But Pop, that doesn't make any sense. If your body is exhausted, sugar only provides a quick, temporary false sense of energy. In the long run, you actually become more depleted." I was very current with all the dangers of white sugar, as my father had just given me several books on the topic. This was long before "sugar free" became a part of the national vocabulary. At the time, the only artificial sweetener was saccharin. Products using saccharin always bore a label warning about potential bladder cancer. I couldn't understand why someone would risk such a horrific disease just for a little short-term sweetness. There was never any sugar in the house, and I had trained myself to not have a sweet tooth for anything other than fresh fruit.

"You're absolutely right. I couldn't figure out what the doctor was thinking. I asked the kid why the doctor had suggested this, and he said that he didn't know. I told him to immediately cut out all that sugar, which was putting additional stress on his liver. I gave him a diet to help rebuild the liver through nutrients, along with another healing. During the healing I found that his spleen was not functioning very well because it was doing a lot of the work of the liver. Due to his extraordinary sugar intake, his adrenal glands were exhausted. I raised the vibrations of all his organs and bodily functions back up to normal. Within a few minutes of the healing, he looked and felt better. Before he left I told him to call me in a week and let me know how he was feeling. Later that evening I called a doctor friend of mine and asked him why the kid was told to eat sugar. He said that because the liver was not working, the sugar would be converted into fat, which the body needs to function."

"Why does the liver need fat from sugar? Shouldn't the fat come from other sources, such as plants, meat, or dairy?" I asked. I knew my father was pleased with my growing knowledge of nutrition. I had started reading books by Adelle Davis and was learning basic biochemistry as a result.

"Of course. We'd all be better off if doctors were taught the basics of nutrition. So listen to this: a week later the woman called back to let me know that her nephew was feeling better than he had in months. After the healing I gave him, he didn't want to stay in the hospital anymore and convinced the doctors just to let him go home. If he was going to die, he wanted to die at home. After a couple of weeks, his doctor called the woman to find out if the kid had died. The mother told the doctor that her nephew was feeling great and getting ready to go back to school. The doctor was shocked and said that the kid should come back for more tests. He told the woman that it was impossible for the kid to be functioning and said that he should have already been dead. So when they tested his liver, they found that it was still not working."

"Wait, his liver's not working and he's running around? How could that be?" I asked.

"That was exactly the same question that the doctors were asking. They were puzzled because they couldn't understand how he was still alive with a malfunctioning liver. According to their tests, the boy should not be alive. After all, if your liver isn't working, what is going to remove the toxins from the body? Otherwise your body will be overwhelmed by poisons. I told the woman I would check him out again.

"When I did a scan on the kid, I kept coming up with a reading that his liver was fully functioning at one hundred percent of its potential. Yet all the tests the doctors had performed indicated that his liver was not functioning. This didn't make any sense, and I just couldn't understand what was going on. I don't usually make mistakes like this, so I rechecked my work and saw that I had done everything correctly. Something didn't quite add up. Finally I realized what was going on. I hadn't asked the question in exactly the right fashion. I had been asking about the functioning of the liver. I had been too general. Instead I now asked, 'At what percentage is the *physical* liver operating?' I got a five percent reading. So his liver was failing, just as the doctors' tests had indicated. Next I asked, 'At what percentage is the *etheric* liver functioning?' That's when I got one hundred percent. The pendulum had given me a reading on his liver, but I hadn't specified *which* liver. Both the pendulum and the spirits require any question you ask to be extremely specific; otherwise you'll receive incorrect information.

"What happened in this case was that when the physical liver began to fail, the etheric liver took over and kept the boy alive. But since the doctors do not know that an etheric body exists, they measure only the physical liver. They would never understand how to properly diagnose the problem or how the boy could remain alive with so little of his liver functioning. The body does not want to die; it wants to maintain itself, so in a case like this, the etheric body takes over the function of the physical body. It's like an emergency backup system."

"So, if ever I get sick, and they can't figure out what's wrong with me, I should tell the doctor to look at my etheric body?"

My father broke out laughing. "Don't waste your time. They'll think you're crazy and lock you up. Eventually today's medicine will be seen as primitive and quite limited. It's going to be another two hundred years before medicine learns how to recognize all the different energy bodies we have. That's when we'll really be able to cure disease, when medicine focuses on realigning energies rather than pounding the body with drugs or sawing the body open and yanking out a precious organ. We are really a collection of magnificent metaphysical energies. To simply treat a sick body as if it is a broken car is so limited. Please don't worry about getting sick; you'll never be in a position where you'll be mysteriously ill. I won't let it happen to you."

Now that I stood in his study, I still wasn't sure why my father had called me in to see him. All his charts spread out on his desk had just been used in the healing, along with his pendulum and the ruler he used to diagnose and calculate dosages of remedies. My father looked up at me and asked, "So what did you think of that lady on the phone?"

I was a little embarrassed that he knew I had been listening to the phone call. I knew he wanted me to say how incredible it was that in a matter of a few minutes, he'd dissolved a clot in the brain of some woman he had never met and who was in a hospital in California.

"Um, I thought it was okay. I guess it was good that you helped that woman. So do you think she'll be okay?"

"Spirit tells me that she will be released from the hospital tomorrow morning. The clot on the brain will begin to shrink. After a couple of days, the doctors won't find anything wrong. She'll live for at least another year."

"How do you know that? If you healed her, why can't she live longer?"

"I always have to work within the laws of karma. This is her allotted time. For example, if someone is near death but has more work to complete here on earth, then I can generally pull her back from the point of no return. However, if there is a karmic debt to be paid or her work here is finished, then there is nothing I can do. I always have to check before I heal to see if there is a karmic debt involved. In certain cases, I have been able to bring back people who have died. I was able to pull the soul back into body before it had cut the silver astral cord. The important thing is that she and her daughter can now repair their relationship. Once that relationship is finally healed, she has completed her task on the material plane and can then leave her body for the next dimension. I'm sure Mrs. Moore will call me as soon as she gets her mother home. Would you like to be able to do this?"

"Do what?" I knew exactly what he was asking but decided to be a difficult, uninterested teenager.

"Heal people."

"Not really." I was more concerned with getting to the beach than removing a blood clot in someone's brain. Pop motioned me to sit down, but I pretended not to notice and continued to stand, hoping to run out of there as soon as possible.

"Philip, to heal someone, to give them the opportunity to walk again or to take away their cancer, is the most important thing you can do with your life. It is very rewarding, a gift from God. There is no more satisfying way to live than to serve others. Arthur has told me that you're a gifted healer. If you choose not to follow my methods, then you will heal in other ways." This was not exactly what I wanted to hear. It was one thing to struggle with learning to live with a supernatural father; it was quite another to know that I had inherited his psychic DNA. As soon as my father delivered this message from Arthur, I knew that no matter how hard I tried, I would never become a normal guy, at least not in this lifetime.

"Oh, by the way, Mark's father had a small accident, and his car was towed. I don't think you're going to the beach today."

"Thanks for telling me," I said with just a bit of unintentional sarcasm in my voice.

"I just thought I'd let you know. I felt it when Mark was trying to get through while I was on the phone. I'm sure he'll call you later." My father had his own form of psychic call-waiting.

"Yeah. I was really looking forward to going to the beach. Oh, well."

"Maybe we could spend a few minutes working with the pendulum. If you knew how to use it, then you could know ahead of time whether or not you are going to go surfing. Once you master it, you can know anything about anyone, anywhere. The pendulum is the central tool in helping you to fully heal people. It can help you determine what modality to use to heal someone and how effective your healing efforts are."

"Ummm, maybe some other time."

Not taking no for an answer, my father picked up his pendulum and said, "Here, let me show you something." As he held it between his thumb and index finger, it suddenly started to swing in a large clockwise circle. "See that?"

"Yeah."

"That's giving me a yes answer."

"Yeah. So? Yes to what?"

"I asked the pendulum if you were having sex with your girlfriend last night, and it said yes."

"Ooops," I thought to myself, "he got me." I wasn't intrigued so much as annoyed that Pop knew embarrassing details about my personal life. He always made me feel transparent. Mental privacy was a luxury I did not know.

"I only asked that question to get your attention. Spying on people is not the purpose of this tool. You can also use the pendulum to retrieve any information you need from the past or the future. Everything is available to you. In the most simplest of terms, our lives and our universe are composed primarily of energy as well as thought, which is a form of energy. Ultimately, everything comes down to this simple concept.

"Using the pendulum will help you learn to train your mind so that you can direct your thought energy anywhere and anyhow you please. Your mind has unlimited power that transcends time and space. Eventually I can teach you to create thought-forms that can cover the planet—or just protect your house from red ants like I did the other day."

Because our property was thick with lychee, banana, and mango trees, there were always ants everywhere—including my bed and underwear drawer. They came in through the windows and cracks in the walls. Every time you opened a kitchen cabinet, ants were crawling all over the dishes and plates. I would sometimes just lie in bed and watch long traffic lines of ants snaking their way up the wall and out through some microscopic opening. Our whole house seemed to be animated with moving waves of ants. There was no need to buy an ant farm for my amusement and education; I lived in one.

"Have you seen any ants lately?" my father asked.

"You're right, there weren't any ants on my toothbrush this morning. Where'd they go?"

"I got rid of them through thought. I built a thought-form around the house that was like a natural insecticide. I imagined a wall of daisies surrounding the house."

"Daisies?" I knew we were heading into nerve-gas territory all over again. Pop would come up with some wacky idea, and eventually science would prove him right.

"Did you ever hear of a powerful insecticide called pyrethrin?"

"No."

"Well, it's made from certain families of chrysanthemums and daisies. By properly visualizing these flowers, I changed the vibration of the house, and as a result, the ants don't want to come in there anymore. It's as if there is an invisible force field around the house that repels them. The ants are now back in the yard where they belong. In the old days, before I developed the thought-forms, I used to have to talk to the ants. I'd tell them that if they didn't get out of the house in twenty-four hours, I was going to spray. They always got out, but in a month or two, they were back. Now, with my new methods, they're gone for good, and I don't have to spend my time negotiating with the ants.

"But there is only one requirement for using any psychic tools or methods. Your efforts and intention must be for the highest good. If you use these tools for personal gain, for revenge, or for harm, it will come back to you negatively tenfold. You can't get away with anything in the spirit world. There are no shortcuts, no get-rich schemes. Once you become a partner with them, they are always watching. They will take care of you, but you have to uphold your end of the bargain. Remember, always ask, 'Is this for the highest good?' This is a question you should ask about anything you undertake. If you do, you'll never go wrong."

The spirit world sounded a bit like the Mafia to me.

"Because I know that you really don't want to be sitting here, I'll make this quick. I'm just going to give you a small lesson on the pendulum, and you can practice whenever you want. Once you get this under your belt, we'll go on to bigger and better things. There is so much for you to learn that will help you for the rest of your life. First of all, the pendulum has no power of its own. It's not magical or magnetic. The pendulum is only a tool to help you communicate with your high-self, which has all the information you are seeking. When necessary, the high-self will go out into the universe and other dimensions to get the answer. Also, by using the pendulum, you will be able to tap into the akashic records, where everything is recorded."

According to my father, the akashic records functioned as a type of ethereal Library of Congress where every thought or action by any living soul in the history of the world has been recorded and stored. I wasn't sure if this endless invisible database also included reruns of *I Love Lucy* or *Perry Mason,* but it probably did. My father had a way of accessing the akashic records to gather information about his patients in order to produce a more accurate diagnosis.

"The important thing is *how* you ask the question. Just like in life. You have to know exactly what you are asking for. For now, keep it simple with just yes or no questions. Go ahead, ask a question, and the pendulum will respond.

"Before I start any work, I say a quick prayer to raise my vibrations so I'll be able to tune in to the proper frequency. I simply say, 'I raise my vibrations to the divine and healing level.' Now say it."

I felt pretty stupid saying this prayer out loud, so I sort of mumbled, "Okay, I raise my vibrations to the divine and healing level." My attitude was, "there, I said your stupid prayer, what else do you want me to do?"

"Philip, you need to feel this as you say it. It has to be real for you. Your superconscious and subconscious minds will hear and understand these instructions and respond accordingly. If you say this properly, you will feel your vibrations rise to a higher frequency. As soon as you say this prayer, your mind will clear, your eyes will brighten, and you will feel a calm alertness. Now say it again. But this time mean it and feel it."

"I raise my vibrations to the divine and healing level." I said it with a clear, strong voice, probably a bit louder than I should have, but I wanted to make sure the spirits heard me.

"That was good. I can tell you already feel better." I didn't want to admit it, but I felt as if I had suddenly woken up. "The pendulum will indicate a yes response by either moving in a clockwise circle or by making a vertical movement. A no response is counterclockwise or a horizontal movement. Now watch."

My father held his hand perfectly still. His wrist was resting on the edge of his desk. All of a sudden, the pendulum began to move in a smooth clockwise circle. "There. That's your yes answer." He must have then given some mental command because the pendulum suddenly stopped and just hung straight down. A moment later the pendulum began to swing in a counterclockwise direction. "You see? That's a negative answer."

"But what are you doing to make it move?"

"Nothing. I'm simply asking a question, and it responds. Try it."

I picked up the pendulum and held it exactly as my father did. It didn't move. I waited. Nothing. Finally I shook my wrist from side to side, which made the pendulum jump all over the place. I looked up at my father. "I can't do this."

He laughed warmly. "You're still thinking about whether Mark is going to call, and if not, then you want to go back in your room and listen to records. Try this, in order to blank out your thoughts: close your eyes for a second and imagine a piece of black velvet covering your mind. It will quiet everything down. Go ahead."

I shut my eyes and visualized a piece of black velvet draped over my head. My head suddenly seemed heavy and nodded. I felt as if I was about to go to sleep.

"Okay. Open your eyes. There. Your mind is still. Don't *try* to make this work. It won't. Just ask a simple yes or no question."

"All right. Am I going to the movies tonight with Maya?" I looked up at my father for reassurance that it was okay to use such a sacred tool to ask such a mundane question. He looked at me and nodded. I held my hand perfectly still. Too still. I was squeezing my wrist and my fingers tightly. There was no movement from the pendulum.

"Just relax. It will come."

I took a deep breath and released the tension in my hand. The pendulum made a small counterclockwise circle the size of a dime. My father's circles were much bigger, maybe the size of a small lime. I looked up at him. "This says no, right? Well, it can't be. We made a date for tonight. I was going to pick her up at seven, and we're going to see something at the Miracle Theatre."

"Well, I guess you're not going. That's what the pendulum is telling you."

"No, the pendulum is wrong. Or maybe I don't know how to work it."

"The pendulum is never right or wrong. The pendulum doesn't know. It just picks up and relays information. I don't think you're going to the movies tonight. Let me check." Holding the pendulum, my father asked out loud, "Is Philip going to the movies tonight, Saturday, with Maya?" Immediately the pendulum swung in a larger counterclockwise direction. "The answer is still no. Do you want me to find out what happened? Maybe she's sick or her mother needed her."

"No, don't bother. I'll just call her. But we had a date. I'll bet she's going out with Scott instead."

"I'm happy to find out."

"No, I'll handle this myself." I did not really want to know if she was seeing someone else.

"Okay. Why don't you work with the pendulum for now? Just keep asking it questions until you feel comfortable that it is responding. It should feel natural, as if you're talking to someone. I suggest you keep track of your questions and the answers you receive in a small notebook, so we can measure your accuracy. This way you will—oh, wait a minute." At that moment, the phone rang. My father answered. "Hello? Just a minute, please. He's right here." As my father handed me the phone, he covered the mouthpiece and said, "It's Mark."

"Hi. Yeah, my father was on the phone. Huh? Your father was in an accident? What happened?"

My father looked at me with a huge smile on his face and whispered, "To be continued." With that, he got up and left the room.

It was now clear that the next phone call would be Maya telling me we weren't going to the movies, just as my father had predicted.

thirteen

•

Another Angry Doctor

I didn't want to tell my father, but since that first lesson, I had been practicing the pendulum a lot. If he knew what I was doing, he'd make me start to study with him even more. I would have to learn how to diagnose and determine remedies—really boring stuff. Instead I used the pendulum to obtain very important information such as "What is the release date for the next Beatles album?" "Is Marcia's mother sleeping with Mr. Stickney?" "Is Julie selling pot?"

For me the pendulum was a great spy tool that made me feel I had an edge over the other kids in school. Unfortunately, my success rate in getting correct answers was not very high; maybe only about 15 percent. Even though I got more things wrong than right, I suddenly felt that I had invincible supernatural powers that protected me against poor grades and teasing by the rest of the student body. Now nothing at school bothered me. If one of the kids harassed me,

I figured I could use the pendulum to find something out about him that would embarrass him, and he would leave me alone.

My SATs were approaching. Not only was I a terrible student but also a disastrous test taker. However, I had hatched an ingenious plan based on my extensive pendulum practice. Since I wasn't planning on studying for the test, I thought it would be a good idea to bring the pendulum with me. I would hold it between my legs so that the proctor wouldn't see me using it. As I read each test question to myself, I glanced down at the pendulum and waited until it swung in a positive direction, indicating the correct answer. So for those questions like "If a train is going sixty miles an hour . . ." I would rely on the pendulum to tell me if the answer was A, B, C, or D.

The phone rang. It was my father calling from next door.

"How's it going?"

"Okay, just hanging out."

"Tonight I'm giving a lecture on healing over at the University of Miami. I'd love for you to come."

"Naw, that's okay, I'm just going to stay home. I think Mom wants me to help her with some things."

"This is going to be really good. Some time ago I healed this woman's mother, and now she wants me to speak to the students to expose them to ideas about psychic healing. It will be fun."

Fun? I couldn't imagine one of my father's lectures being fun. Besides, I had been to enough of them and had heard it all. All this stuff about healing, about spirits, blah, blah, blah. I knew it all by heart.

"No, I don't really feel like it. I'm kinda tired."

"By the way, I think it's great that you're doing all the work with the pendulum. Unfortunately, no matter how hard you try, it's not going to work for your SAT tests."

"It's not?" I couldn't understand why it wouldn't; it seemed to be a perfect use of the pendulum to gain information from unknown sources. After all, that was the purpose of the pendulum, wasn't it?

"No. And do you know why? Because it's not for the highest good. You need to get the test answers from your own mind."

"But you told me that I could tune in to anything in the universe."

"Yes, but I didn't tell you that you could use the pendulum to cheat on a test."

"It's not cheating."

"Yes it is. Come over to my house at six-thirty and we'll drive over to the university."

At six-thirty we both climbed into his big gold Toronado and headed off to the lecture. I had put my pendulum in my pocket in case I had some sort of emergency and needed information immediately. Lecturing at the University of Miami meant a lot to my father; it was a sign of legitimacy. This was a far cry from his earlier talks given in nearly abandoned churches, in people's living rooms, and at psychic fairs. He was still struggling to have his work accepted so that he could pass on the unique information that his spirits had taught him.

My father truly wanted to help people and believed that his work could eliminate a lot of physical and mental suffering. Everything he did was based on the simple notion that we are all spiritual beings with tremendous powers. Until we recognized this, nothing would change—there would continue to be wars, disease, and anger. My father wanted to be able to teach everybody—nurses, doctors, policemen, and the man in the street—how to heal. He felt this power was innate to all humans, and he dreamed of the day when there would no longer be a need for hospitals, doctors, or pharmaceuticals with dangerous side effects. Instead there would be legions of healers who could eliminate disease through concentrated thought and prayer.

Whenever he met a doctor in a social situation, Pop would begin an almost Talmudic argument with the doctor as to why the medical profession was doing more harm than good and how physicians could truly heal people if they understood the wisdom of the body and the spirit. Despite the constant accusations of quackery by the medical profession, there were those rare doctors who supported my father's work and quietly believed. While they would never publicly come to his defense, they readily agreed to be taught his methods as long as he never identified them publicly. They acted as if they were living in the seventeenth century and afraid of being turned in by their neighbors for practicing witchcraft. Nurses would secretly practice his laying-on-of-hands method with their patients, or doctors might use the pendulum in private to diagnose difficult cases. My father worked with several doctors who would call him from time to time for consultations about patients who, no matter what they did, just never got better. Within minutes, my father would give the doctor a complete diagnosis and a list of either alternative treatments or standard pharmaceuticals to use.

Of course, some of this has finally changed with the arrival of the twenty-first century. There are now healers working alongside medical doctors in the operating room. These doctors are seen as the vanguard of the new frontiers of medicine. It was in the context of imagining such a future that my father welcomed the opportunity to lecture at the University of Miami. If he couldn't immediately change the medical establishment, at least he could begin to plant the seeds of change with a new generation.

We parked on campus near the Lowe Art Gallery. As we walked through the breezeway to the student union, I noticed that photocopied announcements of my father's lecture had been taped up on the columns and the walls: "Come Hear Famous Psychic Lew Smith." Upstairs, a room had been set aside with about fifty chairs. When we arrived, the room was empty. I figured that about ten people would show up. A woman in her mid-thirties walked in and greeted my father.

"Reverend Smith! We are honored that you came to speak to us this evening. I know a lot of people are interested in what you have to say. We should have a nice crowd. I think the students will be very curious about what you do. There may be one or two doctors from the teaching hospital dropping in. Is this your son?"

"Yes, this is Philip. Philip, this is Miss Orson, who asked me to come and speak."

"Hi. Nice to meet you."

"It must be wonderful having a father that can do such great things."

"Yeah, I guess so."

Getting only a bored response out of me, Miss Orson turned to my father and said, "Reverend, why don't you make yourself comfortable, and we'll get started in about fifteen minutes."

"But there's no one here," I said with a trace of annoyance.

"Oh, don't worry, they'll come."

By the time my father was ready to start his lecture, every seat was taken, and about twenty students stood in the back of the room.

Miss Orson introduced my father. "Welcome. Thank you all so much for coming for this very special evening. Tonight I have the pleasure and the honor of introducing Reverend Lew Smith, a spiritual healer. Is that the right terminology for what you do, Reverend?"

"Yes. Spiritual healing, psychic healing, absent healing, vibrational healing—they all entail the transference of healing energy from the cosmic source to the patient."

This "Reverend" thing always embarrassed me. I hated when people called him Reverend. All of this Reverend business was actually Arthur Ford's idea. My father was constantly getting thrown out of hospitals for healing people. The doctor would walk in while Pop was waving his hands over a patient, and security would immediately be called to evict him. I guess they were afraid that he was pulling out their IV tubes or unhooking them from the life-support machines. Sometimes the police were summoned and threatened to arrest him for "practicing medicine without a license."

One morning Arthur Ford came through with a message suggesting that my father become an ordained minister. With these credentials he could practice healing without being harassed. After all, he was doing God's work, and there's nothing illegal in that. The next day, Pop sent off a check to some mail-order ministry, and in return he received a certificate stating that he was now Reverend Smith. He then incorporated Temple of the LOGO (Light of God's Order) and was now a man of the cloth. As a Reverend, he would flash his official minister ID card to the hospital staff or the police, and they would leave him alone. If they inquired any further about his activities, he described what he was doing as a "prayer service." That fifteen-dollar check not only saved him a lot of future attorney's fees, it probably saved a lot of people's lives as well.

Miss Orson continued, "I first met Reverend Smith last year when my mother was diagnosed with kidney problems. The doctor told us that she would have to be on dialysis for the rest of her life. Fortunately a friend of hers told us about the miracles that Reverend Smith was performing, and my mother thought she had nothing to lose by going to see him. Reverend Smith quickly diagnosed her problem and performed a healing on her. He suggested that she wait a week and then call her doctor and request that he rerun her tests. Initially the doctor refused, as he was certain of his diagnosis. When my mother threatened to change doctors, he finally agreed. Her new tests came back negative, which meant that her kidney problem had completely disappeared. It is now a year later, with no signs of any kidney problems, nor has she had dialysis. The doctor can't explain it. In fact, he doesn't even try. His attitude is, 'Look what a great job I did. Your mother is fine, that's all you need to know.' However, none of this would have been possible without Reverend Lew. I truly believe that my mother would have been dead by now if it weren't for his help. It has been nothing short of a miracle. I'm sure you will find this lecture fascinating. And now, please welcome my dear friend Reverend Lew Smith."

Applause rippled lightly through the audience. It was made up mostly of college kids and about ten middle-aged people. There was also one hippie couple with matching Indian dhotis; I hadn't seen that in a couple of years. I couldn't figure out why all these college students came to hear a lecture by my father. Weren't college students supposed to be out getting drunk and having sex with their girlfriends on a Saturday night? Most of the time, my father's audience was composed of elderly people looking for cures that they could not obtain from the medical profession. Maybe these college kids thought that he was going to read minds or do card tricks; probably they had no idea what a psychic healer was. But then again, here *I* was listening to my father, just as they were.

I was hoping that Pop didn't introduce me to the audience, which he did from time to time. I didn't want people looking at me like I was some sort of freak for being the son of a psychic. My father approached the lectern and began his speech.

"I'm very pleased to be here tonight. Thank you so much for coming. I am glad to hear that Miss Orson's mother is doing well. I should tell you that she is the norm and not the exception of people that can be successfully healed through psychic means. Most of the people who come to see me are the people that the doctors say are terminal, hopeless, and incurable. I don't believe in such words as *terminal, hopeless,* or *incurable.* Every patient who comes to me, I see in perfect health. That is my starting point.

"I believe that all illness begins in the mind. Stop for a moment and really think about what our mind does: it makes sure our heart keeps beating; it makes sure that we keep breathing when we are asleep; it calibrates our eyes to see in both bright light and low light; it turns that hamburger you ate for dinner into blood and nutrients to feed your body. It does all of this without any interference from our conscious mind. It knows perfectly well how to run the body at optimum performance. However, the mind also knows how to make us sick—and it can do a great job if we let it. We don't get a headache or a stomachache or cancer simply by accident. It comes from somewhere. We make a decision to become sick for any number of reasons. Maybe we feel guilty, or we want someone to take care of us, or we have a karmic debt to pay off. We can also correct our thinking and make a decision to get well and to heal ourselves.

"Unlike doctors, who look only at symptoms, I look for the cause of the disease. If you just treat the symptoms, they'll come right back, and the person will never get better. This is why so many doctors have patients with chronic conditions. They don't know how to treat the true cause of the disease, only the symptoms. You always need to get to the root cause of things to create a real healing.

"Initially, I began healing by simply laying on of hands. I would say a prayer, ask for guidance, open my hands, and spirit would direct my hands to where they needed to go. While my hands were open, energy would pour out into the person. I never felt that it was me actually healing the person; I simply channeled the energy from God or whatever you want to call it.

"Over the years, I have been instructed by the spirits on new and advanced healing methods that have never been seen before on this planet. They taught me how to send powerful healing energy in just a matter of minutes to anywhere in the world. It didn't matter if the patient was in the room next to me or sitting in a cave in Tibet. The psychic energy that I use is not limited by the boundaries of time or space."

Pop seemed to gloss over his spirit connection. He didn't mention Chander Sen or any of his other psychic friends. I think he was concerned that in this university setting, he would seem too kooky if he started talking about his spirit guides. I looked around the room and noticed that people were extremely focused on what he had to say. No one was reading, yawning, or doing the crossword puzzle.

"I have also been extremely successful in diagnosing patients. Oftentimes people come to me because their doctors cannot find what's wrong with them. Despite all the tests—X-rays, blood tests, GI series, cardiograms—their doctors still can't figure out what the problem is. Usually in a matter of minutes, I can give a complete and accurate diagnosis that they can take to their doctor and get confirmed."

When he mentioned his diagnostic ability, it reminded me of the time the doctors had misdiagnosed my grandmother and told her that she was about to die. They had found blood in her urine and suspected kidney cancer. She was undergoing tests in a hospital 1,500 miles away in New York City. The doctors had informed my aunt and uncle that most likely my grandmother's prospects were grim. They claimed that, at best, she had six months to live, and that was after surgery and chemotherapy.

My aunt Sedell called me from New York to let me know about my grandmother's dire condition. After I got off the phone, I went into my father's study. I was extremely upset. I loved my grandmother very much and as a child had spent many summers with her in New York. Originally from Czechoslovakia, she still retained many of her traditional ways, including baking her own bread. "Pop, I just got a call that Grandma has cancer. She's going to die."

My father didn't answer me immediately. Instead he shifted his eyes away from mine, looking out into space as if his mind had wandered.

"I don't think so. They're wrong. They are making a hasty diagnosis based on nothing. But let me check it out," he responded.

Sitting down at his desk, he took out a couple of his diagnostic charts, along with a copy of *Gray's Anatomy*. To start the diagnostic process, he simply held a pendulum in his right hand and asked, "Does Ida Rand have cancer?" The pendulum seemed to hang motionless for longer than usual. Slowly it began to swing in a counterclockwise direction, indicating a negative response.

As if his pendulum had access to the world's most brilliant oncologist, he looked up at me with a smile and shrugged his shoulders. "See, she doesn't have cancer. They made a mistake."

"So what do we do? They're going to operate in the next day or so."

"Then they'll definitely kill her. Let's find out what's really going on."

With his right hand, he held the pendulum over *Gray's Anatomy* as he slowly turned the pages. The pendulum remained absolutely still as he passed the muscular, skeletal, endocrine, and cardiac systems. When he came to the female genitourinary system, the pendulum began to swing clockwise, indicating that this was the area to look for the answer. He held the pendulum over the urinary tract and asked, "Is there cancer in the urinary tract?" The pendulum swung counterclockwise, indicating no.

Refining his question, he now asked, "Is there an infection in the urinary tract?" The pendulum swung clockwise, indicating that this was the location of the problem.

"Is surgery necessary?" The pendulum swung counterclockwise.

"Will medication be helpful?" The pendulum swung clockwise. "Should the doctors use antibiotics?" Again, the pendulum indicated a yes answer.

"Are there any further problems with the patient's anatomy?" The pendulum swung clockwise, indicating that the diagnosis was not complete.

Still holding the pendulum in his right hand, he continued through the anatomy book page by page. As he opened the section picturing the kidneys, the pendulum began to indicate a positive response. He asked, "Do the kidneys have cancer?" The pendulum swung counterclockwise. No.

"Are the kidneys infected?" Yes.

"Is this infection causing blood in the urine?" The pendulum quickly swung clockwise.

"I think you should call your aunt back and tell her that Grandma is going to be fine. She has a kidney infection that is causing blood in the urine. They should do some tests and then give her an antibiotic to clear up the infection. She needs to drink more water to flush this infection out of her system. I think it's better if I leave it at that. If they follow my advice, she'll be released and home in no time. I don't want to get too involved in this one."

My relatives in New York were not terribly fond of my father since he'd jumped ship from reality and left my mother in an emotional free fall. "I don't think they're going to believe you," I said.

"Well, you need to make them believe me. Otherwise they're going to cut your grandmother open for nothing, and she'll die. She's too old to survive the operation." My father closed his eyes and sat quietly for a minute. "Wait, there's something else: the doctors are going to schedule a large number of tests, and then, without any explanation, at the last moment they will postpone them for one day. Tell your aunt that when they suddenly cancel the tests, she'll know I'm telling the truth. Once she realizes this, she needs to prevent them from operating on your grandmother."

I called Aunt Sedell. "Pop says that Grandma is going to be fine. She does not have cancer, she just has a kidney infection. This is what is causing the bleeding. The doctors will eventually just give her some antibiotics and send her home."

"What other good news does your brilliant father have for us?" My aunt was not amused by her psychic—or as she would say, "psychotic"—brother-in-law. They were already expecting the worst and did not want to entertain false hopes for their mother, especially when the messenger was my father.

"It's really important that you stop them from operating. Grandma doesn't need surgery. They'll kill her if they operate."

"They told us it's our only hope. We have to do it to save her. How can we not listen to them and let her die?"

"Well, here's how you'll know that Pop is telling the truth. The doctors are going to order a large number of tests—"

My aunt interrupted me. "They already have. All doctors order tests; what's so amazing about that?"

"Let me finish. Without any explanation, the doctors will suddenly postpone all the tests for one day. When they do that, then you'll know Pop's right, and that's the sign that you must stop them from going any further."

Even though I found my father's psychic abilities highly intrusive in my personal life, I knew from experience that he was overwhelmingly accurate in his diagnoses. I hung up and hoped that I had convinced my aunt to intervene.

Two days later the phone rang; it was my aunt. Her tone of voice was excited and somewhat humbled. "Philip, you were right. Monday morning they were supposed to do some final tests before the operation. Late in the afternoon, I called the doctor to find out the results.

He said that they were going to postpone the tests for another day. They would be performed on Tuesday, and they would operate on Wednesday."

"*I* wasn't right about the tests, Pop was. I'm not the healer around here." I felt that I had to stick up for my father.

"Well, it doesn't matter. Anyway, once the doctor told me about postponing everything I knew that I had to stop them from operating. So I told him that my mother does not have cancer, that it's just a kidney infection, and that she didn't need surgery. Instead, what they needed to do was give her antibiotics. The doctor asked me how I knew this. I told him 'from a psychic in Miami.' He told me not to waste his time and hung up on me. I immediately left work and went to the hospital. The doctor wouldn't meet with me. So I went over to the administrator and the social worker and told them they had to stop my mother's operation. They asked me if I was a doctor."

"Yeah, that's what they say to my father all the time. I keep telling him to print up business cards that say 'Lew Smith, MD, Internal Medicine' and just flash them at people whenever they stop him. But he won't do it."

Sedell continued, "Finally they called the doctor in. I warned him that I would call my lawyer, if necessary, to have the operation stopped. I demanded that he examine her kidneys to see what was going on. The idea of the lawyer scared him. So he agreed. The next morning he called me at seven to tell me that they had rechecked some of the initial tests and that your grandmother has a bad kidney and urinary tract infection from not drinking enough water. He's prescribing strong antibiotics that will hopefully clear up the situation. He said she should be able to go home tomorrow."

"So did he say anything about having to reverse his previous diagnosis?"

"Not a word. He made it sound like this was the diagnosis all along."

"Maybe you should give him Pop's number anytime he wants to check a diagnosis before surgery."

"He won't listen."

"They never do." I was relieved that Grandma was not going to die of cancer or unnecessary surgery. Later, when I relayed the whole story in detail to my father, he simply said, "I know." His diagnosis had been quicker and more accurate than the doctors', despite all their machinery and fancy tests. He had saved her life.

My reveries about my grandmother were interrupted by the sound of laughter. I looked around the room and saw that everyone was laughing at something my father had said in his lecture. I stopped daydreaming and began listening again.

"My diagnosis doesn't come from a Ouija board. This is not voodoo or magic. There is a method to what I do, and this can be taught to anyone. Anyone in this room can be a healer. And that is the greatest thing you can do with your life. To be able to help someone when medicine has failed them is one of the most satisfying things you can do. Too bad they don't teach healing here at the University of Miami. You would all make my job so much easier if you graduated with degrees in healing and went out into the world to help people."

When he said this, I overheard the student behind me say to her neighbor, "Wouldn't that be cool, to walk around healing people and have magic powers?" My father made healing sound like a noble and romantic undertaking. But to me it was just what my father did.

"Tonight there isn't enough time to go into much detail about my healing systems, but I will try to give you a brief overview. Basically, we live in a world of energy patterns. Anyone here that studies physics knows this to be a fact of life. All things in our physical environment, including our own bodies, are just different packets and bundles of energy. To really simplify things, what I do is to tap into this energy and direct it to where it is needed. In this way I bring everything in the body up to its full energy potential. Let's say that someone has a weak heart or his eyes don't see as well as they used to. It's as if a battery has run down. I can put energy back into the heart or into the eyes and bring them up to their full functioning potential.

"How do I do this? Depending on the patient, I use various

modalities to heal them. Someone might need a specific dose of color radiation or the Bach Flower Remedies or homeopathy or just an energy transfer. Some people are possessed by negative entities, some have karmic debts that need to be removed, and others have structural problems with the body that need to be resolved. All of these remedies are sent psychically by thought. I never give anyone so much as a sugar tablet, since that would be prescribing medication and practicing medicine. Nor do I ever touch my patients. Each one of these methods would require several hours for me to discuss in detail. I guess we'll have to plan a series of lectures to cover all this material." About a dozen people clapped, indicating that they would like my father to return.

"But I would like to take a moment to talk about a small tool I use in all my healings called a pendulum." Pop pulled out his pendulum and held it up for everyone to see. I was sitting toward the back, and it was hard to see what the pendulum really looked like from that distance.

"This little pendulum is merely a tool that reveals the required information my consciousness has tuned in to and collected. In some ways, the pendulum functions as my own hospital. Without any X-ray machines, blood tests, or operating rooms, I can diagnose, run tests, and send medication to patients just with this little bead attached to a string. All of this occurs through the power of thought."

I overheard the middle-aged woman next to me whisper to the man sitting next to her, "This guy's nuts. He thinks that little bead on a string is an X-ray machine. Let's go." As they stood up to leave, they made it a point to talk loudly to each other as they walked out right in front of my father. No one paid any attention to them.

Pop continued with his lecture as if nothing had happened. "Thought is basically an electrical impulse similar to radio or television. You can't see the signals in the air and you can't feel the signals, yet when you turn on the television set, you can see or hear your favorite program. Pretty amazing, if you think about it. Yet this is exactly how psychic healing works. The body is like a two-way radio that sends and receives electrical energy. I am able to read and interpret these signals. When necessary, I can adjust them for the patient's benefit.

"Because I work with this invisible energy, I can heal anybody anywhere in the world. This energy is not restricted by time or space. Many of the people that I heal never talk to me or even meet me. I am able to locate and tune in to their bodies through my consciousness.

"The pendulum can analyze these energy patterns that surround us and operate the functions of our body. I can measure deficiencies in these energy patterns and determine what amount of remedy I need to send to correct that deficiency. The pendulum also enables me to look into the body and check the vitality of each and every organ.

"Let me give you an example." With that, Pop picked up his pendulum and let it hang perfectly still. He took a deep breath and watched the pendulum. I saw it swing counterclockwise, giving him a negative response. I wondered what he was asking. No one else in the room knew what he was doing; they sat quietly watching. Pop stopped the pendulum and waited. Again it gave a negative response. At this point, people were beginning to shift in their seats; they wanted something to happen. Once more Pop stopped the pendulum and waited. This time it swung clockwise, giving him a positive response. His brow wrinkled for a minute as if he was trying to understand what the pendulum was telling him. Finally he looked up at the audience and cleared his throat.

"There is a man here tonight whose wife is very ill. She has breast cancer, which has now spread throughout her lymphatic system. For the past three weeks, she has been undergoing chemotherapy but is getting worse. I have been asked to talk to him." The room was extremely silent. Pop looked around as if he had just announced the winning numbers for the lottery and was waiting for the lucky ticket holder to come forth and claim his prize. No one said a word. People were looking to see if this mystery man was sitting next to them. No one moved. It seemed as if my father had made a wrong call. I did not want him to fail in front of this audience. I was embarrassed and felt bad for him. This was at the university, and word would get around that he didn't know what he was doing. I felt like standing up myself and saying that my wife had breast cancer, but I don't think too many people would have believed that from a seventeen-year-old. When my father saw that no one was coming forward, he picked up his pendulum to double-check his findings.

While he waited for the pendulum to respond, a middle-aged man sitting toward the back of the room stood up slowly. Everybody turned to look at him. He stood there for a moment or two, knowing that he was getting the full attention of the room. "I am Dr. Michaels. How dare you stand here, in an institution of higher learning, and spin these fairy tales of psychic healing, which we know is an impossibility and does not exist? How can you walk around spouting nonsense that keeps people from receiving the lifesaving medical treatment that they require? You are only hastening their death and spreading ignorance. I don't know who let you speak here tonight, but I will find out and make sure that this does not happen again. Tomorrow morning I intend to contact the proper authorities to do whatever they can to prevent you from spreading your lies. I shudder to think how many people you have killed by your parlor tricks."

People sat bolt upright in their chairs. The doctor's accusations had created a tangible tension in the room. There was a long pause before my father responded. "Dr. Michaels, why are you allowing your wife to suffer the pain and indignity of chemotherapy when she is so close to death? You know that the cancer spread very quickly from her breast to her lymphatic system and then to the rest of her body. It's now in her brain. You know that there is absolutely nothing you can do to cure her, yet you continue to pump her full of poison that is worse than the cancer. Right now she is so sick from the chemo, there's no turning back. You need to let her die with dignity and not as a failed medical experiment. I only regret that you did not come to me last year when all of this began. I could have helped."

Dr. Michaels stood silent. He didn't say anything, but his face became bright red with anger and then he exploded. "You charlatan!

You faker! You called the hospital and had me checked out before you came here tonight. They told you about my wife. This is just the kind of pathetic magic trick that you use to sucker the hopeless and take their money. I'll make sure you don't get away with this."

The audience was astonished by this outburst. They didn't know who to believe.

My father responded calmly, "You know as well as I do that hospitals cannot release that kind of information. I never met you until just now and had no knowledge that you were going to be here. The information I relayed to you about your wife was given to me by one of my spirit guides. I told you this in an effort to help you open your mind and consider that there are other avenues of healing and that yours might not always be the only or correct way.

"Look, I am not against the medical profession. Doctors perform a wonderful service. But the people who come to me are the rejects of the medical profession. They are the ones that you could not help or that you made worse with needless surgery and toxic medications. Rather than make empty accusations, I wish you would take the time to meet with me. I am sorry to tell you that your wife will pass over by the weekend. There is nothing anyone can do now; she is too far gone. You need to be with her, to express your love to her, and help make her transition smoother. I know she will forgive you."

"*Forgive* me? Forgive me for *what*?" By now the doctor was screaming at my father.

"I don't want to say it here in front of everyone. You know what has transpired between you two. Now is the moment to settle that past history between the two of you. I know how painful it will be to admit that you were wrong and that you hurt her, but you must. She will be gone soon, and it will haunt you the rest of your life. I would like to—"

At that point, Dr. Michaels, who was sitting in the middle of the row, just started bulldozing his way out of the room. He turned to my father and said, "Mark my words, you have not heard the last of me." With that, he left.

I hated when people threatened and confronted my father. Pop

took all this anger and aggression as just part of the job. This was
one of the main reasons I didn't want to become a healer. Not only
did I not want to deal with all the sick people, but more important, I
didn't want to deal with all the people who would scoff at what I was
doing.

My father turned to Miss Orson and said, "I'm very sorry for the
outburst. He is in a lot of pain. His wife is going to die very soon, and
he needed to hear what I had to say. It was the only opportunity of
repairing the past."

Miss Orson didn't know how to respond to what had just happened. She was clearly upset by the fireworks from a prestigious member of the hospital. She turned to the audience and with a forced smile
said, "Well, this has been an interesting evening." It was evident that
she wanted to end the lecture as quickly as possible. "I want to thank
the Reverend Lew Smith for his time and all the wonderful work he
is doing, and I hope you have all learned something. Are their any
further questions?"

One of the male college students stood up and said, "My mother
has been diagnosed with multiple sclerosis, and the doctors aren't
helping her. Is there anything you can do to make her better? The
doctor says there is nothing he can do."

"There is a lot that we can do to help your mother. I would be
happy to see her at my house, or if you want to have her call me, I can
work with her over the phone. I will know in a matter of minutes how
to best diagnose her condition and what form of treatment I would
use. It's quite possible that her dis-ease is due to a karmic debt from
a past lifetime, which we can address, or the issue could be hidden
emotional causes. It could be a physical manifestation. There are many
causes. Remember that just because we name a dis-ease does not mean
that this is the cause of the problem. After we're done here tonight, I'll
give you my card. There is no charge for my services."

Another student, a young woman, stood up and asked, "Um, I
think I'm getting, like, an ulcer. And you know, I have stomach pains
all the time and—"

My father interrupted her. "Your diet is the problem. You drink coffee constantly, smoke cigarettes, and eat French fries. You'll end up with colon cancer if you keep going this way. You need to reduce your stress and stop taking so much pressure from your parents. If you call me, we'll work with spirit to remove all the pressure you're under and get you on a healthy diet. I'd like to see you undertake a series of high colonics to clear out the waste from your intestinal tract so that you can get a fresh start."

"Oh my God, oh my God, how'd you know I eat French fries? Oh my God, that's, you know, all I eat. This is so incredible. Oh, this is so weird. I don't believe this. Wow!"

People started laughing. My father was the only one in the room who took her seriously. He said, "Please don't hesitate to call me; you need to make these changes. You may pay a huge price for your bad habits later on. Better you should correct the imbalance now."

She had broken the ice. Now there were about a dozen hands in the air of people wanting to ask questions. My father pointed at another student. Before the woman could ask her question, Miss Orson leaned over to the microphone and said, "Unfortunately, we have run out of time. I promised the booking office that we would be out of here by nine o'clock. Let's thank Reverend Smith for his time and his wonderful lecture on psychic healing."

With that, there was an enthusiastic round of applause. As the students began to file out, a few stopped to talk to my father and ask questions. He handed his "Reverend Lew Smith, Temple of the LOGO" calling cards to quite a few people. I was looking for the young man whose mother had multiple sclerosis. I expected him to come up and get a card. He didn't.

When everyone left, Pop said, "Let's go eat, just the two of us."

"Aren't you going to invite Miss Orson along?" I was surprised that we were going to eat by ourselves. Usually we left each lecture with a crowd of curiosity seekers.

"No, just us."

We walked over to a Denny's restaurant across the street. As I looked over the menu, I pulled out my pendulum. I thought I would use it to decide what to have for dinner. I asked, "Should I have the turkey combo or the spaghetti?"

Pop started laughing. "I'm just having eggs and toast."

Suddenly I got embarrassed that someone in the restaurant might see me with the pendulum, so I put it back in my pocket. "I guess I'll have the same."

"Thank you for coming with me tonight. It was nice to have you there. What'd you think?"

"It went well. Everyone seemed really interested in what you had to say except for the doctor. He really went a little nuts."

"Well, what do you expect? The man's wife is dying, which he doesn't want to admit, and he doesn't know quite how to deal with the fact that his medical knowledge has failed. Sadly, for certain people, what I do is very threatening. It's really a shame. If they had come to me earlier, I could have helped that woman and saved everybody a lot of pain. I don't know why people can't see that by opening their minds they have nothing to lose and everything to gain."

"Well, I think you handled him really well. I wonder why he bothered to come if he doesn't believe in this stuff?"

"I think spirit sent him. In his mind, he decided to come to the lecture to try to debunk me. But I believe that spirit wanted him to hear what I had to say so that he could make amends to his wife before she died. Who knows, maybe his experience tonight will open his mind to new possibilities."

Just then the lights blinked three times in rapid succession.

"Oh, Arthur's calling. I wonder what he wants?"

Kiddingly, I said, "He probably wants to give his critique of your lecture."

With that, my father took out a pen and began to write down Arthur's words. I kept eating my eggs. So much for dinner with just the two of us.

"Arthur tells me that you are applying for colleges," my father said. "I'm sorry to say that you're not going to get into any of the schools you want. Arthur says he'll give me a list of where you'll get in."

"Yeah, Mom wants me to go to school in the Northeast. She says the universities in Florida are terrible. Maya is going to the University of Florida. The problem is that my grades are very bad, and I don't think I'm going to do very well on the SATs unless I use my pendulum. So I guess you'd better get that list from Arthur of the schools I should apply to."

"Well, why don't you stay and go to school here in Miami?"

"No, I think it's better that I go away. I'll have some new experiences."

fourteen

•

The Goddess Debuts

The cold metal pressed hard against my forehead.

My eyes felt as if they were bulging out of my head. Even though it was approaching midnight, the kitchen seemed to suddenly brighten with a harsh, brilliant light I had never seen before. Everything appeared in stark, high relief. I felt as if I was seeing out of every pore in my body.

Bob was crying as he pushed the gun harder into my head. "You're going to die. You deserve it."

I couldn't breathe.

"And then I'm going to die."

As he said that, he closed his eyes and started to cry. He was leaning heavily on the gun pressed against my head to support himself. To my surprise, I had enough of my wits about me to quickly step backward. As Bob fell forward, I grabbed the gun and threw it right through the window, shattering the glass. The noise startled him. As his eyes opened, he seemed unsure of where he was or what had just happened.

Because Bob had probably been spending time with his two close friends—vodka and Valium—he offered no resistance as I shoved him hard against the wall and ran for my life down three flights of stairs and into the street.

Certainly I had been eager to leave home and be on my own. But this was more than I had bargained for. This was my first year at a liberal arts college in a small New England town. I had settled into a top-floor apartment of an old wooden house off campus and at the age of eighteen endured my first winter without Cuban *tostones* or fresh sugarcane juice. It wasn't easy—cold weather and steam heat didn't come naturally to this tropical native.

Having volunteered as photographer for the school paper, I attended all the lectures, seminars, and cultural events at the college. One day the official school photographer, Bob, started kidding me about being his "competition." I just wanted to take the pictures and get out of there. Bob, who must have been in his early forties, told me that his wife worked as a bank teller and would not be home until around five. He invited me over to their house for a drink. I was new at school and hadn't really made any friends. "Wow," I thought, "the school photographer is inviting me over to his house for a drink." I was honored and also too young or stupid to know that married men with kids could also be gay. Our interactions consisted of drinks and darkroom sex and lasted all of a few weeks until he broke into my apartment to try to kill me.

After I left the apartment, I ran three long blocks to the college dean's house. I banged on his front door until I woke him up. Out of breath, I told him what had just occurred. Through triple-thick glasses that magnified his eyes, he stared back at me in shock. He had known Bob and his family for fifteen years. Here was a sordid accusation of attempted murder and homosexuality that was impossible for him to digest.

I knew immediately from the way he looked at me that either he didn't believe me or, if he did, it was all my fault, and I needed to be gotten rid of.

"What do you want me to do?" he asked.

"I guess call the police and put Bob in jail."

"No, I'm not ready to do that."

"I can't go back to my apartment. He knows where I live. He'll come back and kill me."

The dean thought for a moment. His enlarged eyes twitched behind his glasses. "It's late. I'll put you somewhere safe for the night. Then we'll see what we are going to do in the morning." I followed the dean across the street to the girls' dorm. There was a maid's room in the basement where I would sleep. I was insulted that I was being put in the girls' dorm. It seemed to be more of a judgment on his part rather than a safety strategy.

At six the next morning, two local cops—overweight lugs—woke me up. I assumed that they would be comforting and concerned. Instead they were accusatory and hostile. They *told* me what had happened the night before without asking for any information. "Why did you make all this up? To get Mr. Malina in trouble? You wanted his job, didn't you? Get him fired, and they'll hire you to be the school photographer. We've never had anything like this happen until you showed up. Wait till the judge hears your story. He will not be pleased. If I were you, I'd pack up now before he gets wind of this. If you stay, we have no choice—you're not too young to go to jail."

I got the message. Briefly, I wondered what my father would want me to do. However, I was too ashamed to call him or my mother for advice. I didn't know how they would deal with my situation with Bob and the police. I had made a huge mistake getting involved with Bob and was now paying the price. With great apprehension, I went back to my apartment, packed a knapsack with a pair of jeans, my checkbook, passport, and toothbrush, and left everything else behind. Summer vacation was just a few weeks away. At this point in the semester, it didn't matter whether or not I attended any more classes. I knew I had to leave and get away.

Not knowing exactly where to go, I went downtown and caught the first Greyhound bus to New York City. I thought perhaps I would simply move there and never return to school. On the way down to the city, I decided that my best plan was to fly to Miami and then figure out what I needed to do. Once in New York, I took the next bus to Kennedy Airport. At the time, Braniff had a midnight special. At one minute past midnight, you could book a seat on one of its planes flying to South America with a stop in Miami. If you got off in Miami, the fare was $49. When I landed in familiar surroundings, I looked for any airline counter open that late. I lucked out: Ecuatoriana was open for business.

"Where do you fly to?"

"Tonight we are flying to Quito. Tomorrow, Lima."

"Where's Quito?"

The woman in the soft navy blue uniform that was intended to make her look like an admiral in the Royal Navy looked at me with some annoyance. "Ecuador."

"Okay."

"Okay, *what*?" She was irritated by this skinny kid in blue jeans with no luggage wasting her time.

"I'll go."

"When would be your date of travel?"

"Now. Do you take a check?"

"Do you have identification?"

"U.S. passport."

"Fine." She typed for a few minutes and then wrote out a ticket by hand, giving me the red carbon copy. "We leave in two hours."

"Okay." I was relieved and, for the first time in days, felt safe. Finally I was going to disappear.

For the next three months, I traveled by myself through the mountains of Ecuador and the deserts of Peru. There I swam in extinct volcanoes, hitched a ride to the Galápagos Islands on a cargo boat, saw Machu Picchu, fended off armed banditos and the policia looking for money from the gringo, sat with shamans, and listened to the monkeys of the Amazon. I had no contact with my father, my mother, the police, or the college dean. I lived on raw foods in the mountains, soups from the marketplace, and whatever simple meals I could find for pennies. For the first time, I felt that I didn't need my father's psychic antimissile shield. My travels took me into many dangerous situations, and I always emerged without having said a special prayer or asking the spirits for assistance. The trip allowed me to finally access much of the inner strength that I never knew I had or needed to use because of my reliance on my father. With my confidence restored, I felt that I was finally ready to go back home.

After the blue and white Ecuatoriana jet landed in Miami, I took a cab over to my father's office. We hadn't spoken in months. I thought I would surprise him. I knew he would be pleased with my adventures. When I walked in, he had a colored pencil in one hand and the pendulum in the other. I assumed he had been interrupted in the middle of designing an interior scheme with an urgent spirit message. Pop looked up at me and said, "Well, welcome back. I didn't expect you until this evening. Your plane got in early." He dropped everything and gave me a big hug. "You're safe now; that guy won't hurt you again. I'm sorry, but things happen in life. You handled it well. Use it, learn from it; it will only make you stronger. I left you alone, just as you wished."

As Pop looked at me, he commented that I now had a very strong chin. This is not something I had ever noticed, but it was his way of acknowledging that I had successfully grown from my travels.

It was good to be home, but I felt that my travels and my experience with Bob had cut the umbilical cord between my father and me. I was becoming my own person.

"I want to hear all about the trip," Pop said, "but I have a little problem I need to attend to first." He pointed to a stack of boxes that almost reached to the ceiling. The sides were marked "Japan." "I don't know why I ordered these beads. They're too heavy to use in draperies. They'll pull the rod out of the ceiling. I've never done anything stupid like this before."

I tried to lift one open carton on the floor. They *were* heavy. Each carton must have weighed at least one hundred pounds and contained sixteen boxes of white beads strung necklace style. They were innocuous, plain-Jane beads that at best could be sold at a five-and-dime for fifty cents a strand. I couldn't figure out why he'd bought these beads either. Probably some closeout deal.

Trying to be helpful, I said, "Well, maybe you can send them back."

"No, they won't take them back. I'll just have to figure out some way to use them. Maybe I'll give them away. You must be hungry; why don't we get going?"

I put my knapsack in the car and was looking forward to getting home. I also had not seen my mother for a long time and missed her. I knew she'd be unhappy that I had disappeared without letting her know, but she would be thrilled to hear about my journey. She'd want to know every detail.

For some reason, Pop took the long way home, driving down Biscayne Boulevard, which was lined with shuttered office buildings like ghosts from another era. We passed the long-defunct stark white Art Deco Sears Tower. Its roof was collapsing from termite damage and the summer monsoon rains. The last time I had been in that store was fifteen years earlier with my mother, looking for "necessities." That was the first and last Sears she ever visited. Mom didn't believe in shopping with the masses. Even though she was now leading a different life than she had envisioned, she maintained her dignity, her character, and her moral compass, and still dressed like a million bucks. I can't imagine how hard it was to have her ex-husband continue to live next door to her. Why neither of them picked up and moved on was beyond me. I guess they both felt they had a right to be there. Perhaps they were secretly hoping that this emotional freeze would eventually thaw, and they would pick up where they had left off.

The car windows were open, and the twilight breeze was coming up off the bay, kissing our faces as we headed down the boulevard. Thanks to Miami's never-ending stream of corrupt politicos, who gave away the city-owned bayfront for bags and bags of sweet, crisp, unmarked bills, this simple pleasure of life is now long gone. Miami's Bayfront Park once featured the odd combination of the pristinely white, marble-clad main library and a notorious cruising ground for pedophiles who lurked behind the lush tropical vegetation for under-age bait. It seemed that Miami pedophiles preferred smart underage children who actually could read rather than the dumb-hick kids who hung out at the rifle range. Or maybe kids who read were less danger-ous than kids toting guns. Eventually the library and the pedophiles gave way to sports arenas and tourist malls with daiquiri bars. Prog-ress.

Just across the street from the Freedom Torch, the eternal flame in memory of JFK, which was unlit due to the continuing local Cuban resentment toward John F. Kennedy for failing to provide air cover during the botched Bay of Pigs invasion nearly ten years earlier, my father pulled up to the curb of an anonymous office building with a white marble lobby that looked like an oversized airport men's room. A woman standing on the sidewalk smiled in an aggressive and al-most painful manner at my father. She was smoking one of those long liberated-lady cigarettes. I disliked her instantly.

She opened the door and climbed into the front seat. I noticed immediately that she was wearing navy blue stockings. This was something new to me. What little I remembered of the stockings that my mother wore was that they were sheer or coffee colored. But blue? Even in the swinging sixties, no one wore blue stockings. Pink, yes. Yellow and fluorescent green were okay. But never, *ever* blue. This must be something that was sold at the grocery store in those egg-shaped plastic containers cleverly called L'eggs. Stockings are not an item that should be sold at grocery stores to begin with, much less *blue* stockings. In a million years, my mother would never buy stockings in the grocery store. In fact, my mother didn't believe in grocery stores, except for staples such as detergent or milk. She would drive miles out of her way to find a butcher or a small fruit stand. But stockings? I think she would have rather faced electrocution or deportation than buy a personal item such as stockings at the supermarket. These blue stockings told me all I needed to know about this woman sitting in the front seat of my father's car.

As best as I could understand, this woman was aiming for a kind of Flash Gordon–a-go-go look. Instead she achieved one of chilling morbidity. There was something about the blue that gave her legs the appearance of a cadaver—dead flesh without circulation. Her legs told me that this woman was all about the wrong place at the wrong time. As she nestled into her bucket seat, she mechanically rotated her head like a ventriloquist's dummy and turned to face me, saying, *"Hiiieeeeeee."* Her lips did not move from her frozen smile as this greeting jumped out of her mouth. What her smile really said was, "I wish you were dead." I was not my father's son for nothing. What little psychic genetic material had been passed on allowed me to read people instantly. I could see right through her.

Not knowing where to look first—at her Rosalind Russell–inspired Auntie Mame bottle-black hairdo with a spit curl lacquered into place on her forehead, or her blue eye shadow and harsh red lips, or her cat's-eye rhinestone-encrusted waitress eyeglasses—I focused on her hand holding that long, thin cigarette. My mom smoked Camels, without filters, like a real man. This mystery woman smoked Virginia Slims, probably because she thought it made her appear ultrafeminine and au courant. Instead she looked stupid and common.

Without taking his eyes off the road, my father made a formal introduction. "Philip, this is Ruth. She is a great psychic and is going to be a powerful healer. I thought it would be nice if she joined us for dinner. I knew you'd like to meet her."

I was a little upset. Here I had been back in the country for just a few hours, and I needed to meet a new friend of my father's? What I really wanted was some private time to catch up with him. I guess my stories about life at the equator would just have to wait.

"Oh, hi, Ruth." That was about all the enthusiasm I could muster.

Somehow my father was not sharing my incisive observations about Ruth and instead was smiling; his face was slightly flushed.

Whatever he was thinking, he was clearly ignoring the lack of reality sitting next to him. Everyone in the car, except me, assumed that I already knew this was my father's new girlfriend. The long drive down Biscayne Boulevard had been a prearranged get-to-know-you kind of thing. It was not working.

We eventually pulled up to Fox's, a lounge/liquor store that had been around since the 1940s. It was known for its martinis and prime ribs even though Miami was turning into a *mojito* and *picadillo* type of town. Fox's was now an anachronism that had not yet acquired the patina of charm or irony. The entrance was from the alleyway, giving the whole place a speakeasy kind of feel. Empty liquor boxes that probably had been gathering for weeks surrounded the door. Painted on the side of the olive green building was a big, slightly naughty fox with its tongue hanging out of its mouth, leering at incoming patrons.

In keeping with its lounge heritage, Fox's was dark inside and smelled of old beer and stale cigarettes. Ruth lit up again, adding to the sour smell. She quickly ordered a baked potato with a salad and, exhaling a lungful of smoke, informed me that she was a vegetarian. She patiently explained to me that she did not eat any red meat, any flesh, or anything that had had consciousness. I smiled and nodded.

I felt like saying, "I know what a fucking vegetarian is, you asshole. I've been one practically my entire life." Something told me that she became a vegetarian about five minutes after meeting my father. Usually when I ate out with my father, we dined at one of the few health restaurants in Miami, ordering brown rice and steamed vegetables. Now, with Ruth in the picture, we are having dinner at a lounge? Certainly an odd choice.

"I'll have the prime rib, extra rare," I said, knowing that I was being extremely obnoxious. My father shot me a look. Actually, I was hurting myself more than Ruth. I had not eaten meat in many, many years. I knew that the meal was going to make me feel slightly ill. My father was already calculating how many high colonics I would need to remove the decaying flesh from my colon. Ruth flashed her big fake smile at me again, as if to say, "I know what you're doing, and I'm going to be the winner of this game." Pop ordered scrambled eggs and a salad.

Like a bad Hollywood movie, Pop asked Ruth, "How was your day?" He placed his hand on top of her nonsmoking hand in a sign of affection. She recounted details from her day as a reservation clerk for Eastern Airlines.

Ruth exhaled another cloud of smoke that I pretended made me cough. I gave her my best judgmental look that said, "How can you, the fairy princess of Eastern Airlines, smoke in front of my distinguished father?" She smiled what I can only imagine was her perfected would-you-like-a-window-or-aisle-seat? smile. Holding it for the Kodak moment that she was living in her mind, she ratcheted her head toward my father, keeping her eyes locked on mine. She turned to me for her opening play and said, "You know, you're lowering your vibrations by eating the dead carcass of that cow."

"Yeah, I know, but my father taught me how to neutralize the toxins, send them to the sun for purification, and then return my vibrations to the divine and healing level. So, in the long run, it really doesn't matter what I eat, as I can still maintain my spiritual purity without being debased by the gross matter that I put in my body." I surprised myself with how much of my father's thought processes I had really absorbed.

Pop had now perfected the ability to change his reality just by thought. I remember that after my parents divorced, Pop decided he no longer needed fancy clothes, and his custom-made suits and Nehru jackets gave way to off-the-rack polyester wash-and-wear. To me this was an ominous sign of spiritual bad taste as well as our dramatically altered economic conditions. As Pop's spirituality increased, his interest in the finer things offered by the material plane decreased. Personally, I stuck with pure cotton, which was more difficult to find, as polyester had become the miracle fiber of the moment. Pop repeatedly told me that "polyester is poison and puts carcinogenic chemicals in your blood. The skin can't breathe when you wear that stuff. This is why there is so much cancer around."

Polyester? When I reminded him of the carcinogenic properties of polyester, he explained his change of fabrics this way: "I'm
able to psychically neutralize the negative effects of polyester and
make the body believe that I'm wearing cotton." Thanks to his elite
spiritual connections, he could enjoy the benefits of wash-and-wear
without any of its potential dangers. While this appeared to be just
a bit frivolous or completely psychotic, it was really an indicator that
my father had moved into a realm where he believed that he could
control every aspect of life on a molecular level. With his psychic
powers, he could reprogram his body to repel the negative effects of
the petroleum-based polyester and wear it with impunity. This was
no different from the way he approached changing the body's energy
systems in order to repel and dissolve metastasized tumors. Eventually he would be able to apply this ability to channel thought and
alter physical reality on a much larger scale. In the meantime, I was
hoping that I could make my body believe that this thirty-two-ounce
prime rib was nothing more than a head of lettuce.

At the time, I rarely practiced what my father had taught me
about marshaling my mental powers. If I did, maybe I wouldn't
have had so many problems. According to my father, by creating
the proper thought-form and surrounding our body with this invisible shield, we could theoretically repel everything from radiation
to speeding bullets and life-threatening insidious germs. With the
correct mental attitude, you could smoke a carton of cigarettes a day
with no repercussions as long as you surrounded your lungs with
the white light of protection and sent any carcinogens to the sun for
purification. While I had been well schooled in the art of repelling
toxic substances from my body, what I was really signaling to Ruth
was, "Don't fuck with me or my father, you low-vibration fraud."

Just then the lights blinked three times. We all noticed. Ruth
perked up and announced loudly, "Ohhhhh, Arthur's here!"

I was stunned. How did she know about Arthur? Obviously my
father had been sharing more than a baked potato with Ruth. Now
she was privy to our top-secret relationship with Arthur. No one

except my father was supposed to have access to Arthur. All of a sudden, this interloper with the blue stockings was talking to Arthur? A line had been crossed. This was treason. I felt angry and betrayed. Arthur had practically raised me, and now here he was showing up while Ruth was around. Arthur should have known better than to be talking to this horrible woman. If Arthur had a message for Ruth, I was going to get up and leave. If necessary, I'd walk home. Ruth flashed me a giggly smile that said, "Isn't this fun? A message from Arthur, wheeee!"

Pop reached for a pen and began writing on his napkin. "The white beads were sent to you for a healing purpose. They are not a mistake. In the next several days, we will instruct you on how to properly energize them with healing energies. Give them away to people. They will continue to emit healing energies that those with disease will find helpful." I was relieved that Arthur's message had nothing to do with Ruth. If it had, I would have personally crossed over to the next dimension and strangled him. I thought to myself, "Nice work, Arthur." This was a message that I could discuss with my father, since I was the one unpacking the beads. Thank goodness Arthur kept it general and didn't reveal anything personal in front of Ruth.

Pop leaned back in his chair and, with a smile, said, "Well, that's a surprise. Here I thought that I had made a huge mistake in buying those beads, and all along it was the work of spirit. I should have known better." He was clearly relieved that he now had a reason for having bought several tons of white glass beads from Japan.

Just as Arthur had stated, my father soon began to psychically energize the beads with healing power. For years he gave them to his patients to hold and absorb the energy whenever needed. I still keep mine next to my bed. It was not unusual to walk into one of my father's lectures and see everyone wearing the same strand of white glass beads.

"Oh, Lew, that's wonderful. See, you need to have more confidence in yourself. Doubt is a negative emotion. You need to be positive at all times. We're going to have to work on that." Boy, was she digging in fast. Ruth loved the fact that Arthur had shown up while she was present. Apparently my father was now willing to have someone share his friendship with the spirits. For the rest of the meal, Ruth was like a little bird, chirping "Oh, Arthur this and Arthur that."

Ever since I'd known Arthur, I was told to keep my mouth shut because the outside world could not know that my father was talking to invisible people. Now Ruth was blabbing to the entire world about Arthur while having a baked potato at Fox's. I was having enough trouble digesting the slab of meat on my plate without having to watch her performance. I kept thinking, "Where did he find this one?"

After dinner we drove Ruth home. She lived a few blocks south of her office, in a 1950s apartment building huddled next to the bridge on the Miami River. There was a constant nerve-grating buzz as cars crossed the iron grate drawbridge. It was a place inhabited largely by forgotten souls who, for whatever reason, never managed to do better in life. While my father escorted Ruth to her apartment, I sat in the car and read the psychic predictions page by Jeane Dixon in the *National Enquirer*.

On the way home, Pop told me that he had met Ruth at one of his lectures just a few weeks ago. She had been having severe back problems and asked my father for a healing through laying on of hands. In front of a room full of witnesses, she got the full treatment and was instantly healed. From then on, they were an item. Shortly after this first meeting, Ruth somehow convinced my father that she had divine powers and they should work as a tag team. Soon ads began to appear in the *Miami Herald* for lectures on healing by Lew Smith and Ruth at the Theosophical Society, and the psychic fair at the Holiday Inn on South Dixie Highway. Ruth spoke of the importance of love and forgiveness, while my father performed actual healings.

After our initial get-together at Fox's, my father began to see Ruth every day. He would bring her back to his guesthouse, often in full view of my mother as she was picking up the mail. If my parents had business to transact, it was done on the front lawn while Ruth sat in the car, glaring at my mother. In my opinion, my father was guilty of conduct unbecoming. There was something so unspiritual about the unfinished business of their marriage. Wisdom and enlightenment did not prevail.

After about two months of serious spiritual dating, my father told me that Ruth had just confided in him that she was about to undergo a very dangerous and potentially life-threatening operation. Personally, I was not concerned. If the surgeon's knife accidentally slipped and severed an artery or two, what was the harm? Ruth pleaded with my father that she would need his full cooperation to ensure a successful outcome. Based on this request, my father assumed that he and his psychic deputies would be on call twenty-four hours a day during the ordeal. However, what Ruth really meant was that she would need the full cooperation of his checkbook as she walked out of her job to prepare for the surgery.

What I did not know was that this was not the kind of operation that insurance would cover. In fact, this was not an operation that would be performed in a hospital by licensed surgeons. According to Ruth, she had been chosen by the enlightened masters to have her brain psychically rewired so she would be able to receive cosmic consciousness. With the operation, Ruth would have the deluxe-psychic-ability-upgrade module inserted into her brain. In addition to being able to see the past and the future and heal the sick, Ruth would also have clairaudience and clairvoyance. Messages from the spirits indicated that she would have "implanted speech" and would travel to different astral planes to give lectures and gather information. Ruth was about to become an all-knowing, all-seeing, nondancing goddess. This delicate operation was scheduled to take place immediately and would last a full two weeks. Ruth was instructed by the spirits not to eat any solid food while undergoing the surgery, as the digestion process would interfere with the rewiring of her circuits. Everything she needed in terms of nutrient support, antibacterial agents, and healing factors would be provided by the spirits in order to get her through this operation. The masters told her she would be able to survive off magnetic energy particles in the air, known in esoteric yoga as prana.

According to the classic texts of yoga, these invisible particles sustain our bodies more than our physical food and water. Some schools of yoga also believe that we are born blank, without a personality, and as a baby inhales his or her first gulp of air, she also inhales her complete personality, contained in these prana particles.

Needless to say, my father was very concerned about Ruth's well-being and directed his full attention to making sure that she survived her elective surgery. Toward the end of the first week, my father called Ruth and let her know that we would be stopping by to assess her condition. As we made our way up the stairs of the catwalk apartment building, Pop and I were talking about where we were going to go for dinner afterward. I voted for Cuban food on Eighth Street. As we approached the apartment door, I heard through the open windows Ruth softly moaning, "Oh please, stop. Stop, it hurts. Yes, yes, I am receiving the knowledge. I see the light. Ahhhhhhh . . ." When we knocked, Ruth told us to come in, that the door was open. We couldn't see anything or anybody other than Ruth lying under a white sheet with her eyes closed, looking very ungoddesslike. Pop touched her hand, and Ruth slowly opened her eyes. "Oh, Lew, thank you for coming. I'm in so much pain. But I know this is something I have to do, no matter what it takes."

My father smiled and gave her hand a squeeze. "Everything will be fine. I'm watching over you and have my spirit guides monitoring the surgery."

"Oh, thank you. Where would I be without you?" I thought I needed to give the two brave psychic soldiers some privacy and left to wait in the car. On the way out, I noticed that her kitchen garbage can was overflowing with empty boxes of cookies and bags of Doritos. This didn't look like the garbage of an enlightened spiritual being.

I felt terribly guilty about disliking Ruth so intensely. After all, my father had often presented me with ideas and events that I thought were crazy and disapproved of, but later I came to accept and respect them. Perhaps I just needed to be more tolerant and open to something new. The important thing I had to remember was that my father was happy in this relationship, and that's what mattered. He really enjoyed having a partner to share his ideas and work with. That Ruth was more than thirty years his junior made him feel young and energized. A lot of women hung around my father, and I would have preferred that he had chosen any one of them over Ruth. But perhaps it was my karmic issue to come to accept Ruth and share my father's happiness. I knew that I was being overly judgmental, which according to my father was a major sin and prevented me from seeing the world in an objective manner.

About fifteen minutes later, my father came downstairs and got into the car. It was still light out. He was shaking his head in disbelief and grinning from ear to ear. "Isn't spirit amazing? For over a week now, Ruth has been living off only the prana in the air, with no solid food. Spirit forbade her to eat, as it would interfere with the surgery, and now she is suddenly gaining weight." He laughed. "Did you ever hear of anything like this? Ruth must have gained at least ten pounds since she started the operation, just from breathing. It's really amazing. That prana must contain some powerful nutrients. She is so advanced that she can just live off the air like that."

"Wow. That's really amazing. I hadn't noticed that she had gained so much weight." Prana indeed. I hadn't realized that prana could be purchased in boxes and bags at the 7-Eleven. It made me wonder if I was missing something or if something else was at work that I couldn't understand. I knew better than to burst his bubble. My father wanted to believe what he was telling me and himself. If dumb-old-humanoid me could see Ruth in all her fraudulent glory, why couldn't he? Pop had clearly turned off his psychic fraud-o-meter so that it wouldn't ring every two minutes and disturb his sleep. He was acting like a pathetic mortal, powerless in the face of love and completely willing to ignore the warning signs that were in full view lit up in neon.

During the long days that followed while Ruth underwent her transformation, my father would receive messages from his spirit guides indicating the progress of the operation. Chander Sen checked in with "We are working on the testings to see that everything is perfect. We are sorry that there is pain associated with the tests. This is due to the openings of new memory implantations, and the pain will soon be over. Lew, we will begin our work with you when we are through with Ruth. There will also be changes in your memory bank. We promise to complete with you as soon as possible, as your work will be minimal. You will both be happy with the results and gratified with your help toward others. Meanwhile be gentle toward each other. This is truly a rough period."

Days turned into weeks as the couple waited for the procedure to be completed. Ruth stayed in bed constantly as the work progressed. In another message, Arthur explained, "You are being kept inactive so that there will be no difficulty with the completion of the work on your head. The time is drawing close now, and there should be no hindrance to the final outcome."

A week later Arthur communicated again with yet another explanation of the delay: "Your head was not quite ready last night, hence the last-minute delay. I thought all was in readiness, but I was wrong—my apologies. I hope it won't be long now." As I read this, I wondered how Arthur could have been wrong. I didn't think that there was any such concept as "wrong" on the other side. Later that night Chander Sen reiterated what Arthur said: "We are very sorry. This is something new to us, and we can't be certain as to time. We are still testing, and we want to be absolutely certain that nothing can go wrong." Now this technique is *new* to them? Something was not right in spirit land. In all the messages that I had read, spirits always seemed to be living in a perfect world where everything manifests through thought, and they are able to travel light-years in a blink of an eye. So why all this uncertainty?

Ruth's condition took a turn for the worse. She was becoming irritable and depressed. My father seemed unable to help her. Chander Sen explained, "Ruth's depression is due to our working on that emotion at the present time. Whatever is happening to her will have no ill effects on her mind; all this is part of our testing. We are very concerned with what is happening to her, and in no way will we drop her.

She should ease her thoughts on that score. Her dislike of you at this time is due to her inability to get out and do things, and your activity seems to upset her. Both of you may relax and know that all is going according to schedule."

A few days later, there was an unusual Q&A message at 3:03 a.m. from Chander Sen in which my father became very confrontational with the Tibetan monk. The transcript reads:

> LS: Why was this promise not kept? Was Ruth ready?
> CS: Yes, but we were not.
> LS: Then why promise?
> CS: We thought we could fulfill it. We were hopeful that the time was right, but we were wrong.
> LS: Why all these head pains if it was not going to be finished to-night? How can another promise be acceptable after all this?
> CS: I cannot give you an answer to this.

Like Arthur, Chander Sen always had all the answers. This was indeed a strange communication from spirit.

Finally a message was received from Arthur that indicated the process was complete. "Ruth received awareness this morning at one o'clock. She can start her lecturing at any time now. The words will come. All her head work has been completed. We are very proud of her, and we will be with her when and as she needs us."

Apparently the procedure was an outstanding success. Ruth was now supposedly having visions, seeing into the body with X-ray vision, and reading auras. She never made it back to work at Eastern Airlines—there were more important issues in life than making reservations to Nassau. After the operation Pop spent more of his days away from the office, consulting with Ruth on psychic matters. They planned how to heal the planet of anger, disease, war, and hatred. Ruth continued to show up on my father's arm at every function, glowing and readily dispensing sage advice. She had adapted quickly to her new goddess position.

Several weeks after the operation, the goddess began to have a little problem. Perhaps one of her newly rewired circuits had not healed completely. I read about this incident in one of Arthur's messages to my father afterward. Ruth was experiencing the unsaintly desire to throw and break things, not unlike a two-year-old. Ruth's carefully crafted peace-and-love veneer was cracking around the edges. Her nirvana shtick was giving way to a burn-in-hell bitch routine. Without any warning, Ruth exhibited an uncontrollable rage that had the velocity of a Category 5 hurricane. She was cursing, screaming, throwing things, overturning chairs, and beating on my father with her fists. *The Three Faces of Eve* was being remade into *The Two Faces of Ruth*.

Seeking help and an explanation, Pop pulled out his pendulum and discovered that the cause of this erratic behavior was possession by some dark force. Using his diagnosis chart, he attempted to raise her vibrations so she could dispel this possessing entity. It wasn't working. Every time he pulled her vibrations up to the divine level, she slipped right back into the lower depths of darkness. No two ways about it: Ruth was deeply possessed by a powerful entity that was unwilling to let go. Usually my father could dispel an entity within a minute or two. But not this one. This dark force was prepared to give my father a run for his money.

Even though I was not the official psychic in the family, I would have bet that this was not the first time that Ruth had been controlled by dark forces. I never felt comfortable with her, and I would not have been surprised to learn that she was either psychotic or possessed by multiple dispossessed entities. Most likely, I believed, Ruth had used what little intelligence she had to aggressively conceal her true mental condition. With great foresight and planning, she waited until she had settled herself nicely into my father's bank account to reveal who she truly was. I would have bet even more money that the possessing entity had never left; it was just taking a little nap while Ruth worked her way into my father's life. For whatever reason, my father had never really done a proper scan on Ruth. Something was always in the way of him really seeing the true Ruth, unlike his ability to instantly see through anyone else. Instead he let his emotions override his brilliant psychic ability and allow this witch to become a part of his life. Or perhaps he had scanned her and decided, "What the hell, I'm lonely, she's not bad-looking, what's the harm?" Whatever the reason, this was the first time in decades he'd acted perfectly human.

In most cases of possession, simply raising Ruth's vibrations to a higher level would have made her body an inhospitable environment for the possessing entity, in the same way that heat kills germs. Dark souls cannot operate in a high-vibration environment. They are repelled by the intense energy of a person vibrating in the 500,000-to-800,000 range.

Since the vibrational approach wasn't working, Pop tried talking directly to the entity. Sometimes this was effective. Pop would reason with the possessing spirit, suggesting that it would be happier being released from the host's physical body. He would explain that it was dead and needed to move on to the next plane; it would never evolve if it remained in this parasitic relationship with a living body. Usually, after this little heart-to-heart, the entity would skulk off, and the possessed person would suddenly recover and reclaim his or her original personality. As horrible as these dark forces were, they were generally cowards at heart. They just didn't want to accept the fact that they were dead and, as a result, acted out like spoiled children, causing all kinds of problems.

Pop opened his attempted dialogue with Ruth's possessor: "We come in peace. I can help you transition to the next level. Let me guide you through this." There was no response, but at least Ruth was taking a breather from turning over tables and breaking glasses. She was lying on the floor and making noises as if she were trying to speak but someone had a hand over her mouth.

Since the dark spirit would not communicate, Pop decided to tap into the entity's identity and learn what he could about this invader. He began to silently ask questions while watching his pendulum for its response. After a couple of minutes, he turned to Ruth and speaking directly to the entity said, "I know who you are. You're Michael

Trainer, born 1823. You died in a fight in a bar. You were shot. Ruth can no longer host you. This is not the place for you. You will be happier on the other side. It is only there that you will be able to realize the full lessons of your untimely death. I am asking you in the name of the Holy Spirit and the Star of David's healing light to please leave. May God bless you."

As soon as he said these words, Pop attempted again to raise Ruth's vibrations. He figured he had an open door. Using his plastic ruler as a scale, he began rubbing the fingers of his right hand in a circular motion on the tabletop. Pop had psychically adjusted the scale on his ruler so that every inch was equal to another 100,000 increase in vibrations. His goal was to reach eight inches, which would bring Ruth's vibrations up to 800,000—the cosmic level. No matter how hard he tried, he could not get beyond the four-inch mark; his hand would stop, as if it were pushing against an unyielding force. This Michael Trainer was a powerful bundle of negative energy. Clearly, Michael did not want Ruth's vibrations raised to a higher level, since that would dislodge him from her body. Pop kept trying to push his hand up the ruler. After several minutes of struggling, his hand finally reached the eight-inch mark; he had broken through. When Pop looked up from the desk, Ruth was suddenly reanimated. Her classic may-I-help-you? smile had returned.

"Hi." Ruth seemed to have no memory of her recent behavior.

"Michael's gone."

"Huh?"

"Michael Trainer."

"Who? Lew, what are you talking about?"

"Michael Trainer. The man who was possessing you."

"What man?"

"Ruth, you have been throwing things and upsetting the furniture for the last two hours. You were possessed."

"Possessed? Me?" She laughed. "That's ridiculous."

"Just look around the room. Who turned over all the furniture? It certainly wasn't me."

"Me, of all people, possessed? By whom?"

"I told you: Michael Trainer."

"But, Lew, I can't be possessed. My vibrations are at the divine level. No entity can get through that. I'm completely protected."

"There must have been a break in your aura. Or sometimes these negative entities come in while you are asleep and are out of your physical body, traveling in the astral body." My father neglected to mention that those with severe mental illness were highly vulnerable to possessing spirits.

"Actually, I'm sure it was your aura that was affected. Remember, you were speaking with Rosemary on the phone, and afterward you complained that you had a headache from her negativity. I think this is the cause of the possession, or at least the initial event that led to you being possessed. Rosemary's low vibration created a weak spot in your aura, and once your guard was down, this Michael Trainer found his way in. You can't be too careful; you should always be testing your vibrations to see what's going on. In any event, he's gone, and I have your vibrations back at the level where they should be."

"Oh, thank you, Lew. I'm so glad you were around to fix this."

As if on cue, the lights blinked. Arthur had been observing this conversation and provided his explanatory comments, which my father wrote down. "Ruth's traumatic experience was one of possession. It was fortunate that you recalled the phone call from her friend. This is the first instance that I became aware of a 'thought-form poltergeist.' You were wise in picking it up. We must be wary of all the negativity that abounds, even from friends on the phone. This is the importance of keeping the white light around us and maintaining an attitude of positive thought and vibrations. We cannot tamper with free will, and it was Ruth's free will and conscious mind that unknowingly accepted the thought-form. Fortunately she had you to seek out the disturbance in her mind of the desire to throw and break things. Your knowledge that you have stored up came to the fore, and you were able to give release and relief. We must teach this knowledge in order to combat the negative attitudes and vibrations around us. This planet can be such a serene and loving abode with all people on a love level. You can do much to bring this about. Your friend with love, AF."

During this time, Arthur continued to dictate messages, the majority of which encouraged my father to marry Ruth. With advancing age, Pop became both spiritually stronger and emotionally more vulnerable. Being the Wizard of Oz was lonely; he wanted someone to share his secrets with, someone to share the stage with. I think he longed to feel human again. He wanted a partner in life, and no one had stepped up and made herself available except for Ruth. And if the spirits had given their psychic seal of approval, who was I to argue with them? Maybe Arthur figured that my father was better off with a fake than alone.

A short time later, the spirits announced that the time had finally arrived—there would be a holy marriage of these two exalted souls whose aim was to heal the planet of human misery. It was all arranged. The stars were in alignment; it would be on an auspicious day that would ensure great happiness for the two divinities.

To get the happy couple off on the right foot, Arthur offered to do the house hunting from above. That would be his wedding present: to find the perfect house where they could fulfill their ministry and heal the world. In one of his messages, Arthur gave my father the name and phone number of a real estate agent named Bob Dwyer, who, according to this message, had the perfect home just waiting for them.

As instructed, Pop called the real estate agent and described his dream house. It should be open to the tropical breezes, quiet, and surrounded by lush foliage. Like any true salesman, Mr. Dwyer immediately said, "I have just the house for you." In this case, he did. The house was located off South Dixie Highway near the Miami Serpentarium, a tourist attraction where they milked cobras for their venom used to treat arthritis. My father and his love had found their new home. The contract was signed that day.

Everything was going according to plan; the only thing left was the wedding ceremony. While planning the event to be held at a local church with a sympathetic minister, my father found out unexpectedly that he and Ruth had already been married. According to a message from Arthur, Ruth and my father had met and married in the late 1800s when she was working at a newspaper in the Midwest.

The marriage in this lifetime was held at a small church in the pines with Reverend Ted Tiemeyer, author of the book *Jesus Christ Super Psychic,* presiding. Ladies dressed in blue gaped in disbelief that Lew Smith was getting married. After the ceremony, the witnesses—believers, assorted clairvoyants, and UFO abductees—shared stories of remarkable healings performed by my father. Ruth smoked and ate cake. I wished the happy couple well as they prepared for their honeymoon: a trip to the legendary Findhorn Garden in Scotland, where forty-pound cabbages grew to the size of houses, and tomatoes were the size of cars. These extraordinary vegetables occurred because the garden was tended by fairies and the wee people who reportedly sprinkled their fairy dust in the garden, and *poof!*—ten-foot cucumbers.

When they returned a couple weeks later, my father was silent about his trip to fairyland. His only response was, "It was cold." When my father was troubled, he grew quiet and measured his words. Something was wrong, and I don't think it was disappointment with the size of the vegetables.

About a week after they returned from giant love land, I dropped by the new house to see how they were settling in. The front door was unlocked. The entranceway to the house was a large screened-in patio with a pool. The living quarters were off to the right and the garage was to the left. I walked in and found my father in the garage. He was leaning over the washing machine, adding soap powder to a load of laundry. I had never seen my father operate a washing machine. I was surprised he even knew how.

Hanging from the ceiling over the machine was a strange molecular-looking structure about two feet in diameter that seemed to be modeled out of blue plastic sticks sprinkled with glitter. On one hand, it looked like a high school science project that never made it to the Westinghouse finals; on the other, it appeared to have intricate connections and strange atomic configurations that I had never seen before. You could sense that it was unlike any existing earthly molecule. As I approached the garage, the molecule was spinning slowly in the morning breeze.

"Hi. What's that?" I asked, pointing to the giant blue molecule.

"Oh, that. That's a force-field emanator. It emanates a force field of energy around the washing machine and repels all negative energy."

"Does that, like, help with the laundry and get the clothes cleaner?"

Pop laughed. "No, it raises the vibration of the room and keeps out dark forces."

"Sort of like one of those electric mosquito catchers people use on the patio."

My father thought for a minute and responded, "I guess you could think of it that way."

"But why in the laundry room? Why not in the house somewhere?"

"We need it here because Ruth was viciously attacked by a negative entity while she was doing the laundry. So I built this thought-form to protect us from this dangerous entity. I don't want her near the washing machine, just in case it happens again."

"So how was Ruth attacked?"

According to my father, they had just spent their first night in the house. The bed had not yet arrived; they slept on a mattress on the floor. The next morning, Ruth went into the garage to do the laundry. Suddenly, he heard Ruth screaming, "Get away! Get away from me! Help! Somebody help me! Please!"

He ran to the garage to see what was wrong. Ruth was thrashing about on the floor, yelling, "Help! Help! Stop! Aaaaahhhhh, I can't breathe, you're choking me!"

"Ruth, Ruth, what's wrong?" My father looked at Ruth writhing and then looked around the garage. There was no one there but her.

"It must be a negative entity. I'll be right back." My father went into his study, grabbed his crucifix, and ran back to the garage. He reached out to touch Ruth, but she kicked him away. Then Ruth beat him with her fists as she struggled to fight off this invisible attacker. Finally extricating himself from her blows, Pop waved the cross over Ruth and started talking to the entity. "You must leave here. This is no place for you. You must go toward the light. Ruth, Ruth, hold on, I'm going to raise your vibrations. Stay with me, it is almost over." Pop said his exorcism prayer: "I raise your vibrations to the divine and healing level and free you from any and all negative energies that inhabit your body. I send them back to the proper plane to free them from attachment."

Within moments Ruth's shrieking quickly died down. It was as if all the air had suddenly been let out of a balloon. She was out of breath. Panting like a dog in the noonday heat, she said, "Oh, Lew, thank you! It was horrible! It was inside of me. I felt as if I were being strangled; I couldn't breathe. I think it wanted to kill me. I've never been so scared in all my life. What did it want? I was just putting the clothes in the washing machine, and this cold darkness came over me. I can't quite explain it. It felt like there were a hundred snakes slithering all over me, choking me. I've never felt anything like this before. Oh my God, it was so . . ." With that, she began to sob uncontrollably.

My father comforted her and helped her up. They walked back to their pink bedroom, and she got into bed. "You should rest now," he said. "You'll be fine. I need to go speak with Chander Sen and find out what's going on. Some negative thought-form must have found a new way to feed off your energy. I'll need to purify the house and build an energy field so this does not happen again."

In his study, Pop picked up his pendulum to diagnose the incident. Moving the pendulum over his finder chart, his intuition was confirmed: a dark entity had attempted to possess Ruth. He closed his eyes and said another exorcism prayer for his wife. At that moment, he felt Chander Sen attempting to contact him. He took out his pen and wrote the following: "The thought-form that inhabited your garage was created in negativity. It was brought in on a vibration of jealousy to harm the female who lived in this house. Since it cannot reason, any female who gets within its vibrational range will receive its negative rays. A negative thought-form alone will not dissipate except through prayer or exorcism. It has now been released and will no longer cause any harm. The energy of a thought-form should be sent to water for purification and to be used for the highest good."

As I listened to my father tell me about this attack, I had no doubt that Ruth had been overcome by a negative entity. I had seen this type of possession many times and knew it was dangerous and very real. However, I thought to myself, "Ruth's always recovering from something: psychic surgery, thought-form attacks. Her vibrations should be high enough so that these things don't happen to her. This stuff doesn't happen to my father because he is a spiritual being, but with Ruth . . ."

In an effort to really understand what was going on, I asked, "So Ruth's not going to be doing the laundry anymore? Shouldn't that emanator thing protect her?" I didn't like the idea of Ruth sitting back and letting my father do everything for her. After all, Pop was in his early seventies, and Ruth was still a young chickee in her mid-thirties. She could certainly help out a little around the house.

"We'll see. I'm sure everything will be fine and this won't happen again, but right now she's still traumatized and needs some time to recover."

"So what are we going to do for lunch?" I asked.

"Let me see what Ruth wants to do."

I knew that Ruth would just continue to lie in bed. There was nothing in it for her to join us for lunch. The most Ruth had done to reach out to me in the last year was to spontaneously give me a small canned ham that she didn't want to eat in front of my father. Me? Canned ham? What was this woman thinking? Why did this staunch vegetarian who had just received cosmic consciousness happen to have a canned ham lying around? Did she find it in the street? What was the lovely thought behind this overwhelmingly generous gesture by Ruth? None that I could think of. My father and I ended up going out to lunch by ourselves.

Ruth worked hard at trying to isolate me from my father. When I was in town during holidays, she would either not be available when my father wanted the three of us to get together or make such demands on my father that he had no time to see me.

My mother was insistent that I return to school even though I felt it was a waste of time. I promised her that I could at least get a degree and then move to New York to pursue painting.

Once I returned to school, my father and I would talk maybe once every three months on the phone. I wrote frequent letters and received occasional replies. Our conversations and correspondence concerned mostly art or which of the many metaphysical books on color healing, magic, kundalini, or orgone theory I had read. Our connection remained our ongoing discussions of the supernatural. Possibly our emotional distance was due not only to the physical distance but also to the natural process of me growing up and being on my own. Or maybe Ruth monopolized all of my father's emotions, and there was nothing left for me. On the surface, we were no longer so intimately involved in each other's lives. I later learned that Pop's distance was probably due to the difficulties he was experiencing with Ruth.

According to written psychic messages from my father's various spirit guides, things were not going well for the couple. There were frequent disagreements, which were compounded by Ruth's manipulative and erratic behavior. What was extremely odd about these particular messages were the repeated scoldings that my father would receive from the spirits. Yet they always excused Ruth's violent outbursts as a normal reaction to my father's uncaring coldness. Until Ruth appeared, the spirits had always been very gentle and protective of my father. If they chastised him, it was only for not working hard enough or seeing enough patients, but never for not being understanding. I came across these documents after my father's death. In reading them, I realized that something strange had occurred in his relationship with his longtime spirit guides. I couldn't quite understand it, but something had definitely changed.

The following message from Arthur was odd in both its tone and choice of words. It seemed curt and lacking in Arthur's usual literacy:

"Your upsetment is a very strong reaction, knowing as you do that Ruth is hardly responsible for her outburst. It is about time that you were able to realize it. Ruth could absolutely not be capable in her right mind of doing the things she does when negative forces suggest the action. Please stop and think before you get angry, so that both of you don't get upset. It won't be much longer now when everything will be smoothed over. Hold on till then, and all will be well, and our problems will have been resolved."

Upsetment? When he was alive, Arthur Ford was an extraordinarily articulate and erudite gentleman. I doubt that death erased any of his verbal skills. Increasingly, messages from Arthur and Chander Sen took on an aggressive and condescending character that I had never seen before.

On another occasion, Arthur castigated my father once again: "Lew, you are being stubborn again. It does not take much to irritate Ruth, so why invite trouble? You are both honed to a sharp edge; just ease back and don't throw darts. Please believe me, I know what I am saying. Your friend, Arthur." As a result of these spirit messages, my father began to question himself and started searching for various ways to become softer, gentler, and more loving toward Ruth. However, whatever he did was never enough. There was always another unexpected outburst from her that was quickly followed by a stern reprimand from his spirit guides.

Without telling me, my father and the divine Miss Ruth quietly divorced. Also without telling me, he then remarried Ruth three months later. Then, eight months later, the happy couple divorced again. This time Ruth sailed into the sunset with a boat captain she met and a chunk of alimony payments from my father. The first time Ruth married my father was for money. The second time Ruth married my father was for more money. Most of the money that he had carefully saved to continue his healing work and research departed with Ruth to fund her next psychotic adventure.

Ruth was an anomaly, a black hole, a blip in the quantum theory of space-time continuum. For whatever reason, the spirits conjured up this witch and put her directly in my father's focus. I can only imagine that through Ruth he had experienced an entire life cycle of emotions—love, courtship, marriage, divorce, longing, marriage, divorce, and betrayal—in the space of less than twenty-four months. At this stage in my father's life, time was precious. This was his last chance to live the life of an average mortal. He had work to do and not long to do it. Now that this compressed roller-coaster ride was over, it was time to get down to the serious business of making miracles in a way that had never been done before and no one could have ever imagined.

Throughout my adult life, Ruth's relationship with my father remained one of those unsolved mysteries that happen to all of us. None of us can ever really know what generates or extinguishes that special spark between two people. We are all outsiders when it comes to other people's relationships. For me this was one of the only incidents in my father's life where I could not comprehend how both he and his spirit guides had allowed Ruth to enter his life and create the damage that she did. Once my initial dislike of her had subsided, I began to simply accept this aberration in my father as a curious flaw in an otherwise remarkable man.

After I finished the first draft of this book, I was reviewing some of my father's papers, and I came across a stack of pages ripped out of a steno notebook. They had been stuffed in the back of a spiral notebook and were held together by a rusted paper clip that included a small piece of paper marked "Imposters." I had no idea what this meant and began looking through the messages. Each page had a red line drawn through it as if it were to be deleted. These messages from the spirits detailed the psychic operation that Ruth had gone through, as well as messages about her depression and irrational behavior. Much of the material I was familiar with—the waiting, the pain, the promises of great psychic powers. As before, the messages seemed odd in their hostile tone as they provided questionable explanations for an array of puzzling events.

One message from Arthur was somewhat defensive, apparently in response to a question posed by my father. "Guardian angels are always sure of what will happen. Spirit doctors and guides are not. We have been working on Ruth all this time with a concept in mind that memory and knowledge can be implanted in the human entity and can be withdrawn at the will of that entity. This makes for an all-knowing human computer. What better means would there be for bringing the 'word of God' to all who will listen? This, my friend, is no hoax. Ruth has been subjected to that before, and you have a right to be wary, but she knows in her heart that she is being programmed for what she has been destined for. We are being supremely careful and cautious, for this has been our greatest undertaking to date. We too had to experiment and learn and develop skills and knowledge before we started with Ruth. Our beginning goes back many incarnations of the present Ruth with foreknowledge of what was to be. Her soul history or destiny has been as a leader. But leaders must be taught if they are to fulfill their missions. Chander Sen and Dr. Berman were the only ones who worked on Ruth. Be a bit more patient; we are almost through." I was disturbed by the word *hoax*. Why would Arthur even raise that issue? My father had no reason to ever mistrust Arthur. I also wondered why the spirits would need to experiment on a human when they had access to unlimited knowledge both past and present. This was the first time that any of my father's spirit guides had been stymied by limitation. These questions bothered me as much as his marriages to Ruth did.

Several pages later in this pile of documents, I finally found the explanation I had been looking for all these years. There was a message to my father that solved the mystery. It was unsigned; I'm not sure who it came from. "We have both been fooled—to be kept from helping others and developing ourselves. The messages have been false because I have been gullible. I took the messages as true simply because I did not question properly. I asked, 'Do you come through Christ?' This left the door open. Negative entities can say they come through Christ but not through Jesus. We both awoke in the morning with a vibration of fifty. We had been pulled down in the astral. Also, the dreams have been bad. Nothing of a spiritual nature. You have been tranquilized to keep you inactive. I doubt if spirit would do this unless absolutely necessary."

A few pages later, there was a clarifying message from Arthur titled "Regarding the Hoax." "There are groups of negative entities that, like the White Brotherhood, who work for good, band together to cause conflict and create confusion among those whose lights are bright. This is their method of preventing the spiritual minded from adding to their ranks. The traps are set for those who seek shortcuts. You must be wary of those by listening to your inner voice and learning how to discern the true from the false. These experiences are lessons that you must learn. The truth is within you. Your soul will guide you if you but listen to the voice within."

After this message the rest of the pages in the notebook are blank. Apparently, for my father, that was the end of the matter. He realized, without ever letting on, that Ruth was not just a fake but a bundle of negative, harmful energy that marshaled up dark forces whose goal was to interfere with his healing work and possibly destroy him. The dark buddies that she hung out with were somehow able to impersonate Arthur Ford and Chander Sen and get through to my father on their particular wavelength while blocking their genuine communications. Throughout the time that he spent with Ruth, he was repeatedly attacked, hindered in his healing, and exposed to false information. Yet he decided to stay with her, knowing her secret. He must have loved her in a way that I'll never understand.

fifteen

•

The Mad Scientist

The phone rang. I wiped the paint off my hands onto the front of my trousers and answered it.

"What are you thinking?"

I was taken aback that my father would even ask such a question. We both knew that he didn't need to ask, since he always knew what I was thinking, whether I liked it or not. We hadn't spoken in over a month.

"Nothing, really." I had been moody the last couple of days. Obviously my father picked up on this and decided to give me a call.

It was now 1980, and I had been living in New York for the past five years. After Bob the photographer tried to shoot me, I half-heartedly skipped from university to university in the Northeast. I honored my mother's wishes and completed my degree. Now I was on my own doing the work I loved.

That week I'd just had a studio visit from Richard Marshall, one of the curators at the Whitney Museum of American Art. The visit had gone well. Richard liked the work and said that he would like to reproduce one of my drawings in the *Paris Review,* which I knew would please my father. Eventually Richard would select my work to be included in the prestigious Whitney Biennial. Any artist would have been thrilled by such events, but I was currently in between gallery associations, and the lack of a home for my paintings gave me a constant sense of anxiety. Museums were happy to look at my work, but galleries were not quite sure what to do with my ten-foot drawings. As the dealer Holly Solomon said to me at the end of a studio visit, "We just can't afford to frame your work." Interestingly, after my father died, I found Holly's name on a small piece of paper in his files. It was a note about her mother, who lived on Collins Avenue in Miami Beach, needing a psychic healing from my father. I could not figure out how Holly came to contact my father, since I never discussed him with her or vice versa.

Having once had a gun pressed to my head caused me to want to live way below the radar. As a result, I dressed inconspicuously, had an unlisted phone number, and became even more invisible than when I lived in Miami and tried to disappear from being the son of a psychic.

My studio loft on the Bowery was housed in a condemned building with no heat. The building was owned and neglected by the city. Several artists had taken over the loft as a place to live and work. The windowpanes were broken. I had glued cardboard over the windows to keep out the wind. For warmth I hung from the ceiling large sheets of plastic that I bought on Canal Street; those "walls" would trap the small amount of heat emanating from my tiny electric space heater. The transparent plastic tarps allowed me to partition out a studio and a bedroom area. A makeshift kitchen had been installed. There were no walls separating the bathroom from the rest of the space. At night I ate dinner under an electric blanket.

Without even a hint from me as to what was going on, my father started right in as if we had discussed my current situation many,

many times. "Well, I wouldn't worry about your art. Just because some gallery hasn't said yes doesn't mean you can't paint. Keep painting and keep writing. Doing the work is what's important; you will be guided. If you want, the spirits can help you with inspiration for the painting. Meditate, and I will send them to you. Your paintings will be unlike anyone else's."

"Thanks, but I'll just do it on my own. Maybe I should have listened to mom and become a lawyer."

"I really don't think you had a choice. I knew very early on that this was your destiny. Remember when I went to the ashram with Dr. Mishra? Well, I had your chart done. I can't even remember how old you were at the time. In fact, I had your chart done by several astrologers who were there. They all said the same thing. Your destiny is in art. It is how your soul speaks."

In my paintings, I was attempting to map out a kind of dreamlike state of consciousness populated by a flood of pictographs not unlike the types of images one might receive during a séance. When I was a kid, my father would drag me to every psychic in town for a reading. They would take one look at me and start describing the images that were appearing before their eyes. In the trance state, most mediums get their information from flashes of mental symbolic pictures, which they interpret for the sitter. For example, a psychic might see a picture of a woman with lots of blue jewelry talking, and he would interpret that as a wealthy woman from the island of St. Bart's coming to give you a lot of money.

Each of the pictures in my image-dense work could operate on multiple levels of meaning and interpretation not unlike a tarot card reading. In some ways, I was trying to emulate aspects of my father's work—he could implant energy or thought-forms into objects or people. What I did was try to implant energy, multiple meanings, and codes into ordinary-looking images. Over time the images in my paintings began to reveal multiple scenarios for the viewer. As a kid, my fascination with archaeology and ancient Egypt seemed to have some impact on the formal construction of my paintings as well.

An astrologer that I saw every year on my birthday as a kind of spiritual tune-up told me that my work was an active form of meditation. He said that during the painting process I entered a metaphysical space. I don't think he was wrong. I usually slept most of the day and painted all night until the morning. My mind was quieter in the middle of the night, and I felt better able to access the more arcane aspects of my mind as I worked until morning. On rare occasions, if I took a break in the middle of the night, I would go around the corner to visit artist Bob Rauschenberg on Lafayette Street.

In the few years that I had been in New York, my work was exhibited at Artists Space, the Drawing Center, and occasionally an uptown gallery on Fifty-seventh Street. I was extremely fortunate in being included in a seminal 1977 exhibition of new artists titled "Pictures." The critic and art historian Douglas Crimp had uncovered a vein of artists who were all working with found media images and were producing a new kind of work that was the polar opposite of the reigning vogue of conceptualism and minimalism. This unique moment produced a new crop of artists that included Robert Longo, Sherrie Levine, Troy Brauntauch, Richard Prince, Cindy Sherman, and David Salle. The "Pictures" exhibition was well attended, widely discussed, and traveled to several museums and universities around the country.

Simultaneously, I was earning a bit of money by writing for magazines such as *ARTS, GQ,* and Andy Warhol's *Interview.* For some reason, writing came to me naturally, as it was not such a different process from the pictographic storytelling in my paintings. My published interviews included artists such as Keith Sonnier, Rauschenberg, Warhol, Jasper Johns, Roy Lichtenstein, Laurie Anderson, and David Byrne, as well as Run Run Shaw, the great producer of martial arts films in Hong Kong, and Morris Lapidus, the long-forgotten, audacious architect who would live to see his brilliant career reassessed by a new generation. Writing gave me an opportunity to have extraordinary conversations with people I might not otherwise have met.

Whenever I turned in an article for *Interview,* I would head up to Warhol's Factory to personally deliver my double-spaced interview that had been banged out on an old portable typewriter. While I'd be talking with Bob Colacello, *Interview*'s editor at the time, Andy would eventually drift over and speak with me in this open-ended, cryptic way that I understood perfectly given my background of listening to disembodied spirits deliver messages. Almost every other Saturday, when the Factory was quiet, Warhol would call me in my studio to chat and catch up. Often I was invited to Factory lunches with food brought in from Brownies health food restaurant, as Andy's tape recorder captured the roundtable conversation for the next issue of *Interview*. Years later, after editor Robert Hayes passed away, Andy would offer me his job. I couldn't paint and edit a magazine at the same time, so, regrettably, I declined the most fun job on the planet.

During my conversation with my father, he kept trying to put a positive spin on my bad mood. "The 'Pictures' exhibition you were in traveled all over the country. It is a very important show and will have a great influence on art for many years into the future. You should be very pleased. It got a lot of attention. People respond to your paintings in a profound way. While they are not for everyone, there is an energy and power in your paintings. If you meditate before you begin work, you can actually put healing energy into your paintings just like Zen monks before they begin their calligraphy. I always wanted you to work with me, but I think you do your best metaphysical work through your paintings. I know you're depressed. Do you want me to remove it? It'll take just a second."

"Naw, don't bother, it'll go away." I was in no mood to be tinkered with. "Besides, isn't depression good for creating? Aren't artists supposed to be tortured and depressed?"

My father laughed. "That is a really stupid idea. I hope you will quickly let go of that thought. Art should come from a serene, wise place that is not disturbed by negative ideas. You know, I've told you this before, you create your own reality through your thoughts. I've taught you so many exercises to improve your thinking so that you are always on an elevated level. You need to be at that high vibration, and only then will you make art that will speak to people over time."

Even though my father was 1,500 miles away, I was sure he could see me rolling my eyes in annoyance at what I thought was a pointless, patronizing lecture. I felt that he just didn't understand the creative process even though his entire life had been one large creative endeavor.

"You need to keep your thinking on the divine level," he continued. "Then true inspiration will come. All the hardships you are experiencing are your own creation."

Oh, man, I didn't need to hear this right now. Happy thoughts were not going to help me complete the painting I was working on. They certainly weren't going to get the Whitney Museum to consider my work for its permanent collection.

"Keep your thoughts pure and elevated. You know how to filter your thoughts. If not, all this negative thinking will only create a negative reality."

"Okay, okay, I got it." I was irritated by his sunshiny attitude when I was involved in the stark and dangerous *life-and-death* struggle of making a painting.

My father believed that every aspect of our reality was first created in our thoughts before it physically manifested. We were the directors of our own movies—not chance, not the guy across the street, not our boss. If you wanted to be covered in white mink, become president of Mali, or invent a flying car, you just needed to visualize it. He had always taught me that by aligning my thoughts with the magnetic properties of the universe, they would attract good or bad events, depending on the content of my thinking. The choice was mine. At the moment, I was being a passive, negative thinker and not in control of my mind.

"You sure?" he persisted. "I could run a quick scan and psychically send you some Bach Flower Remedies to correct your current imbalance." My father's intentions were good. He hated to see me suffer.

In addition to being able to heal the physical body, my father was able to heal and remove mental blocks, emotional traumas, insecurity, phobias, neuroses, and obsessions almost instantaneously. He could collapse ten years of psychiatric care into about three minutes. As his healing talents evolved, he would now begin every healing with diagnosing and treating the mental state, as he believed that all disease originated in the mind—be it the superconscious, conscious, or subconscious mind. Once the mind had been healed, the body would more readily follow.

This breakthrough in his technique came when he discovered the work of Dr. Edward Bach, an English surgeon from the 1930s who felt that there had to be a more intelligent way of treating illness than cutting and sawing our precious bodies. Bach, who eventually became one of my father's spirit guides and communicated with him on a regular basis, left his lucrative practice and followed his intuition into the fields to pick specific flowers that had mental healing properties.

When Dr. Bach held a particular flower in his hand, he would intuitively sense and then physically experience the very condition that the flower could cure. For example, certain flowers would make him feel anxious or fearful or depressed. When he experienced these mental states, he then knew that this flower could heal that emotion. Once he had discovered a specific remedy, Dr. Bach would then distill the flower's essence and use it medically. Based on his research, he developed the Bach Flower Remedies, a therapeutic system composed of thirty-seven remedies used to correct an almost unlimited range of mental disorders and imbalances. As Bach states in his book *Heal Thyself,* "Disease will never be cured . . . by present materialistic methods for the simple reason that disease in its origin is not material . . . Disease is in essence the result of conflict between the Soul and Mind and will never be eradicated except by spiritual and mental effort."

Over the years, Pop had created detailed charts of the entire range of human emotions and corresponding methods of balancing and correcting them. Not only did he believe that negative emotions were often the basis for most disease but he also needed to be able to check out if there was emotional resistance when one of his healings didn't take. Like many of his other healing methods, these techniques had come from Arthur, who told my father, "It's time you got busy and work on the charting of attitudes and emotions. You will need that information to determine what your patient is thinking and his attitude of acceptance regarding the healing you are giving him." With one of these charts and a minute or two with the pendulum, Pop was able to know every detail of a person's past, present, and future emotional makeup. By going down this chart with his pendulum, he was able to develop a detailed diagnosis of his patient's mental condition as well as determine the correct remedy.

Part of me wanted to let my father do his mind voodoo on me so that I would be rid of this painful depression. I had no doubt that he could release the blocks and negative mental attitudes that I was experiencing. But I felt that would be cheating. It would be like some father buying his kid into college even though the kid had a D average. I wanted do it on my own and experience life free of outside psychic interference.

My father did his best to make me feel better. "Look, the important thing is making work that's true to your soul. Don't worry about whether anyone likes it or not or if a gallery wants to represent you. Those galleries don't know anything. The artist always comes first. I know your work will eventually be in many museums, but that really doesn't matter. Use your art as a kind of meditation and as a way to advance your soul. Everything else will take care of itself."

He shifted the subject. "So, when are you coming to visit? I'm doing a lot of exciting new healings with different kinds of energy that spirit is teaching me. I'd love to share it with you. Just yesterday Arthur came in and told me, 'Remove fifty percent of a patient's energy, energize it, and shoot it back to him after rebuilding the vibrations to full potential. Request that the molecules, atoms, and crystals are energized to full potential before sending it back. Ask that the blood be revitalized.' You should see the results that I've already gotten with this method. I had a woman here today who was so lethargic, her head kept dropping down. Before I began the healing, I did what Arthur suggested, and she perked right up. She was a new person. It made the rest of her healing that much more effective. I'd really love you to see this in action. I also want to teach you to do it; it would be very helpful for you."

No doubt this would have been a handy trick for me to learn, especially when I would stay up all night working and did not leave the house for weeks on end. Interestingly, I later found out that the medical profession in Europe was doing a somewhat similar procedure known as plasmapheresis, where doctors would remove the "dirty" blood of an ill patient, filter it, and then put it back into the body. My father was rejuvenating the body in a similar fashion but on a subtle energetic level.

"I don't know, let me see how things go. It's awfully cold here, and I do miss Miami a lot. I don't think I was meant to live where there is snow."

"Or unheated buildings."

"How'd you know?"

My father just laughed at the stupidity of my question. "I'll leave you be. You'll get over this—it's just temporary—but I'm always here if you need me."

"Thanks, Pop, I know."

For someone who had been raised by a decorator, surrounded by the tropical color of hibiscus, bougainvillea, bird-of-paradise, and poinciana, I was making paintings that were basically black-and-white drawings. New York had drained all the color out of my work. As my art became increasingly minimalist in line and color, my father had begun to use color as another means to heal people. About ten years earlier, he had started placing small squares of colored plastic cellophane over a lightbulb in order to project colored light onto patients. He would use his pendulum to determine what color and how much exposure they required before he would bathe them in healing colored light. Eventually he gave up using actual lightbulbs and simply visualized the person surrounded by a particular colored light.

Physics tells us that each color has its own frequency or vibration.

For my father, each individual color was not unlike an individual vitamin. Someone might be deficient in vitamin D or E and require supplementation. By projecting these specific vibrations created by the colored light, my father could realign and normalize both mental and bodily functions. In the most simplistic of terms, red was energizing, blue was calming, green strengthened the immune system, and yellow could do everything from induce diarrhea to increase alertness. One could heal others or himself simply by visualizing the appropriate color targeted to the ailing organ.

Pop taught me to put large glass jugs of water in the sun to absorb the full energy spectrum. This was especially important to do during the winter. Water, he told me, should always be exposed to the sun to be energized. All of our water comes to us from dark underground pipes, and so it is devoid of the vital light energy that our bodies need. By capturing all the different invisible wavelengths contained in sunlight, this "color water," as he called it, could revitalize our bodies. After it had absorbed the sun's rays, Pop told me to sip it daily, like a fine brandy. He also insisted that I practice color breathing. If I was low in energy, I would close my eyes, inhale red, and visualize it infusing my entire system. I'd then pull another all-nighter.

Several weeks after this phone call, the New York winter got to me. I took up my father's offer and headed home. My first night back in Miami, Pop invited me to observe one of his new healing classes. As I sat in his living room, watching the class, the warm, balmy air felt good on my skin as it drifted through the living room.

"Who wants to dematerialize?"

My father held above his head a small one-inch blue cardboard square with some writing on it in white ink.

Scattered around the living room was a group of seven people looking nervously at the piece of cardboard. If they raised a hand, would they disappear into the ether, never to return? The room was still, with a heightened silence. No one was volunteering. They were waiting for the punch line that this was some kind of joke. My father's hand remained frozen in the air as he looked around the room for someone to sign up for the journey to another dimension. He was not smiling.

What these people did not realize was that my father wasn't kidding. He was willing to show anyone in that room the exit door from three-dimensional reality. Buckle your seat belt and have a nice flight. I had no doubt that anyone who placed the piece of cardboard on their forehead would have slowly faded to black and disappeared from the material realm. My concern was, would he be able to bring them back? He didn't mention anything about *re*materialization or a return ticket.

Personally, I'd had enough space travel in my lifetime and was perfectly content to remain earthbound for the time being. I declined when my father offered me a small blue square to place on my forehead.

This was one of his first classes on the projectors, a new healing technique that over the years he had developed in collaboration with his spirit guides. Chander Sen had been the head of the "project development team."

Pop told me that Chander Sen was able to split his consciousness into millions of individual entities, like drops of water in the ocean. It was in this way that Chander Sen was able to be in so many places at once.

There was something astonishingly elegant about the simplicity behind this broad-spectrum healing system that combined the look of a kindergarten arts and crafts project and the thinking behind quantum physics. I had never seen my father actually make one of these projectors—no one had. Usually Pop was very generous in sharing his healing methods. This time he was not. Now that he had finally perfected it, he guarded this methodology as if he had the formula for the atomic bomb. It was one of the many secrets that died with him. He believed that these projectors were too powerful and too effective to risk misuse by ill-intentioned people. Their energy seemed to be unlimited.

Chander Sen warned him to carefully guard the secret process of creating the projectors: "The projectors' power can be destructive to the sender if misused. Be careful that it does not fall into the wrong hands, for none but the pure in heart should send forth its light. Its primary purpose is for healing, and it is guided by universal law to fulfill its purpose in all of its facets. It should be created for a specific purpose, and the effect will be instantaneous. Its power will not be dissipated but will lie dormant until projected."

What little I knew about the creation of the projectors was from what my father told me and what I read in his messages from the spirits. The process began with Pop analyzing a specific disease or its remedy from a pure energy perspective. Once he obtained this information, he would then take this energy "DNA" and create a type of psychic "vaccine" and mentally imprint it as a thought-form onto these small cardboard squares. At times, in order to create these projectors, he might also use his pendulum as if it were some sort of spectrometer to analyze the information he was receiving about a particular disease's energy matrix.

Once Pop had placed the specific thought-form onto the cardboard, he wrote the name of the ailment or organ that it addressed on the outside and then sealed it with tape. On the back of each projector was a code number, which he used to organize the projectors into elaborate healing systems. When he would diagnose a patient, the pendulum would indicate the number of the specific projector that the patient needed. It was a bit like ordering from a Chinese menu: "I'll have a number 234, 'Thyroid Cells,' to start; and then a 345, 'Remove Fear,' and for my main course, I'll have a 665, 'Reye's Syndrome.'"

Over the last several years, Pop developed projectors for over four hundred different conditions. These small cardboard squares were designed to heal everything from the adrenal glands, bladder infections, and blood infections to realigning the chakras, curing herpes, and repairing bad teeth. In addition to healing specific conditions, the projectors were able to regenerate not only cellular structure but organs in the body.

Pop would organize the projectors alphabetically, starting with *Abundance, Acne, Allergens, Asthma,* and *Astral Trip* to *Hemorrhage, Heparin, Herpes,* and *Impotence,* all the way through *Tranquillity, Vagina, Zinc Sulfate,* and *Zone Irritation.* He then placed them in small cardboard folders that banks give children for holding small collections of dimes and quarters. When the bank refused to give him any more, he would get them from the church, which passed them out to the parishioners for their weekly offerings. They featured a realistic portrait of Jesus on the cover.

After years of research and development, the projectors were now standardized and reproducible. It was almost as if Pop were franchising himself by inventing objects and symbols containing specific healing energies that could be used by others for when he wasn't around. In this way he could multiply the number of people who could deliver his healing energy.

In one of Chander Sen's many messages to my father on the subject, the monk observed that the projectors had an almost miraculous ability to regenerate damaged organs in the body: "The projectors are adding a new level of communication and therapy to spiritual healing, and you have only scratched the surface. You will now start tuning in to the different states of consciousness and correcting misalignments of the various bodies and levels of being in man. Now we can regenerate any cellular structure or organ in the body. If a lung is working only at twenty percent, we can regenerate that lung and put new cells and new air sacs in there to function at one hundred percent." Pretty powerful stuff.

The projectors were a new way to utilize the invisible energies of the universe. Great leaps in culture have always been made whenever invisible energies were discovered and harnessed, such as X-rays, atomic energy, television, radio, electricity, and microwave communication, among others. Perhaps Pop's initial discoveries of these subtle energies will eventually be used for healings that could include organ regrowth and reduced cellular aging, which could lead the way to an immortal body.

In his healing room, he kept the most frequently used projectors attached to the wall above his desk. Many times he told me that while he was diagnosing a patient with the pendulum, individual projectors would suddenly fall onto his desk one by one in a specific sequence. This happened only during a healing; the projectors never fell at any other time.

After this happened a few times, he asked Chander Sen why the projectors would fall only during healings. Chander Sen responded that it was his way of handing my father the specific projectors that he needed during that healing—not unlike a nurse handing tools to a surgeon during a procedure.

Back in the healing class, there were no takers for the free chance to dematerialize into the ether. Pop handed out different projectors to each student so that he or she could feel the specific energy packed into this little square of cardboard. I watched as his students sat quietly, absorbing energy from their small squares of colored cardboard pasted to the middle of their forehead. Despite the strangeness of the scene, an unusual calm pervaded the room.

"Be careful, don't leave the projector on your forehead for more than three minutes, or you'll overdose," Pop warned. "These things are very powerful. I don't want you to do any damage. Donna, what did you feel?"

"Lew, I found myself breathing very deeply, but then I got a pain in my head. I had to take the projector off. I got scared."

"What is written on your projector?"

Donna removed the projector from her forehead and turned it over. The word *oxygen* was written on it.

My father continued. "Let me explain what happened. You're a shallow breather, right?"

"Yes, I am."

"The projector opened up your air sacs so you could take in more oxygen. You're not accustomed to this rush of oxygen. The pain you felt was your body telling you that you couldn't handle this much oxygen even though you needed it. That's why you took it off. You will have to acclimate. You need to breathe slower and deeper. Do you get migraine headaches?"

"Yes, terrible ones."

"Here, put this one on. You'll feel it very quickly."

"Hmmm, I feel myself swaying, so peaceful," the young woman exclaimed. "I can hear words. Someone is talking to me."

"The projector is giving you exactly what your body needs. Your air sacs are opening up at a slower pace now. This is the amount of oxygen you require to better regulate your system. It's amazing that this is just a piece of cardboard, yet it can have such an effect on you. Why? Because of the power of thought—there is nothing more powerful than the ability to control and send thought. Whenever a new medicine is discovered, I am able to distill its essence and create a projector for it. This way we can use the true benefit of the medicine to treat illness without any of the side effects. That is the beauty of this system."

My father used Donna's experience to tell the class about his own problem with being overoxygenated. "This reminds me of what happened back in 1972 when the spirits started raising my vibrational levels. They wanted to elevate me quickly so that I would be able to do more powerful healings. The problem was that they took me up the scale too quickly, and I was gasping for air. I was dizzy and out of breath. I felt like I had just climbed a mountain. I told them I couldn't handle it. So they lowered me back down to the physical level. It took them a full two weeks to bring me back up to the divine level at 220,000. Now, of course, I remain at the cosmic level, which is 800,000, with no problem. I had to adjust to living at this higher level. All of us in this room can eventually be at the cosmic level. Donna, over time your body will also acclimate to the positive increase in oxygenation.

"Let me show you how to choose what projector you need. Open up your booklets containing the projectors. Now, take your pendulum and either hold it over each one, or use a pointer in your other hand and point to each one and ask if you need it. When your pendulum moves in a clockwise motion, then you need the energy from that particular projector.

"These projectors heal not only the physical but the mental. The projectors go into the consciousness to program the mind, which then directs the body accordingly. By using the appropriate projector, we can do a complete psychological healing in a few minutes that would take a psychiatrist years. We can totally reprogram consciousness so

that people change their destructive thought patterns or heal their psychiatric problems. We always need to get the patient into a state of mental harmony. When one is not in mental harmony, you can pick up any kind of disease. Okay, now I want you to use your pendulum to choose what projector you need. Let's start."

All the students held pendulums over their books of brightly colored cardboard squares. Their pendulums were registering at different speeds the various projectors that they needed. They picked out projectors with names like *past-life pain, inner sight, no smoking,* and *tranquillity.* This exercise continued for about ten minutes. Then all of a sudden everyone's pendulum stopped at exactly the same time. It was as if there'd been a power failure during an electrical storm or someone pulled the plug on the pendulums' energy source. They just hung limply, and the room became very quiet. One by one the students looked up at my father.

"What's wrong?" he asked, suppressing a smile.

Jack said, "My pendulum stopped. It's dead. What's going on?"

"Mine too," said Marie. The students looked nervously at one another to verify that they each had the same problem.

"I shut off the power to your pendulums. This is to teach you a lesson. This power is not to be taken for granted. It can be used only for the highest good. I created it, and I can turn it off. You can never use these projectors for personal gain or for evil. I can take the power away, and if I don't, then Chander Sen will."

This was an impressive display of my father's psychic power. It certainly had awakened the class. There was a sense of alarm in the room. If my father could shut down their pendulums and projectors, what else could he do? The class was now much more alert and respectful. Just then the doorbell rang. Pop motioned for me to get the door. I opened it, and standing before me was a woman slightly hunched over with a look of pain on her face.

"Is Lew here?"

"Yeah. He's in the middle of teaching a class. Are you in the class?"

"No, I'm in a lot of pain, and I need a healing fast."

"Okay, let me see. Come on in and wait here and let me ask him. What's your name?"

"Janet."

When I went back to the living room and told Pop about his visitor, he asked me to have her come in.

Pop greeted her warmly, then introduced her. "Everyone, this is Janet, who just stopped by for a healing. I'd like for you all to watch so that you can learn a bit more from this case. Janet, what can I do for you?"

"My back has been hurting, and it's just getting worse. I was in the neighborhood and thought I would just stop by."

"Okay, let's see what is the cause of the problem." Pop held the pendulum in his right hand while he silently asked questions about Janet's condition. "There is a slight deformity in your spine that makes one leg shorter than the other. Once we adjust this problem, you will no longer have any backaches. Why don't you just stand up, right in front of me? Now, just relax and close your eyes. You will feel something gently pushing you forward or backward. Go in that direction. Don't be afraid—you won't fall. The body is telling you what position you need to be in to receive the healing."

Janet stood up and within seconds started swaying forward as if she was drunk. Since her eyes were closed, Pop told her what was occurring. "You're going forward. Okay, that means that the body wants you to lie down on your stomach because Chander Sen is going to work on your back. Every vertebra in your spine will be adjusted. Don't be alarmed; you will feel as if someone is poking his fingers into your back. That will be Chander Sen working on you. I will not be touching you."

Janet lay on her stomach while my father stood over her. Her head was turned to one side, and her eyes were closed. The room was quiet as the students watched the process. Janet appeared to be asleep. Every once in a while her shoulders twitched, and her hips would sporadically roll slightly from side to side. Occasionally her eyes would

scrunch up as if someone had touched a sore spot. Nothing much seemed to be happening. It was hard to imagine that this woman's spine was being completely reworked and adjusted.

After a few minutes, Pop said, "All right, you should be coming up now." Janet opened her eyes, blinked a few times, and stood up slowly without saying a word. "How does your back feel?"

"I feel like I've grown a couple of inches; it's much straighter. I hope it stays this way. I've never stood so straight in my life."

"Well, you certainly look like you're standing straighter," he said. "Sit in this chair and hold your legs straight out." My father stood in front of her and looked down at her legs. "Can you see that one of your legs is shorter than the other? Look at the difference."

"Oh my God, I never noticed that."

"Well, this is the cause of your problem. You are constantly pulling your back out of alignment because of this difference. This affects your entire nervous system and every organ in your body. Now I'm going to equalize your legs. Don't do anything to help me. I'll lift them up." Pop put his hands on top of her feet and lifted her legs straight out. Slowly he slid his hands up her feet until his thumbs rested on the inside of each of her anklebones. With his hands, he brought her legs together so that they were touching. His right thumb was about an inch and a half higher than the left thumb. This clearly showed how uneven her legs were. "Janet, look where my thumbs are. See the difference? I have them on your ankles, but one is higher than the other, and they are not matching up. Now watch your legs come together. They'll move by themselves. Just watch."

A minute passed, and slowly Janet's left leg seemed to be sliding back into her hips while her right leg remained stationary. The movement was slow and effortless. "I can't believe this, my leg is just gliding into place," she said. "I don't feel any pulling or anything. This is amazing. Lew, if it wasn't you doing this, I wouldn't believe it. I've never seen anything like this in my life. This is impossible."

Talking to the legs, Pop said, "Just a little bit more . . . almost . . . c'mon. Okay. Thank you. Look," he said to Janet, "now they are perfectly even." To prove this, he again placed his thumbs on her anklebones and used his knuckles as a measurement. They now lined up perfectly. "There," he said. "Now you'll walk more easily, no more backaches.

"I want to do one more thing before you leave. Please lean forward, just slightly. I want to do an overall healing starting at the top of your head and working all the way down your body. You should feel the energy going in through your head. First I need to normalize the lymphatic system." His hands were resting about three inches beyond her shoulders.

"Okay, now I'm going to adjust your circulation system. We need to get your blood flowing a bit better. It's somewhat stagnant; your pressure is not as strong as it should be." He slowly moved his hands over the outline of her body without ever really touching her, as if he were smoothing bumps in the sand. She took several deep breaths, as if reaching for additional oxygen. When Pop pulled his hands away, her eyes opened. At first she didn't speak but just sat there staring into space. The look on her face seemed to indicate that she didn't quite remember where or who she was.

"I feel as if someone rebuilt my entire body while my eyes were closed," she said. "All the pain in my back is gone. I've had that pain for years, and it was constant, twenty-four hours a day. No medication ever fully took away the pain. But now I feel brand new. This is amazing."

"No, this is not amazing at all," he said. "This is how healing works. It's very straightforward." Turning to the class, he added, "This is what I am teaching all of you. Each one of you will be able to do this and more. Janet, take a minute, catch your breath, and when you are ready, stand up. Now, let's get back to the projectors."

Janet waited for about two minutes, stood up with a smile, and walked toward the front door without saying a word. I opened it and let her out.

I observed my father as he taught. He was alert and sparkling with a clear, calm energy. Something had happened once Ruth left the stage.

The klieg lights went on, and the director called, "Action!" Dress rehearsal was over. The cameras were rolling. Pop had punched—no, ripped—a hole in the widely accepted construct of the universe. He had found a different kind of electrical outlet to plug into.

One of the offshoots of creating the projectors was that my father had refined his ability to build energized thought-forms that could be utilized for almost any situation. With this new skill, he began to create a universe of invisible structures and functioning ethereal machines that served to protect him, energize him, nourish him, discourage intruders, and keep him safe from automobile accidents twenty-four hours a day. If you can imagine a comic-book mad scientist whose proton energy fields could repel asteroids and other invaders—that was my father. He had now entered the realm of science fiction and completely erased the boundary between imagination and reality. What he imagined became real, whether it was visible or not. Pop accepted, without any doubt, his ability to create a new reality at any given moment just through focused thought and energy manipulation. He switched seamlessly between the seen and the unseen without missing a beat. His world of the imagination was now completely activated, and he had forever erased any remaining mortal limitations.

His spirit guides were training him to utilize his energy for even larger projects. Now just curing leukemia or deafness was suddenly small potatoes. He had bigger fish to fry. I heard him tell one of his classes, "I have brought people back from the dead. I have had many cases where the soul is already out of the body. It was way down the tunnel to die. No matter what the doctors think or believe, it is the soul that determines whether the body shall live or die. On many occasions I have reasoned directly with the soul. But first I have always checked with the higher powers as to whether or not I am permitted to bring it back. If the soul still has work to do, I will ask it to please come back to its body and accept the responsibility of the work it has to do. They came back and were revived, much to the doctors' amazement, even though they were clinically dead." All in a day's work for my father.

And if raising the dead wasn't enough, he also told his students that with guidance from Chander Sen, he had resolved the dangerous hydrogen bubble that contained radiation at Three Mile Island. "I can stop the radiation from leaking out of nuclear plants. I did it for Three Mile Island. When that radioactive bubble of hydrogen occurred, they said it was going to create a meltdown and spill radiation all over the community. It was too dangerous for anyone to go into the nuclear plant. Fortunately Chander Sen came through and told me that radiation can be neutralized by using the violet ray. And that's what I did. I surrounded Three Mile Island with the violet ray and was able to eliminate the radiation. After I did that, the bubble dissipated, the radiation cleared, and then workers could go in and clean the place up."

When he wasn't bringing people back from the dead or containing radiation spills, Pop continued to perform everyday healings, which often included assorted celebrities as they breezed through Miami. During one of my visits home, I took my father to the Miami Film Festival for the premiere of Brooke Shields's new film *Tilt*. After the movie, we were invited to the opening night party at a Deco mansion on one of the private islands just off of Miami Beach. The teen actress was coming down with a cold—something she didn't have time for, as she was about to open the film nationwide with numerous guest appearances. She looked unusually pale with a touch of green-gray. My father was introduced to Brooke as someone who could fix her cold. The two of them retreated to a corner of the room for about fifteen minutes, where my father performed his magic, and Brooke returned symptom free, ready to greet her public.

The projectors provided a new type of psychic technology that allowed my father to enlarge the scope of his powers. His correspondence school with the spirits was now training him to look beyond healing sick people and to treat larger phenomena, such as weather patterns, political events, and even whole societies. A new crew of spirit masters was now communicating with him from even more subtle dimensions.

One of the instruments in which they were training him was a series of complex geometric diagrams that looked a bit like Tibetan mandalas. The spirits would implant the finished design in his brain, which he would then dutifully copy onto individual index cards using a pen and a dime-store compass. Each diagram was created to emanate a highly specific force field. It could be used individually or in conjunction with other diagrams for a greater synergistic effect. On the back of the card was written an identifying code, such as "Phase II, #4 Hilarion."

Apparently, the force of these diagrams was so powerful that my father used them only under spirit supervision. The spirits would contact my father with detailed instructions as to which specific numbered cards to place on his "sender board" at what time of day and for how long. Let's say there was a hurricane brewing in the Atlantic, or the Everglades was low on water. My father might receive a message to place a certain sequence of four or five of these cards on his "sender board" for twelve hours and then replace them with other cards as the storm weakened or rain fell on the Everglades. In his notebooks there are detailed notations of these directions from the spirits.

In some ways the sender board operated a bit like the Buddhist stupas and prayer wheels that I would see many years later during a visit to Nepal. High in the Himalayas, the monks would string brightly colored prayer flags from a tall dome-shaped stupa, which to my mind functioned like a satellite dish for sending the prayers out into the universe. Surrounding the enormous stupa was a circle of brass prayer wheels, which you would touch and spin as you walked along the path. The spinning wheel would create a dynamic energy that would send your prayer out to the attention of the necessary gods or guardian spirits. Just like the monks in Nepal, my father was constantly beaming out silent corrective energy to protect and heal the planet.

If it seems as if my father was losing his grip on reality or that the constant impingement of spirits on his mind had created an advanced psychotic state, the truth was that he had never been more down-to-earth or shown a greater presence of mind. Everything seemed very simple for him. All he had to do was follow the instructions of the spirits. With his nose to the metaphysical grindstone, he no longer had to search for meaning, struggle for answers to large questions, or wonder if his powers would leave him. He simply did as he was "told." And the results were, more often than not, miraculous.

Looking at these mysterious geometric drawings, I realized that the best way to really understand my father was to simply accept the fact that he was three hundred years ahead of the rest of us. This thought gave me great patience in dealing with his incomprehensible ideas and behavior. It was clear that I would never fully comprehend what my father actually did or how he did it. I now understood that it must have been a great effort for him to try to explain these advanced, ethereal thoughts that the spirits had implanted in his brain to plain mortals such as me. Therefore if he was willing to make the effort to try translating these supernatural ideas, I should be patient and nonjudgmental in meeting him halfway. It was evident that Pop had traveled to an unseen dimension, gathered information, and brought it back in order for us to hopefully advance our consciousness.

I had no doubt that one day in the future, many of his fantastic discoveries would become reality for a new race of more advanced, enlightened humans. And why not? All human achievements, from skyscrapers and heart transplants to sending a man to the moon, first emanated from our thoughts. Although, in my father's case, his thoughts were actually coming from other dimensions. For reasons I will never comprehend, my father was chosen to bring this information forward.

sixteen

•

Mister Magic

Ever since I was a kid, my father had trained me to always remember my dreams. Next to my bed was a pad of paper, flashlight, and pen in order to record that evening's dream sessions the moment I woke up.

For my father, dreams were not just the idle musings of a sleeping mind but another reality with its own logic. Back in 1925 he kept a detailed diary of his dreams. From one of his first entries, it is clear that Pop was already aware of the power of dreams to provide access to other realities. He writes, "I must train myself to remember my creations of sleep. I must put my conscious mind in touch with my subconscious. There is something in it. People awaken their unknown and latent qualities and powers in just such a way." Perhaps my father was anticipating some of his future spirit guides with this: "Dreamed last night of a funny person, or rather a peculiar one of a dark green hue with feelers on his head and balls at the end of them which shone and glistened with lights and colors like a spotlight." In another, he may be having his first out-of-body experience: "Dreamed I saw all the planets as planets close-up and not as stars." But one dream stands out as the first indication of his nascent psychic abilities: "Dreamed of fire and freight train just before I awoke. First thing I saw after I woke was the morning newspaper with a picture of fire and freight train wreck on the front page." Being able to dream of the next day's headline in advance was quite a feat for such a young man. Clearly he had never forgotten this first experience of premonition, and it explained why he was so adamant that I preserve, treasure, and understand my dreams.

Pop would tell me that before going to bed, I should plan out my dreams as if they were storyboards for a movie. If I needed to solve a problem, I was to instruct myself while falling asleep that the solution would appear to me in a dream. If I didn't like a dream's outcome, he told me to go back to sleep and act as the director to re-create the dream to my liking. This was a psychological and spiritual training exercise. If you could sharpen your mental abilities to the point where you could direct your dreams like a computer game, you would easily achieve control over the events in your waking life as well.

This training had played an important role in the creation of my paintings. Before I started any painting, I would first go to sleep for an hour or so with the intention of dreaming. I'd wake up a little groggy, my head filled with remnants of surreal dreams, and immediately start to work. I felt as if I was painting while still in a sort of trance, and as a result, the hallucinatory images that poured forth on the canvas were more documentations of my subconscious mind than anything else. I could never work after I came home from a dinner party or even from the grocery store, as my mind was filled with the ephemera of real-time reality, which I found encumbering to the creative process. I needed the resonance of my own dreams to generate paintings.

It had been years since I'd had a bad dream. This particular dream didn't panic me, it just bothered me. In the dream, I saw my seventy-seven-year-old father in a subway station at Broadway and Lafayette.

As he climbed the stairs, he would pause to catch his breath. The entire dream ran just a few seconds, but it left me slightly rattled when I awoke. For some reason, I didn't bother writing this one down and went about my day. The dream stayed with me the entire day, resulting in an uneasy feeling that wouldn't go away. I hadn't dreamed about my father in years.

Why should I worry? After all, my father was immortal. How could he not be? He healed the sick and raised the dead. He convinced souls not to leave their bodies, removed demons from possessed bodies, and neutralized nuclear radiation. He had superhuman powers not seen since the time of the alchemists. But all of this was just not enough to prevent the universe from skipping a beat.

"Something has happened . . ." Lisa, my father's latest girlfriend, was on the phone. "I don't know how to say this. Your father is dead."

Silence. I had never had a phone call like this before and didn't know how to understand what I was hearing. For an eternal moment, I completely disconnected from reality. During those few seconds, my mind went into "pause," if not complete meltdown.

Somehow the cosmos had made a mistake. This wasn't supposed to happen. When my mind and body finally resumed operation, I reverted to the exceedingly polite young man that my mother had raised, and with great warmth in my voice said, "Thank you so much for calling, I really appreciate it. Good night." This was the default response for unknown situations.

Suddenly I was shivering. I had moved from the Bowery and was now living in a nearly abandoned turn-of-the-century brownstone that had been originally owned by the Astors during the 1870s but had mutated into a heroin den. The first night I moved in, I spent hours cleaning used needles out of the burners on the stove.

A few minutes later, the phone rang again. "Uh, hi, it's Lisa."

"Yes, Lisa."

"Well, what are you going to do?"

"About what?"

"Well, uh, your father."

I never knew anyone who had died before. My father had taught me that no one who surrounded himself with the white light ever died. That was the purifying magic cure-all.

"Well, doesn't he just get buried?" I asked, assuming that some company just showed up and took care of this.

"Yeah, I guess so, but who— I mean, you need to come here." She was becoming unraveled.

"Why?"

"Well, you have to take care of everything."

"Like what?"

"Like burying him."

"Bury him? I don't know how to do that."

"Well, I don't know what to do either."

"So, what do I do?"

"I don't know, but you need to take care of this."

"But I'll have to fly down to do this."

"Yes."

"Okay. Good-bye."

After I hung up, I was overcome with rage. I started running around the house screaming at him, *"You weren't supposed to do this! You made a big mistake! This is really stupid! You better fix this right now!"*

Breathless from screaming, I stopped and quickly tried to think if I knew of any technique to bring him back from the dead. I tried to remember everything he taught me but I had refused to learn. I knew he told me about how he would talk to the soul before it left the body, check its karmic record, and then reunite the soul with the body. I wasn't sure where to begin. I didn't know where I had put the pendulums he had given me. They were probably in a box in the basement. If it had been awhile since he died, it might be too late to get him back into his body. I didn't really know what the expiration time frame was on this particular technique. If I waited too much longer, he would have left the physical plane and would have difficulty finding his way back. Immediately after physical death, there was a period of disorientation as the spirit adjusted to being free of the body. If there was no one there to meet it, then the soul supposedly floated around for a while until it got its bearings.

I started to call Lisa for the estimated time of death but hung up. I didn't want to talk to her. God, if I could only remember what I saw him do hundreds of times.

For the first time ever, my father had goofed in a major way. For some reason, he wasn't watching for just that one split second when the universe snuck up on him, opened wide, and swallowed him whole. In the blink of an eye, it was all over, and he was gone. Who would protect me? Who would stop the evil spirits from attacking me? Who would talk to Arthur for me? Who would make all the bad stuff magically go away? There was no one else who could do these things. It's not like my father was a lawyer, and if he died I could call another attorney to represent me. He was irreplaceable. Suddenly my safety net had been ripped out from under me. For the first time in my life, I was now completely human and vulnerable. My gifted slide through life was over. I could feel the hard whoosh of life's vagaries coming at me fast. I would now be exposed to disease, harm, toil, and trouble like every other human on the planet. My precious InvisaShield was gone. But most of all, I missed the man whose existence made me more special than I was. It was his exploration of other dimensions that allowed me to live in a world defined by magic and miracles.

All night I paced around my apartment hoping for a sign, something that I could do. If I had died, my father would have known exactly what to do. But no, I had to smoke pot and run around with bad kids when I could have prevented this from happening if I had only paid attention. I was so stupid. In fact, I was the stupidest person on the whole planet, in the whole universe, and in all dimensions. Ever.

As Lisa requested, I took the first flight the next morning to Miami. When I stepped off the plane, the sun hurt my eyes, and the humidity made me nauseous. My native weather had suddenly become

hostile and unbearable. Even though my world had completely collapsed, I looked around and saw cars moving, people talking, yelling,
smoking, eating. Didn't they know what had just happened? The
world had just ended, and all these people acted as if this was just like
any other day.

As my taxi approached his house, I saw that a crowd had gathered
in front. Some of the people were talking, some were crying, while
others just stared into space, their faces filled with pain. I sensed that
they were waiting for my father to appear, just like I was, to disprove
the unbelievable news they had heard.

When I got out of the cab, they rushed up to me and begged for
me to heal them and their loved ones. Crying with pain, they said,
"Please, please, my daughter is in the hospital and needs your help!
Your father said you had the power."

"My sister has breast cancer. You can save her!"

"My father has had a heart attack. We need your help!"

In that brief instant, I now saw what my father went through
twenty-four hours a day. It was overwhelming—a responsibility I
could never have handled. Being a doctor, where you see sick people
day in and day out and helplessly watch them die, is bad enough, but
having to be a nonstop miracle worker would have been impossible.

This was now the moment to become my father, to make him
happy, to continue his work. Somewhere inside of me, I knew that
even though I was a bit rusty with my healing techniques, I probably
knew enough to help these people. Whatever I did, no matter how
clumsy, it would be better than doing nothing. Even though I didn't
listen or really pay attention whenever he tried to teach me, I had
watched thousands of healings. I knew the drill backward and forward, but I had never done it on a real person. This is what Pop had
always wanted. He knew he had a once-in-a-trillion-lifetimes gift, and
he wanted me, who carried his DNA, to continue his work. It was as
if my father's sudden death was preordained to create this succession.
I could feel invisible hands pushing me to start healing immediately,
while I, Philip, wanted no part of this. I knew that once I performed

just one healing, it would open the floodgates. Just as they had for my father, they would line up around the block, call at all hours of the day and night from around the world to be freed from the pain, ravages, and threat of disease. What I really wanted more than anything was for these people to go away. How could they bother me now? I had nothing to offer them. Certainly there was someone else they could call to remove the tumor or stop the bleeding. That's what the yellow pages are for. Look up "Twenty-four-hour Tumor Removal" or just call "1-800-TUMOR."

The truth was that there *wasn't* anyone else to call. Besides, these people had already seen every possible doctor, who had told them, "I'm sorry, but there is nothing else we can do." That's why they were now willing to trust the lives of their loved ones to someone like me. My father was dead, and I was in no mood to assume the position of chief of psychic surgery at the Lew Smith Supernatural Hospital.

Without much, if any, thought, I made the definitive decision: I knew nothing about healing, and I didn't want to know anything about healing. As far as I was concerned, my father's powers died with him. There would be no passing the torch and no inheriting the mantle. As I made my way through the crowd, I muttered vaguely, "No, sorry, call someone else; sorry, come back tomorrow."

Once inside the house, I started to worry about practicalities. Was there a will, burial instructions, or some psychic message waiting for me? For my father there had always been a sign or an indication as to what the next step was. When he was alive, the universe was more than happy to reveal its inner workings, to answer his questions to point him in the right direction. The universe was his ally. Now that door had been slammed shut and the plug pulled on the ever-present blinking neon sign that said Welcome, Open All Night.

I realized that there was another matter I had to deal with: no one had told me where the body was. Was he still at the hospital, the morgue, or the police station? All this happened without me, and now I was supposed to fix it.

I walked into his healing room, hoping that I would find detailed instructions not only for the burial but for the rest of my life. The room looked as if he had just stepped out for a moment to go to the post office. An air of suspended animation pervaded it. I wanted to find the "on" switch so that I could make time move forward or backward—anything but this awful pause that I experienced. It felt as if he had been kidnapped. There was no note, but perhaps there was a secret cassette tape that once I played it would self-destruct. Nope. Nothing. No father, no instructions, no tape. I was definitely on my own.

The light on his answering machine was blinking impatiently. I started to listen, hoping that there would be a clue. Maybe someone from the hospital had called, maybe the funeral home had called—or maybe my father had called. Instead there were endless calls from endless strangers requesting endless healings. Everyone on that tape was sick or dying. Impatient, I fast-forwarded through the tape, making them all sound like cartoon characters leaving cartoon messages. I didn't want to hear any of the details. Each one of these messages was about someone's life in need of immediate assistance and repair. Were they all going to die without my father around to help them? I didn't want to know the answer. My attitude was, "Sorry, too late, you should have called yesterday."

Lisa was hiding out in their bedroom. We had not formally met yet. I walked in and thanked her for letting me know that my father had died. She didn't quite know how to deal with me. Our initial discussion was awkward. I was not prepared to ask the details of what had happened. She muttered something about being sorry. I told her I needed to make some coffee.

In the kitchen, I saw that she had a white plastic Mr. Coffee machine on the counter. This told me everything about her that I didn't want to know. Having grown up on Cuban espresso, or at the very least coffee made with a Brazilian *colador* that looked like a white cotton sock stretched over a wooden handle, I felt that Mr. Coffee was appropriate only in the domain of the unenlightened. Mr. Coffee had no place in my father's house. This woman had to go. I certainly didn't like her before my father died. But now, having seen the Mr. Coffee,

I blamed her for my father's death. I'm not quite sure why, but I felt that she'd killed him.

I refused to drink from Mr. Coffee and made some ginseng tea instead. While it brewed, Lisa mentioned that she would like to continue living in the house and continue my father's work. "Fat chance," I thought. If anyone carried on, it would be me, and I didn't think that would be happening anytime soon. I think she'd known my father all of about six months. There was no way that she could have learned about healing or anything else about his work in that amount of time.

While I drank my tea, she handed me a large, ugly blue plastic bag as if it were some kind of peace offering. It was a horrible blue; the kind of thoughtless blue that they might use in making potties for the infirm or rubber sheets for the gurney. I couldn't stand touching the bag; it felt hot and dirty. There was something profoundly unpleasant about it.

As I opened the bag and peered in, my face was hit by an exhalation of warm, humid air. I blinked to protect my eyes. It was as if this bag held my father's last breath. When my eyes refocused, I was looking at the remains of my father from his ride to the hospital. His glasses, his watch, his ring, his crucifix with a Star of David superimposed on it, his wallet, and a dental bridge—all lying in a jumble at the bottom of this ugly blue bag. That was it? That was all I got? This was all there was of my father? His whole life added up to an indecent blue plastic bag filled with trinkets? The objects felt contaminated, as if they had touched something bad, something not my father. Something called death. I lifted my head, looked at Lisa, and said nothing.

She now volunteered, "All I know is that I was watching TV, and your father was in his study on the phone with one of his students, Ray. For no apparent reason, he began to have shortness of breath. He asked Ray to send him a certain kind of healing energy to open up the air passageways. They were on the phone for about forty-five minutes. Afterward, your father came out to the living room and began nervously pacing around. He was very agitated and said he wasn't feeling well. You know your father never got sick. I offered to call the paramedics, but he said no. When he collapsed, that's when I called. They got here as soon as they could. When they began to work on him, I saw your father leave his body. He was standing there watching everything that was going on. His expression was 'So this is how this is done.' Then they took him to the hospital. He died on the way."

I didn't believe anything she said to me. None of this made any sense. Something was very wrong with her and her story. How could my father be so stupid as to spend forty-five minutes on the phone with one of his students and not get to the hospital? Who was this Ray person? I had never heard of him. Forty-five minutes is a long time to be on the phone trying to get one of your students to relieve your chest pain—and not one of your stellar students, at that. Ray was clearly incompetant when it came to his basic healing skills. My father must have known he was having a heart attack. I know he always told me that a healer could never heal himself, in the same way that a surgeon could not operate on himself. But still, he could have done something, called someone. Something didn't add up.

My father had devoted the last years of his life to healing people, to picking them up after the medical profession had dropped them. Unfortunately, I also knew that he would never have put himself in doctors' hands and asked them to save him. Most likely he would rather die. And he did.

The phone had not stopped ringing. Each time the answering machine picked up, it repeated the same haunting message: "This is Lew Smith . . ." I didn't want to listen to the callers or the messages they were leaving. I thought about all these people who were home waiting for my father to call them back, to save them, to heal them. With my father gone, the funeral homes would probably notice a sudden uptick in business.

Back in the kitchen, I spotted a small orange prescription bottle on one of the shelves tucked next to my father's vitamins. I had never seen a bottle of drugs in his house, ever, and was surprised. Under no circumstances would my father have taken a prescription medicine.

I picked up the bottle and noticed that it belonged to Lisa. I read the label. One hundred tablets of Synthroid that had been filled two days earlier. When I opened the bottle, only three of the original one hundred tablets remained. Where did they all go? I needed to know more about Synthroid. I immediately went into my father's study and pulled out his *Physicians' Desk Reference.* Synthroid was normally prescribed for low thyroid condition. However, there was a small warning that adverse reactions could include hyperactivity, nervousness, heart failure, and cardiac arrest.

Where were those missing ninety-seven pills? I couldn't ask Lisa; she would lie to me anyway, so what was the point? Increasingly, it seemed that this woman who had suddenly appeared in my father's life was somehow involved in his sudden death. Was it for money? Or was it to take over his healing practice for the power and the glory? Or was she one of those female serial killers who preyed on elderly men in the hope that they would leave everything to her in their will?

Since childhood I had always been comfortable with conspiracy theories to explain the unexplainable. I'm not talking about those general mass-market theories that implicated the U.S. government or the Communists in the killing of JFK, but rather the more esoteric ones such as the use of magnetic waves by the Soviets to control our minds to create a sympathetic environment for them to assume control of America. My father's death created an ideal situation in which to manufacture reams of mental documentation to explain his mysterious expiration. How could there be any other reason for his demise other than by nefarious means? Perhaps Lisa had won over Arthur through some strange psychic/tantric/sexual initiation, and he had turned on my father and assisted in his killing. Or maybe Lisa had poisoned my father and discouraged him from calling the paramedics while she watched him pace nervously around the living room as the poison constricted his arteries. This way he would die, leaving her what she imagined to be his millions. Or how about this: Chander Sen decided that he urgently needed my father on the other side for advanced healing instruction and accidentally ripped his astral body from the physical body? As a result, my father was unable to reunite his bodies and disappeared from the physical realm. I was comfortable with any of these theories. Given time, I would continue to build much more elaborate explanations for his sudden death.

In an effort to play detective, I copied down all the information on the prescription bottle and drove over to the supermarket, where I could use the pay phone without Lisa listening in. My first call was to the pharmacist at Super X drugs. "Can you tell me when prescription number 794627481 was filled?" I asked.

"December eleventh, two days ago."

"And was it filled for one hundred tablets?"

"Yes."

"Um, I have this bottle, and now there are only three tablets remaining. I think my father may have been given these pills or something."

"What do you mean?"

"Well, my father's dead, and all these pills are missing. Maybe he was killed with these pills."

"Oh, I don't think so. The pills could be anywhere. Someone could have put them in another bottle or poured them down the drain or—"

"But I read in the *PDR* that this could cause a fatal cardiac event."

"I'm not sure. I can look that up. Just a minute, please . . ."

"Thanks for your help. Bye." I was afraid he was going to put me on hold and call the cops. Lisa had probably called him by now and told him not to say anything. I'll bet she knew what I was up to. She was probably busy covering up her trail fast.

Next I called a friend's father and asked for the name and number of an attorney. When the attorney answered, I gave him my name and began my story. "I think my father has been murdered. See, there were all these pills, and now there are only three left, and this pill can cause heart attacks, and there is this woman in the house who I don't know, and I think she wants his money because she says she's going to live in the house and—"

"Did you have breakfast?"

"No."

"I think you're just upset and need some food. Go get some pancakes. It'll be fine. I'll talk to you tomorrow." *Click.* As usual, I was having trouble getting people to believe me. This was no different than the rare occasions when I mentioned to someone that my father had this dead friend named Arthur. I was always met with the same wall of disbelief. My murder theory was not playing well either.

After the pharmacist and the attorney, I called directory assistance and asked for the number and address of the medical examiner's office. I pretended that I was in a movie and doing exactly what the son of a murder victim would do. I was writing the script as I went along.

"County medical examiner's office."

"Hi, my father has just been murdered, and I need to get an autopsy."

"Yeah, just a minute." The operator barely covered the phone when she yelled out, "Jorge, I got one for you!"

"Detective Perez."

"Yeah, my father's been murdered, and I need to get an autopsy done before this woman leaves town." Perez took a deep breath filled with annoyance. I was obviously disturbing his *cafécito* break. I continued, "Well, there were all these pills, they were just filled a few days ago—one hundred tablets—and now there's only a few left, and my father's dead. And I read that these pills can give you a heart attack, so that's what happened. Now I need to get an autopsy before—"

Perez wasn't buying. "What'd you say your name was?"

"Smith. Philip Smith."

"Okay, Mr. Smith. Here's what I think: I think you're overreacting a little bit, and you need to calm down and maybe think this thing through a bit more."

"Yeah, but I need an autopsy, because I know you'll find the drug in his body."

"But we're not going to do that. See . . ." Detective Perez was determined not to be helpful at any level. I hung up and got in the car and headed to police headquarters downtown.

At the police department, they just shuffled me around. I had already told the receptionist that I had a murder on my hands and needed to talk to the chief detective. All I got was an "uh-huh." The receptionist pointed me to a room with scuffed-up bitter green walls and gray furniture to just sit and wait. There were another six people waiting along with me. Just one look at them, and I knew they had much worse problems than I did. About an hour later, Detective Gonzalez appeared—a compact guy with a crisp white shirt who didn't like to get his hands dirty. I pitched the Synthroid story one more time. He nodded. "We got one little problem here. Synthroid is instantly metabolized by the body, and the autopsy isn't going to show anything. Bury your father and call it a day."

"Oh. I thought an autopsy could find anything."

"Nope, only certain key drugs. Sorry." He stood to leave.

What a dumb fuck. He lied to me, and I believed him. He was just too lazy and didn't want to bother to fill out the paperwork to do the job. I should have known better than to assume that this $16,000-a-year detective knew anything about medicine, much less pharmaceuticals. I was still a kid in many ways and didn't know how to push my way through the system.

Many years later, I told this story to a brilliant pathologist friend of mine, who said, "Of course Synthroid would show up in an autopsy. You can find anything if you bother to look for it."

No one was helping me. I was wasting my time with the police and decided to head back home. As I drove up to the house, there were even more people waiting outside wanting to know when I was going to be raising my father from the dead. It was unbearably hot for December, and I could hardly breathe. I felt as if I were underwater and very close to drowning. Over the next several hours, the doorbell continued to ring. People stopped by to tell me that they just heard this terrible rumor that my father is dead and it just isn't true, is it? The bell rang again. I opened the door.

"Well, hey there, Philip." I was looking at a slightly disheveled but overly perky southern blonde with a thick accent and a beaming, wide-mouthed smile. I recognized her but couldn't remember her name. She had been at the house many times before. Her claim to fame was that she had a bit part on a TV sitcom from my childhood, *Car 54, Where Are You?*

"Someone told me that your daddy was dead." She broke out laughing, slapping her thighs. "Why, I never heard anything so silly in my entire life. Fact is, I just saw him up at the Winn-Dixie supermarket buying those Stella D'Oro cookies he likes so much. So I just wanted to stop by and say hey. Now, you give a big kiss to your daddy when he gets home. Hear? Bye now!"

Others would stop by with similar stories. In the twenty-four hours after he died, my father's various appearances hovered somewhere between Christ rising on Easter morning and numerous Elvis sightings. Aside from these few witnesses of resurrection and eternal life, my father's death brought out scores of mourners dropping by or calling to tell stories of how he had saved their lives. Tears filled their eyes as they related their rescue from terminal diseases and emotional distress. These were astonishing moments, as I listened to the endless miracles he performed.

During the last several years, I had been so caught up in my own life, as well as my father's magical mystery tour, that I had not communicated that often with my mother. I called her to let her know that my father had died. This was the cue she had been waiting for to reenter my life. She took a deep sigh and asked how she could help. I just started crying. With my father gone, she felt she could now reclaim her right as my parent, which over the years had been usurped by him and his various spirits.

Days went by, and still I could not locate my father's body. No one knew where it was. I called the hospital; someone there said that he was never admitted, since he died on the way, in the ambulance. Lisa was not helpful. She couldn't remember where the ambulance took him. After calling all over town, I finally located my father at the hospital morgue. Apparently, one arm of the hospital doesn't speak to the other. I asked if I could stop by and take one last look. The nurse told me, "Trust me, honey, you don't want to take a look at that body." I wondered what that meant, and my paranoia began generating ideas of how he had been stabbed and cut up by Lisa or used as an anatomy lesson for residents.

"Just tell us what to do with him." When she said this, it reminded me how all of this was just a terrible mistake and that he wasn't supposed to be dead. Besides, I had no idea what to do with him. I had never visited a local cemetery in Miami. I didn't know who to call.

After that phone call, I figured I'd better get a jump on things and begin casket shopping. As much as I enjoyed shopping, picking out a casket is truly one of the most horrific and unaesthetic activities in existence. I made the assumption that my father would like to be buried in a plain wooden box. Nice and simple. The salesmen looked at me with disbelief when I asked if they had any plain pinewood caskets. No such thing. One went so far as to respond, "You're joking?"

Every "showroom" I entered had hideous shiny metal boxes with upholstered red or baby blue velvet that made them look like pimp Cadillacs for the dead. I was shopping for a casket as I would a nice suit—simple lines, nice fit, understated color, nothing too flashy. It should be so easy not to be buried in bad taste. I made a mental note that when I got back to New York to call Calvin Klein about coming out with a line of designer caskets—something simple in elegant monochromes such as dove gray and tarragon—appropriate for traveling to the next world in style. If the Egyptians figured out how to design for death, why couldn't we? After two days of looking, I still could not find a plain wooden casket and was contemplating making it myself with a few sheets of plywood, nails, and a handsaw. At this point, all I wanted was something simple, elegant, and comfy.

While I continued to mentally design the best possible casket, I decided to begin packing up Pop's office. Too many people were coming by asking for mementos, and I didn't want anything disappearing. I was also concerned that as word of his death spread, the authorities might show up with a subpoena in order to claim his papers.

As I started cleaning off his desk, I accidentally leaned on what I thought was just the side of a cabinet. It was actually a false panel that gave way and revealed a hidden, small safelike area with black metal boxes filled with various legal papers and recent diaries. I opened the one marked "1981" and noticed two small but very telling entries. The first, dated July 24, 1981, stated simply, "I received mastership today 1,500,000." Less than a month later, on August 18, 1981, a second entry stated, "I reached the disciple level today. Vib. 2,000,000. Work with high spirits." These strange notations indicated that just a few months before his death, the spirits were moving him up the ranks very quickly. Clearly, something was up. In the yogic traditions, when someone reaches ascended masterships, he can leave the body at will. He acquires unusual powers that rival those of comic-book superheroes, such as levitation, being in two places at once, and the ability to materialize whatever one thinks about. For these masters there is very little difference between life and death, as the body becomes less important. Reading these entries made me think that my father's recent death was due to him being transferred for service in another dimension.

Also in this cabinet was a copy of his will. I didn't even know he had one. Seeing his signature on his last will and testament was unsettling. It was as if he had signed his own death warrant. His instructions were simple: he requested to be cremated. Burning his body made me uncomfortable; it seemed so brutal, but at least it eliminated the problem of an ugly coffin.

As I was reading the will, the phone rang. Barton Johns, a longtime friend of my father, called to inquire if I'd "heard" from him. Barton expressed his surprise and disappointment that there had been no clairvoyant message from my father announcing that he had reached the other side. As he said this, it made me feel inadequate as a son *and* as a son of a psychic—I couldn't even pick up the signals emanating from my dead father. In my defense, I mentioned to Barton that it takes a period of time for the dead to transition to their new situation of being without a body. They have to learn how to navigate in their new etherlike environment. Once they settle in, they eventually figure out how to communicate with the folks back on earth. Plus, I was in such a state of shock, I was not in any condition to receive a Western Union from the next world.

To change the topic away from my failure as a junior psychic, I mentioned that I had finally found my father's will and his wish for cremation. Barton became very excited, as if telling me about a white sale at Macy's. "Yeah, we've checked it out. We want to be cremated too. Buena Vista, only $299 for everything. This is the way to go." Barton would know. He was an engineer who claimed to have developed a long-standing relationship with a group of aliens whom he hung out with whenever they visited planet Earth. No matter what time of day or the circumstances, almost every other sentence out of his mouth started with, "When I was on the mother ship . . ." Barton said that he had witnessed all of the alien advanced technology used for healing the sick. Once prodded, he would describe in exacting detail the aliens' astounding abilities to rejuvenate organs, repair wounds, and create new body parts. He felt that my father's techniques for healing were far simpler than theirs but similar in that they both harnessed the power of invisible energies. Barton was confident that my father learned all his healing methods after having been abducted by aliens, put to sleep on the mother ship, and having had a chip implanted in his brain.

After our conversation, I began to worry about how the cremation people would know which were my father's ashes or someone else's. At $299, I seriously doubted that they would properly separate the different bodies to provide individualized service. I assumed they waited until they had a critical mass of bodies, dumped 'em in the oven, and gave you back the dust of that day's body burnings all mixed together. Or they probably made more money by dumping the body in a landfill out by the airport, then went to the quarry, smashed up some rock, handed it to you in a plastic bag, and said, "Here's your wife, Mr. Fester."

Based on Barton's enthusiastic recommendation, I had Pop booked into the nearest Buena Vista for his cremation. Since I did not witness the delivery of the body or the cremation, who knows what they did. Two days later a cardboard box arrived containing the "remains" in a plastic Baggie tied with a twist. These days I'm sure they've graduated to the added convenience of Ziploc so that nothing can leak out. As I looked at the bits and pieces of gray and white chunks in the bag, I thought about his whole life reduced to just a handful of dust. His brains, his eyes, his teeth, his laugh, his hands—all concentrated in a bag filled with what looked like gray bread crumbs.

I called Buena Vista and asked what I was supposed to do with the bag. They suggested I come on down to their showroom to select one of their "memory vases" to store the ashes. This seemed like a practical idea. Unfortunately, the urns looked like the kind of vases that you see in hospital rooms with those ordinary flower arrangements of a few carnations and a tired yellow chrysanthemum. Thoughtless and beyond depressing. If I wasn't going to bury him in an ugly coffin, I certainly wasn't going to pour his ashes into something that looked like it came from Sandi's Flower Shoppe. I thought maybe Pop had an old jar of olives lying around that I could rinse out and put his ashes into.

The solution for his ashes' final resting place came years later, during one of my visits to India. On this particular trip, I was a guest of the Indian government, which had wanted me to write an article on Bollywood, which at the time was largely unknown in America. The government had arranged a special visit to the Taj Mahal during a full moon. This was an unusual honor, as it required special governmental clearances. My guide was excited that I was going to have this privileged experience. As we approached the mausoleum, he turned to me and said, "The Taj at full moon; you will have a very special dream tonight."

There were only about ten of us on the grounds. The immaculate white edifice glowed in the moonlight. I was running a bit of a fever, and the guide said, "You need gin to cool the body. There are many herbs in gin that will make you better." At the time, I didn't drink, as Barton Johns had warned me that the space people said that humans should never consume alcohol because it destroys brain cells. After years of youthful indiscretion, I was working hard to keep my brain intact. However, the idea of something naturally medicinal was alluring. After my first gin and tonic, I headed for bed.

That night, as the guide predicted, I had a memorable dream. In it, the phone rang. It was my father calling. "I just want you to know I'm okay; I have a lot of new friends and am keeping busy. Everything is okay here." *Click*. When I remember dreams with great clarity, it is because they *are* important and need to be paid attention to. The dream was extremely comforting. I had no doubt that it had been a direct message from my father.

The next morning, my guide took me back to the Taj for a final tour. Seeing the Taj in the daylight was less magical but even more impressive. As I studied the detailed inlay work throughout the building, I was told that the descendants of the original craftsmen still practice these intricate design and inlay skills inherited from their forefathers. We drove out to the small town and met a man who represented a group of workers. I explained that I needed to make a container for my father's ashes. Several of his men followed me back to the Taj. There we copied floral and geometric patterns that I wanted reproduced on the urn in semiprecious stones. On a piece of paper, I drew the overall design for the box. It would be a vertical rectangle of the same pristine white marble used throughout the Taj.

Even though Pop's body had been cremated and an obituary published in the newspaper, I continued to receive calls and letters from people asking to be healed. I needed to provide some sort of final notice that my father no longer lived on planet Earth. A memorial service seemed to be the answer. I called the synagogue where I had been bar mitzvahed to see if the current rabbi would be able to officiate at his memorial. I didn't know the guy, but I figured that there would be some consideration for someone who had such a long history with the synagogue. While talking to me, he checked his schedule over the next several days and found that his calendar was filled. "Let's see, I have golf with the Bernsteins on Tuesday, Wednesday the Hadassah lunch, and I'm playing tennis in the afternoon with my wife . . . So how about next Wednesday at four—wait, no, no, I have something penciled in. Could you call me back in a couple of weeks and see how I'm doing?" I told him never mind; I would conduct the service myself.

Fortunately the Church of Religious Science agreed to host a memorial service. Pop had been a key figure at the church, holding a weekly healing circle that saved a lot of people from medication and surgery. The pastor let me know that they would give me the hall for free, but I would have to pay for the organist. Apparently a free hall for a memorial was an extremely generous gift. I was continually shocked at how much everything costs when you die. I guess I thought that people would feel sorry for you and pick up the tab for everything.

I spoke with the organist and asked her to sing "On A Clear Day (You Can See Forever)," from the Barbra Streisand movie in which she plays a nutty broad with psychic powers. My father loved that movie because it was one of the few times that someone with ESP was portrayed in a film. In my grief, I imagined my father hovering above us, having clear days and seeing everything, everywhere. The organist said no and insisted that she play the theme from *The Rose*. *The Rose?* What did that have to do with my father? I tried to negotiate.

"Okay, how about 'Oh What a Beautiful Morning'?"

"I want to play 'The Rose.' It was your father's favorite song."

"It was? Well, okay."

After her serenade, I ascended to the pulpit. Hundreds of people were there. All eyes were filled with unspeakable loss. I looked around the hall. Many people were wearing his white healing beads or holding a pendulum or some other artifact that he had given them.

They looked to me with the hope that I would tell them something that would make their pain go away, something that would replace my father in their eyes. Here was a group of people that had come in contact with a man like no other. His disappearance from the physical world was unthinkable and, for many, unbearable.

I struggled to hold back the tears and began, "Very few people, including myself, fully understood what my father did. To cure fatal disease or heal mental illness just through thought and invisible energy seems incomprehensible. According to the world of science and medicine, what he did on a daily basis was not possible. Ask any doctor, and he will quickly tell you that no human can wave their hands, close their eyes, and dissolve a cataract or repair a punctured lung. If, during his life, my father had simply cured just one person of cancer, that alone would have been a miracle. But the fact that he did this day after day was an extraordinary achievement.

"In cooperation with unseen spirits from another dimension, my father devoted his life to creating the future of medicine. He struggled against official ignorance and prejudice in the hope that he could show doctors a safer and more effective way to treat disease. We may not even begin to understand what he did until the next century. But hopefully, one day medicine will move beyond treating symptoms with chemical poisons that may heal one part of the body while killing another or surgically treating the body like a broken plumbing system. When my father healed, he addressed the intelligence and the miracle of the body. He was able to cure when pills wouldn't and surgery couldn't, in ways that seemed strange and simplistic yet achieved remarkable results."

I hoped my father was listening to how proud I was of his extraordinary accomplishments. "Once my father perfected his own healing methods, he sought to teach everyone that they too can heal. He never felt that he was in any way different or better than anyone else because of his abilities. His goal was to awaken the innate healing power in as many people as possible in order to improve human consciousness and help us all understand the living miracle that we all are. This healing power is within all of us. I know that he would want his work to live on and continue to bring health and end suffering whenever, wherever possible."

Afterward, at a small reception, people were smiling and laughing. The sound hurt my ears. My mother had joined me at the memorial for moral support. I was grateful for her being there. She had not lost her passion for social intrigue, though, and asked me in a loud whisper, "Which one is his girlfriend?"

"Mom, this isn't a cocktail party. Pop's dead. *Please*." She gave me one of her "Well, aren't we spoiling the fun?" looks, which put me on notice to lighten up.

Throughout the reception, I heard constant stories of how my father saved someone's life through a remarkable healing. People stopped me, interrupted me, tugged at me to let me know how my father had cured them or a member of their family. It was gratifying to hear the sheer volume of stories about how he had helped so many, many people.

My uncle Ron, who was married to my father's sister, came up to me and said in his best Brooklyn mafioso voice, "Hey, what about paying back that fifteen hundred dollars I lent your father?" My father never, ever, *ever* borrowed a dime from anyone. At that point, I'd had enough. I walked away without saying anything and decided to go home. People asked to come back to the house with me and just sit "in his aura." I needed time alone.

The house was painfully quiet; a heavy stillness hung in the air. I tried to accept a death that I never thought possible. I started checking off all the areas of my life that my father would no longer be involved in. There wasn't going to be much of my life left once I finished the list.

I hit the power switch on his radio for some background noise as I continued to pack up his healing room. Not knowing the local stations, I left the dial exactly where my father had previously set it. Some sort of call-in show was in progress. After a couple of commercials, I heard the announcer say in a choked voice, "I have just received news that Lew Smith has died," and she began to sob uncontrollably. She immediately cut to the show's theme song, "Good Vibrations" by the Beach Boys, thereby indelibly associating that song in my mind with my father's death. Eventually the announcer returned. "I apologize. It's just that Lew meant so much to me and has done so much for me, especially when I was sick. I can't believe it. If any of you have had an encounter with Lew, please call and share."

Speaking was Micki Dahne, Miami's well-known psychic astrologer. Micki had brilliantly combined her psychic abilities with a bit of showbiz. She could entertain and foretell the future. Her headline-grabbing predictions were often published in the *National Enquirer*. During her weekly radio show she dispensed psychic advice for problems concerning love, health, and money. Despite the program's regular half-hour format, this particular show was extended for an additional hour as the switchboard lit up with so many people calling to share the miracles my father had performed to save their lives. The stories were all testimonials to the extraordinary healings by my father—from getting this one off dialysis, and finding someone's lost dog in Hialeah, to healing someone's mother of pneumonia, saving a daughter from unnecessary surgery, curing heart failure, schizophrenia, testicular cancer, diabetes, allergies, and on and on and on. These calls served as the most wonderful and powerful memorial I could have ever imagined.

For years after my father died, I tried to locate Micki Dahne, with no luck. She was not listed in the phone book, and as her public presence had died down, I assumed she had passed away. Fortunately, while I was writing this book, my mother came across a brief article in the *Miami Herald* about Micki in which they published her Web site address. I wrote Micki an e-mail explaining that I was Lew's son and that I was looking for anecdotes about my father. Two days later she called and told me the following story:

"About twenty-five years ago, some friends of mine called to tell me that their son was in the hospital with cancer. The doctors had given up all hope and expected him to die that evening. They had asked me to stay with them at the hospital. I remember that for some reason, the kid was having trouble voiding; they kept changing the catheter, thinking that was the problem. The doctors couldn't understand what was going on and had just given up. Needless to say, the poor kid was in tremendous pain.

"At some point, your father walked into the room. I had never met him before. He ran his hands over the boy's body. He told everybody in the room that the kid was healed. The kid certainly didn't look any better to me. Then your father took two strands of heavy white glass beads out of his pocket. He placed one around the kid's neck and the other one around my neck. He said to me that I should go home and go to sleep, as there was nothing else I could do. Before I left, he told me that in the middle of the night these heavy glass beads would burst—they would explode after they absorbed all the disease. This would be a sign that the kid had been fully healed.

"So what else was I going to do? The doctors said the kid was going to die that night anyway, so I went home. About three o'clock in the morning, I woke up terrified by a noise that sounded as if someone was shooting a machine gun in my bedroom. Then I looked down, and the white beads were exploding like popcorn around my neck. Minutes later the phone rang. It was the kid from the hospital. Just like your father said, his beads had exploded, and he had wet the bed. His systems had started working again.

"The next day, the hospital released him. Two days later the kid was canoeing and having a great time. I'd never seen anything like this happen before, and, believe me, I've seen a lot. Your father had a gift that no one else had. Such a good soul, he gave so much to so many people. There was no one like him. By the way, he was an Aquarius, wasn't he?"

"Yes."

"Was he buried?"

"No, I cremated him."

"Oh, good. I'd hate to see an Aquarius mixed up with all that earth. It just doesn't work."

"Well, those were his instructions."

"See, he knew what was the right thing."

Her comment made me smile. Only my father would have known someone like Micki, who knew the correct burial method for each astrological sign.

Several weeks after Pop's death, I was back in New York, having lunch at the Factory with Andy Warhol. Before we sat down, Andy wanted me to photograph him for an article I was doing on him. As I began to shoot, Andy started to sneeze. I put down my camera to wait until he finished. Andy called out in between sneezes, "Keep shooting, don't stop!" This was one of the greatest art lessons I ever received: all reality is equal in interest and just as valid.

While we waited for lunch, Andy and I chatted, as assistants brought in *Marilyn* and *Cow* prints for him to sign. Over the years that I had visited the Factory, Andy had heard about my father from various people, and he was always fascinated by the idea of a psychic decorator. Andy knew a lot of decorators, but none that could place furniture *and* heal appendicitis. He and his assistant, Ronnie Cutrone, would constantly crack jokes about my father that were hysterical.

After he finished signing the prints, Andy turned to me and asked, "Uh, so what's new?" I told him my father had recently died. There was a long moment of silence. I could tell that he was having trouble processing this information. He looked at me with a bit of surprise and in his cryptic but insightful way offered his condolences with, "Oh, but . . . but I thought he was magic."

And that he was.

Epilogue

"It was a mistake. Your father did not have to die."

Frank Andrews looked up from the tarot cards spread out in front of me. This man had never met me before. I hadn't said a word since I sat down at his table, and he dealt the cards. It was 1991, the tenth anniversary of my father's death.

A friend had suggested that I visit Frank, a well-known psychic whose clients included John Lennon, Perry Ellis, and Princess Grace. Frank lived in a small Federal townhouse on Mulberry Street across from a church graveyard. His house was decorated with rare Biedermeier furniture, Tibetan skulls encrusted with rare gems, and a legion of small, yapping dogs.

As Frank uttered these words, I felt a burning knife enter my body. I had always known that there was something unanswered about my father's sudden death but had chosen to bury that idea as deep into my subconscious as possible. But now a total stranger had confirmed what I had always suspected. I did not need to hear any more details, but Frank continued without any prompting.

"What happened was that your father got up from his nap and, while he was still slightly groggy, accidentally grabbed the wrong bottle. He took some of his girlfriend's medication instead of his vitamins. The medication induced a heart attack. Because he didn't know what was happening, he waited too long to call the paramedics. It took him by surprise. I also see that he had something to do with the spirit world. I'm getting that the spirits tried to contact him and help, but he was too confused to recognize their signals. The sad thing is that it was all a mistake. This should not have ever happened. He'd be alive today if he hadn't taken those pills. But sometimes things happen for reasons we can't understand, no matter how much we try. I can have you talk to your father. We would have to go upstairs, but you must never tell people what we did."

Something in the way Frank said this scared me. As much as I would have given anything to talk to my father, I imagined there would be blood sacrifices, animal sex, and horrible noises. I declined.

Several years later, when I mentioned this offer to Frank's sister, Terry Iacuzzo, also an extraordinarily gifted psychic, she said, "Oh, that must have been in the early nineties. At the time, Frank had all these weird spirits around him. He would go into trance, and suddenly jewels the size of eggs would materialize in his hands from thin air. All kinds of strange things were going on with him. There was a flock of spirits around him that temporarily gave him extraordinary powers. He would have definitely put you in touch with your father. I don't know about now, though. Something happened between him and the spirits. It got too crazy, and they left for another dimension."

The reading with Frank had opened up a long-closed wound. For the past ten years, I had put my father in mental cold storage. It was too painful to think that he was no longer around. I had effectively put a wall around that part of my life and sealed it off with barbed wire and heavy cement. Despite this dead storage, I tried to carry on the best way I could.

That evening, in an effort to distract myself from Frank's revelation, I decided to see the new Charlie Chaplin film biography directed by Richard Attenborough. The timing seemed serendipitous. As a young man, my father had worked for Charlie Chaplin and Samuel Goldwyn. I thought that watching this film would serve as a nice remembrance of my father's life.

Only on a few occasions had he ever told me the story of his early days in Hollywood. Pop never liked to talk about the past. He made a real effort to live only in the present, given that he had lived through a lot of hard times—especially as a child in Poland, watching whole villages being burned because Jews lived there. As a result, it was rare when he brought up any of his memories. But the Chaplin story was the rare exception. He told me this story with great pleasure.

When my father was just fifteen, he worked as an office boy for Samuel Goldwyn, who at the time went by his real name of Goldfish. Pop's main job was to ceremoniously usher visitors into Mr. Goldfish's office as well as cash the movie stars' paychecks so they wouldn't have to stand on line at the bank. Goldwyn loved my father, and when he left his job, Goldwyn told him that if he ever needed anything to just call him. Eventually, Goldwyn would move to Hollywood to found the Samuel Goldwyn Studio.

When Pop turned twenty-one, he wanted a bit more adventure and hitched rides on the cross-country freight trains with the hobos to see how far he could travel on no money. I remember him telling me, "From time to time, the train would stop, and a conductor would come along and throw us off the train. We slept in the desert and made campfires. A lot of these guys were really scary. I jumped off the train in Los Angeles and started looking around for a place to stay. The police let me sleep in the jail for two days but then told me to move on. Somehow I found Grauman's Egyptian Theatre. They were promoting the movie *Ben-Hur* and had placed these two huge chariots out in front of the theater. I was exhausted, so I crawled into one of the chariots and fell asleep.

"One morning I decided to go see Douglas Fairbanks Sr. to ask for a job. I found his famous house. As I approached, he was just leaving to go to the studio. He asked if I'd like a ride into town.

"Fairbanks was going to meet Charlie Chaplin and Mary Pickford at his studio. I asked Fairbanks if I could get a job there, and he told me to come over and talk to him at the studio. When I asked for the address, he said, 'You found my house, find my studio.' Fairbanks dropped me somewhere in town, and it took awhile for me to find my way to his studio. I told the guard I had an important package to deliver to Mr. Fairbanks. All I was carrying, besides my camera, was an empty box that I had found on the sidewalk. When I got there, Mary Pickford, Charlie Chaplin, and Douglas Fairbanks were out front talking. Fairbanks recognized me from that morning. Since I had my camera with me, I asked Chaplin if I could take his picture. He agreed and told me that this would be the first picture that he ever posed for outside his studio while in makeup. He was in the midst of shooting *The Gold Rush*. Then Chaplin asked if I would like to tour the sets for the movie. I knew right then that I wanted to be in the movie business.

"After the tour I went to look for Mr. Goldwyn's studio. I decided to see if he remembered me from New York and ask him for a job. When I found his office, I told the secretary that I wanted to see Mr. Goldwyn. She raised her eyebrows and gave me this look like, who the hell are you? I told her, 'Tell him Lewie is here.' You should have seen her face when Mr. Goldwyn said, 'Send him in.'

"Mr. Goldwyn greeted me warmly and asked what he could do for me. I told him that I wanted to make movies. He made a few calls, and by that afternoon I was on the set of *The Gold Rush,* and they were training me as an assistant cameraman. Eventually I did various things on the set, ran the camera, helped design and build sets. I worked on several Chaplin movies."

Hollywood was an exotic paradise compared to the bleak, hardscrabble streets of New York's Lower East Side, where he had grown up at 64 Suffolk Street. His family lived in a one-room tenement with seven kids sleeping on the floor. There was a tub in the kitchen, and all they could afford for breakfast was a teaspoon of milk in a glass of hot water. Pop's father was an electrician who helped Lewis Comfort Tiffany fabricate his famous lamps. Eventually the family moved to more comfortable quarters in Brooklyn.

With friends like Goldwyn, Chaplin, and Fairbanks, his future in Hollywood seemed bright. Then, one day in the middle of a shoot, an urgent telegram arrived (just like in the movies): MOTHER DEATHLY ILL STOP COME QUICK STOP. Grabbing the next train back to New York, he said au revoir to Hollywood. So long glamour-pusses, boring Brooklyn here I come. Pop arrived back in Brooklyn to find his mother smiling and in perfect health. The telegram had been a motherly ruse to bring her son back home—she missed her little Lewie. Even with six other siblings, Pop was the favorite. If I'd had a choice in the matter (and many of the best gurus in India say that I did), I would have preferred being born the son of a Hollywood director rather than the son of a Miami decorator—though these days they are almost one and the same. Unfortunately, we all have our karma and our crosses to bear.

Of all his stories about being in Hollywood, my favorite one was about the photograph he had taken of Chaplin, Pickford, and Fairbanks. On the few occasions that he mentioned this photograph, it was always with a great deal of pride about the uniqueness of the circumstances surrounding the taking of this picture. Watching the Chaplin movie reminded me of this mysterious photograph. Even though I had been through all of his papers when he died, I'd never found the picture. I began to wonder if that photograph ever really existed. Why hadn't I ever found this precious memento?

The next morning, I called my mother to see how she was settling into her new apartment. She had just moved that week. We talked about where she was going to put the sofa, how she loved the view, and that the cable guy hadn't shown up yet. During our conversation she mentioned that the night before she was up very late, unpacking boxes of books.

"Something strange happened last night. I was putting my books away on the shelf, and all of a sudden one of my cookbooks fell off the shelf and landed open on the floor. When I went to pick it up, I noticed that there was a small brown photograph tucked into the spine. What do you call that? Oh, a sepia photograph. It's just a tiny photograph, sort of wallet sized, all brown. I never saw this photograph before in my life. I have no idea who these people are, but there are three of them standing around talking."

"Maybe the people in the photograph are relatives of yours?"

"No, I don't recognize them. I don't know how this photo got in one of my cookbooks."

"Maybe it was one of the books you bought at a yard sale. You should probably just throw the picture out."

"You're right, I probably will. Oh, I forgot to tell you that on the back of the photo someone wrote in brown ink, 'Charlie, Mary, and Douglas.' "

I was stunned. "Mom, take a closer look at the picture. Tell me if you think that the man in the photograph is Charlie Chaplin."

"I can't really tell, it's so small. Let me put my glasses on."

"I think this must be the missing photograph that Pop always talked about. Please don't throw it out. Last night I went to see that new movie about Charlie Chaplin. It made me wonder where this photograph was and why I had never seen it. Now suddenly it appears out of nowhere. You know, it's ten years since Pop died."

"Ten years? Oh my God, that long?"

"Wait a minute, how come you have this photograph? I didn't think you had any of Pop's stuff."

"Why would I have anything from your father? We divorced a long, long time ago. I must have bought this cookbook just a few years ago and never even used it. Even when we were married, I never saw this picture. I don't know how it got here. This doesn't make any sense. I'll save it for you and give it to you next time you come down."

Pop was saying hello—loud and clear. And of course he would

have chosen a tangible object that involved an image so that I could not have dismissed his communication as simply the meanderings of my own mind. The existence of this photograph would always be a reminder of his continued presence.

At that moment, I realized that he was still with me, guiding and protecting me as he always had and always will. Even though I couldn't see him, he was still watching my every move. But unlike before, I was delighted to have him spying on me.

Acknowledgments

With Thanks . . .

Unlike my usual solitary experience of making a painting, this book involved a legion of dear friends and generous associates. I am grateful to all those mentioned here as well as to many more who lent ears, support, and time to this very personal project.

First and foremost, Eric Schorr for his constant brilliance, patience, and extraordinary kindness.

Diane Coffield for telling me decades ago that this book needed to be written.

Max and Sedell Rand for remembering long-forgotten stories.

Bruce Deitchman, for friendship, facts, and more facts.

Dirk Wittenborn, Eric Konigsberg, and A. M. Holmes, a talented posse of esteemed writers and friends who each patiently and generously advised me on the nature of making a book, especially when the finish line seemed impossibly far away.

Manuel Gonzalez, who has rightly insisted that whenever possible I should mambo through life—but especially when writing this book.

Patrick Lilly, Gabriele Fiorentino, Kirsten Wittenborn, Helen McEachrane, and Guido Apicella for their very thoughtful and valuable input.

Al Zuckerman, who immediately loved my father's story and became a great ally in making this book possible.

Judith Curr, a gracious and remarkable true patron of the arts whose magical ideas and endless curiosity are always inspirational.

The astute and visionary Michael Selleck, who was intrigued enough with my story told to him over dinner to spend his vacation reading the manuscript. Michael, you have made a dream come true, and my father has asked me to personally thank you.

The extraordinarily talented Mr. Peter Borland, a true gentleman and a scholar. Peter has been the devoted guardian angel of this book. His delightful, insightful, and brilliant guidance made these words tell an even better story than I ever thought was possible.

For my many new friends at Atria, you are all so kind, generous, and patient.

And finally, at a loss for words, I bow my head with profound gratitude and endless appreciation to Kaicho Nakamura; my debt for all your precious wisdom can never be repaid.